FACTS, FRAUDS, AND PHANTASMS
A Survey of the Spiritualist Movement

Facts, Frauds, and Phantasms

A Survey of the Spiritualist Movement

GEORGESS McHARGUE

DOUBLEDAY & COMPANY, INC., GARDEN CITY, NEW YORK

For all the blithe spirits
in B.F.Y.R.
especially T.G.A.

1. Egyptian pyramids, courtesy of the National Archives, Washington, D.C.
2. Egyptian mummy, courtesy of The Metropolitan Museum of Art, Rogers Fund, 1912.
3. Yakut shamans, New York Public Library Picture Collection; from *Il costume antico e moderno* by Giulio Ferrario, 1838.
4. Mesmer's *baquet*, New York Public Library Picture Collection; from *Les Merveilles de la Science* by L. Figuier, 1869.
5. The house at Hydesville, from *The Missing Link in Spiritualism* by A. Leah Underhill, 1885, p. 477.
6,7,8. Margaret Fox (Kane), Kate Fox (Jencken) and Leah Fox (Underhill), *ibid.*, pages 122, 465, and 475.
9. Andrew Jackson Davis, from *The Magic Staff* by Andrew Jackson Davis, frontispiece.
10. Daniel Dunglas Home, New York Public Library Picture Collection; from "Brittan's Journal."
11. Ira and William Davenport, from *An Encyclopedia of Occultism* by Lewis Spence.
12. William Stainton Moses, from *Spirit Teachings* by M. A. Oxon (pseud.), frontispiece.
13. "Katie King," photo by Sir William Crookes, 1874.
14. Sir William Crookes, courtesy of the British Information Service.
15. Eusapia Palladino, from *Personal Experiences in Spiritualism* by H. Carrington, fcg. p. 128.

16. Eusapia's cabinet, *ibid.*, fcg. p. 144.
17. Title page, *Revelations of a Spirit Medium*, original edition.
18. Eva C., photograph by Baron Schrenck-Notzing, Paris, 1912.
19. Bishop James A. Pike, photo courtesy of Executive Council of the Episcopal Church.

CONTENTS

CHAPTER I   Spirits and Shamans   1
CHAPTER II   Saints and Somnambules   19
CHAPTER III   Mr. Splitfoot and Friends   31
CHAPTER IV   "Curiouser and Curiouser"   49
CHAPTER V   The Poughkeepsie Seer
                in Summer-Land   65
CHAPTER VI   Mr. Home or Mr. Sludge?   85
CHAPTER VII   Too Many Cooks and
                Professor Crookes   109
CHAPTER VIII   Many Phenomena, Only One
                Palladino   131
CHAPTER IX   Spiritualists Get Together   159
CHAPTER X   The Decline of Mediumship, or
                How to Fake a Séance   177
CHAPTER XI   Laurels and Latin, or
                How Not to Fake a Séance   207
CHAPTER XII   More Mummery and Some
                Modern "Miracles"   233
EPILOGUE   The Bishop's Tale   255
GLOSSARY OF TERMS   275
BIBLIOGRAPHY   281
INDEX   285

CHAPTER I

SPIRITS AND SHAMANS

To most people the meaning of the term "spiritualism" is rather vague. It suggests "ghosts" or "mediums and that stuff," or it may even be confused with any part of the occult world in general, including astrology, drugs, witch cults, the Tarot, crystal gazing, reincarnation, phrenology, water divining, flying saucers, and ESP (extrasensory perception). Actually, spiritualism has very little to do with most of these topics, although it has some relation to ghosts and ESP. "Mediums and that stuff" comes fairly close after all, but is hardly specific enough for a definition. Probably the most exact way to describe spiritualism is to say it is the belief that the individual personality survives after death *and can communicate with the world of the living*. The last part of the sentence is the most important. By itself, belief in the immortality of the soul does not make one a spiritualist. It is the idea that the soul or spirit can still take part in human affairs, either through communication or through direct action, which is essential to spiritualism and which explains the importance of spiritualism's central figure, the medium. Most spiritualists agree that not everyone has the ability to make contact with the spirit world. The medium is a special person who is in some way "sensitive" to the spirits and through whom they can pass on their messages to the rest of us. And although there have been places and times when it seemed that mediums grew as thick as grass, the general case is that mediumism is a rare phenomenon—about as rare, say, as having six fingers.

Today there are spiritualists all over the world. Spiritualism has its own societies, its own newspapers, and even its own religious groups. And though the movement's rate of growth is perhaps not so spectacular now as it was in the nineteenth century, its success is impressive in view of the fact in its present form spiritualism is only a little over 125 years old.

That is to say that before the middle of the last century there were no professional mediums and no "spirit circles"—groups of believers who gathered together for the purpose of getting in touch with the spirits. Such spirit circles are the backbone of modern spiritualism and we shall see later that their appearance on the scene was both sudden and spectacular. However, it would be a mistake to imagine that spiritualism sprang up out of nowhere, for the ideas on which it is based are very ancient, perhaps older than the human species to which we all belong.

At some time in the history of our remotest ancestors, those two-legged, club-wielding, roving hunters whose picture has been drawn for us by the anthropologists, the process of evolution must have produced the situation in the brain that we now call consciousness or rationality. Animals, of course, are conscious in the sense they may become unconscious as a result of illness or injury, but not in the human sense of *self*-consciousness. Somewhere the ancestors of man acquired the understanding that they were all separate individuals, each with his own unique experience of life and death. Death. The realization that every individual must die is inseparable from the idea of individual life. We do not know whether there was ever a time when men or pre-men accepted the coming of death with the simplicity of animals; our knowledge of our own species does not go back that far. It seems all too natural to us now that death should be regarded as the most fearsome and mysterious fact of life. Some might even say that the fear of death is part of the definition of mankind, that we would not be human if we were able to think of our own disappearance as a matter of no importance.

Fear, awe, and a little curiosity—those are the emotions that dominate our idea of our own death. And when the death is that of someone close to us, we also feel sorrow and a sense of loss. It is these feelings that probably gave rise to man's first ideas about an afterlife. For if something called the spirit survived, it would help the living to handle many of their doubts and fears.

First of all, if the spirit survived, one would not have to feel that the dead were gone forever. They might still be present invisibly, watching over those they had cared for in life. This was the attitude that developed into ancestor worship.

Second, one could look forward to a day of reunion with those who had died, a very comforting thought for grief-stricken survivors. Perhaps, then, death was not so frightening as it seemed. The life after death might be a better one, free of the pains and fears and challenges of what we call the real world. Perhaps the spirit could even come back again in another body, for what can be left can also be entered. Thus arose the idea of reincarnation.

Yet there was also another side to the picture. Suppose the next world were much the same as this one? Suppose one could be hungry there, and cold, and alone? Perhaps it would be as well to provide for the possibility. The idea that "you can't take it with you" is only a relatively recent one.

To find the very earliest evidence of belief in the survival of the spirit we must go back beyond the beginnings of history, perhaps beyond *homo sapiens*, the human species itself. We must go back, in fact, to Neanderthal Man, the low-browed cave-dweller who today makes his home mainly in comic strips. The real Neanderthaler, who may or may not have been classifiable as *homo sapiens*, was not an amiable oaf with a fur tunic and a pet saber-tooth. Beginning about two hundred thousand years ago, he lived and hunted in the glacier-chilled lands of Europe, Asia, and the Near East, a wanderer on the edge of humanity.

Sometime between seventy-five thousand and twenty thousand years ago the Neanderthaler disappeared, probably driven to extinction by brainier and more efficient types like Cro-Magnon Man. But before his disappearance the Neanderthaler had left behind his bones and tools and weapons as a record for those who came after. Much of what is known of him comes to us from burial sites in France, Germany, and elsewhere. For even the Neanderthaler did not leave his dead to be eaten by wild beasts.

Nor did he simply shovel them into a hole in the ground. He put them into carefully dug graves, sometimes laid out so as to point east and west, and often he buried objects along with the bodies. The things the Neanderthaler chose to leave with his dead were so simple that it is almost hard to think of them as possessions—shells, the bones of food animals, a few stone tools. But the message was clear. Death is only a door to another existence. Somewhere beyond, the dead will again have need of the things they once valued.

The pattern set by Neanderthal Man is one that persisted through thousands of years of human history. The shape and arrangement of the graves and the kind of articles they contained changed often; the basic idea did not. When pottery was invented, it was bowls and beakers that went into the graves, to the gratitude of future historians. After men learned to plant crops for food, burial sites might contain rice, barley, or maize for the nourishment of the spirit. And when metal-working was discovered, bracelets, diadems, finger rings, or utensils of gold, bronze, or silver were placed in the graves of the rich and powerful. There is hardly a single ancient civilization that did not provide for the future life in some such way, whether its tombs were stone beehives, earthern mounds, or underground chambers.

It was probably in ancient Egypt, Sumeria, and China that the practice of providing for the future comfort of the dead reached its most elaborate form. In their enormous, pyramid-shaped tombs, the Pharaohs of Egypt were equipped with food, clothing, musical instruments, ornaments, games, and complicated books of instructions on how to behave in the next world. They were

also the object of efforts to preserve the one thing that
no amount of magic or religion had ever been able to
save for man—his body. The practice of mummifying the
body by means of natron, bitumen and other preserva-
tives (whose effectiveness was much enhanced by the
dry climate of Upper Egypt) undoubtedly reflects the
conviction that the welfare of the spirit was dependent
on that of the body, perhaps even that the soul would
one day re-enter the body.

The great size and fantastic luxury of Egypt's tombs is
without equal. However, the concept of the afterlife was
carried one step farther in the royal tombs of Sumer
and China. There the furnishings were just as rich and
beautiful, but the spirit of the ruler also took with him
into the next world a whole retinue of human beings—
slaves, musicians, charioteers, all apparently sacrificed at
the time of the king's funeral. The king on earth was still
to be a king in the afterlife.

Gifts "sent with" the dead in this fashion are only
one expression of man's ideas about the relations of men
and spirits. In some cases it was fear that came to
dominate the picture. The dead were thought of as
malevolent, jealous of the living for the very fact of their
being alive. Dead spirits might come back to revenge
wrongs done to them in life, to do general mischief to
mankind, or even to steal the spirits of the living. Then
the ceremonies attending death were designed to turn
away the anger of the dead and sometimes to prevent
them from returning to trouble the survivors. The body
might be tied up tightly, weighted down with stones, or
pierced by a stake so that the spirit could not "walk."

It was this attitude that gave rise to belief in ghosts—

spirits in at least partly visible form which return to avenge a wrong or pay for some crime. Ghosts are hard to differentiate from the spirits called up by mediums, for some believers maintain that ghosts cannot appear without the mediumship of a living person, even though the medium may be unaware of his function. Perhaps the best way to distinguish the two is to say that ghosts *haunt* something or someone and generally seem unaware of observers, while the spirits of the séance room are less concerned with past events, less likely to be visible, and more ready to communicate with the living. In any case, fear of the dead in the form of ghosts has often acted as a deterrent to spiritualists and others who seek to communicate with the spirit world. At the back of the mind there is always the unvoiced thought: What if the dead "return," what if they refuse to go back when we are through with them, *what if they try to take us with them?*

However, even in the most extreme cases, the dead are not thought of as totally hostile. This is often especially true of the spirits of one's ancestors, who are supposed to wish to see the family prosper. Hence the very widespread custom of making periodic offerings to the dead, either at the grave site or at an altar in the home. The offering may be anything from a bowl of milk to one hundred bullocks, but its purpose is always to convince the departed spirit that since the living still show it due honor it should look kindly upon the survivors.

In a great many societies, ranging from the simplest to the great civilization of ancient China, the ancestors were expected to respond to the attentions of their descendants with more than visible protection. For since the ancestors were in many cases very old and were thought to have superior wisdom, their advice and consent were sought before the family or tribe took any important action.

Here for the first time we encounter the matter of direct communication with spirits. It seems that the most popular means of accomplishing this is through dreams, and, when one thinks of it, that is very natural. How often in ordinary life do we dream about friends or relatives whom we haven't seen for years? Dreams are as immune to the limitations of time as are our memories; in both, the living and the dead mingle freely. One does not need to be a psychologist to see how impressive it can be to receive dream advice from a departed relative, especially if the person in the dream is someone who had great influence during his lifetime and whose death was a great loss. We know that psychology says dreams are produced by the unconscious mind and frequently represent things we *wish* would happen. In times of stress, the desire for wise advice may actually produce its own answer in the form of a dream. Nevertheless, the fact that the dead were often seen in dreams was always one of the chief reasons for belief in spirits. It seemed that figures seen in this way must have existence somewhere, that they could not simply have vanished forever.

But although dreams are both taken as evidence of spirit return and used as a means of communication, they are in many ways unreliable and unsatisfactory. First of all, dreams tend to be highly symbolic and capable of many interpretations. If you dream you see your grandmother in the form of an antelope attacking a snake, does it mean you should give your daughter in marriage to the village wood-carver, or not? Furthermore, dreams cannot be had at will. Sometimes the ancestors seem to refuse to speak.

Perhaps this is the reason why many different societies developed devices that would help to clarify the messages of the spirit world. Such devices are not to be confused with the many similar objects used for divination or foretelling the future. Almost anything can be, and probably has been, used for divination—crystal balls, doves' livers, playing cards, dice, pools of water, feathers, pebbles, tea leaves, spilled wine, the flight of birds, cloud patterns, forked sticks—the list is endless. However, divination is not thought of as being guided specifically by the spirits of the dead, nor does it usually spell out a verbal message. Instead, it is seen as a *symbol* of future events and must be carefully interpreted, usually with divine inspiration.

The contrary is true of devices such as the planchette. In its oldest form the planchette was found in ancient China. It was a triangular or heart-shaped piece of board that rested on wheels or rollers at one end and was supported at its apex by some sort of writing instrument such as a piece of charcoal, chalk, or (later) a pencil. When the operator placed his hands on the board it would, if conditions were right, move over the writing surface in such a way as to write out a message. The modern form of this device was invented by a French spiritualist named Planchette (whence, of course, the name) in 1853.

Another type of mechanism spelled its messages by pointing to the various letters instead of writing them out. The Greek philosopher Pythagoras and his followers were using something of the kind in the sixth century B.C. Instead of a writing instrument at one end, this device had a pointer that indicated various Greek letters carved on a slab of stone. A modern equivalent is called the ouija board, the name being derived from the French and German words for "yes," *oui* and *ja*. The ouija board is set up so that it can point to words or phrases such as *yes, no, I don't know,* and *goodbye* as well as to the letters of the alphabet. It is usually a wooden tripod on rollers that moves over a polished board when a hand is placed on it. Like the planchette, the ouija board operates without conscious control and can be worked by almost anyone who is interested, although more coherent results come with practice.

There have been many other mechanical means of spirit communication. They range from moving dolls to stones suspended over the circular alphabet, but like dreams they will not always work on demand. They also have the drawback of being quite slow and tedious to use unless the operator has had a good deal of practice.

For this reason many people resort to the third means of getting in touch with the spirit world, which is to consult a medium. Probably one of the earliest accounts of a mediumistic séance is the biblical story of King Saul and the woman of En-dor. In English that lady is most often described as a witch because that is the word used by the translators of the popular King James version of the Bible. To anyone familiar with mediumism, however, the story of the events at En-dor is unmistakably that of a séance, and later translations of the Old Testament have changed the word from "witch" to "medium." It is worth noting, before we examine the story itself, that already in this ancient period (around 1056 B.C.) mediumism was looked on with suspicion and had in fact been prohibited by Saul himself. Now, however, Saul was frightened and willing to seek help from any source.

When Saul saw the army of the Philistines, he was afraid, and his heart trembled greatly. And when Saul enquired of the Lord, the Lord did not answer him either by dreams, or by the Urim (a device for divining the will of God) or by the prophets. Then Saul said to his servants, "Seek out for me a woman who is a medium, that I may go to her and enquire of her." And his servants said to him, "Behold, there is a medium at En-dor."

So Saul disguised himself and put on other garments, and went, he and two men with him; and they came to the woman by night. And he said, "Divine for me by a spirit, and bring up for me whomever I shall name to you." The woman said to him, "Surely you know what Saul has done, how he has cut off the mediums and wizards from the land. Why then are you laying a snare for my life to bring about my death?" But Saul swore to her by the Lord, "As the Lord lives, no punishment shall come upon you for this thing." Then the woman said, "Whom shall I bring up for you?" He said, "Bring up Samuel [the prophet and adviser of Saul's youth] for me." When the woman saw Samuel, she cried out with a loud voice; and the woman said to Saul, "Why have you deceived me? You are Saul." The

king said to her, "Have no fear. What do you see?"
And the woman said to Saul, "I see a god coming up
out of the earth." He said to her, "What is his appearance?" And she said, "An old man is coming up;
and he is wrapped in a robe." And Saul knew that
it was Samuel, and he bowed with his face to the
ground, and did obeisance. (I Samuel, XXVIII, 5–14
in the *Revised Standard Version*)

The end of the story, in which the spirit of Samuel
prophesies correctly to Saul that he will be defeated
and killed in the coming battle, need not concern us here.
Much more relevant to the topic of spiritualism are some
of the details of Saul's experience. Its general tone and
atmosphere were to remain typical for the next three
thousand years, although it is a little odd that no mention is made of the medium's going into a trance, which
is almost always the rule at séances of this sort.

Nevertheless, Saul's servants had certainly done well to
send him to En-dor. Few mediums before or since have
been so successful at producing, on command, both the
right spirit and the right message. It is much commoner,
but no less characteristic, for the medium to establish her
good faith by revealing something the sitter has not told
her—in this case, the fact of his identity. And finally,
there is the description of the appearance of the spirit,
which must be recognized by the sitter before the séance
proceeds. Presumably Saul's confidence was won by the
correctness of the revelations about himself and Samuel,
though it should be noted that the description of the
latter is pretty vague. What else would one expect a

prophet to be but "an old man . . . wrapped in a robe"? Still, we must admit that the medium has given a very creditable performance in this instance.

Though mediumism was frowned on in ancient Israel, there were many places where it was accorded the greatest veneration. Some of the famous oracles of Greece were mediumistic in nature, particularly the one at Delphi. The Pythia, as the priestess of the Delphic oracle was called, always went into trance before delivering her messages. The trance is an unusual state of consciousness that seems to be between sleep and waking; the conscious mind is suspended while the unconscious mind is awake and aware. Most trances are purely mental in origin, but some scholars have suggested that the Pythia induced her trance by means of drugs or perhaps by breathing the volcanic fumes that rose through cracks in the floor of her cave.

If the tales and myths are to be believed, the Pythia had many more talents than would come within the strict definition of mediumism, for she was both a prophet and a seer (one who can perceive events at a distance, a clairvoyant). The Pythia probably enjoyed the greatest prestige of all the Greek oracles, as is indicated by the anecdote in which King Croesus of Lydia decided to test all the great oracles of his day. To each one he sent a messenger with the instruction that at a certain hour of a certain day he was to ask the question, "What is the king doing now?" Only the Pythia replied correctly, if gruesomely, "He is cutting a tortoise and a lamb into pieces and boiling them in a brass cauldron." The tale is of special interest because, although it does

not deal with a spirit message, it seems to show that
Croesus was history's first methodical researcher into
psychical phenomena. If others had followed his example
—if, for instance, Saul had asked the woman of En-dor
to tell him the color of Samuel's eyes—modern investigators might have more reliable evidence from which to
work.

The truest forerunners of modern spiritualists are not
to be found in Western cultural tradition at all, as it
happens. Instead, they go back to places far removed
from either Delphi or En-dor and to a time more ancient
than either. All around the northern rim of the globe
and in certain parts of North and South America are
found peoples of hunting tribes whose religion and daily
life are deeply bound up with a practice called shamanism. Having spread out from Siberia at some time in
prehistory, their way of life has remained unchanged for
tens of thousands of years. Whether they call themselves
Voguls, Ostyaks, Ona, Eskimo, Samoyeds, Tungus,
Yahgans, or any of several other tribal names, their views
of the relationship between men and spirits and the procedures they use for communicating with the other world
are quite similar. Usually the man who deals directly
with the spirits is called the shaman, and he or she is
one of the most powerful persons in the tribe.

Though at first glance the shaman's role might be
mistaken for that of a priest, magician, or "medicine
man," it is in reality very different. Like the medium's,
the shaman's power is thought of as a highly individual
gift that can be reinforced by practice but cannot be
learned by any amount of study. In the development of
shamanism we can see the search for guidance through

dreams carried one step farther. It is almost as if the shaman is appointed to dream for the whole community. Here is the way the process of becoming a shaman, or Holy Man, was described by a chief of the Oglala Sioux more than sixty years ago.

> To the Holy Man comes in youth the knowledge that he will be holy. The Great Mystery makes him know this. Sometimes it is the spirits who tell him. The spirits come not in sleep always but sometimes when man is awake. When a spirit comes it would seem as though a man stood there, but when this man has spoken and goes forth again, none may see whither he goes. Thus the spirits. With the spirits the Holy Man may commune always, and they teach him holy things.
>
> The Holy Man goes apart to a lone tipi and fasts and prays. Or he goes into the hills in solitude. When he returns to men he teaches them and tells them what the Great Mystery has bidden him to tell. He counsels, he heals, and he makes holy charms to protect the people from all evil. Great is his power and greatly is he revered; his place in the tipi is an honored one. (Natalie Curtis, *The Indians' Book*, pp. 38–39)

Here, except for the deliberate attempt to bring on visions and visitations, is a fine description of the onset of mediumism as it might occur today. And here too is a good approximation of the functions of modern mediums, who have often undertaken healing with the advice of the "spirits," have given counsel, and have written lengthy books of spirit teachings, even if they do not do much business in "holy charms to protect the people from all evil."

In addition to having special knowledge and powers of healing, the shaman was frequently gifted with other allegedly supernormal abilities. From the Ona people of Tierra del Fuego, the extreme southern tip of South America, we have a detailed account of shamanistic magic. On this occasion the performance had no particular purpose since the narrator, Lucas Bridges, had simply asked for a demonstration by the celebrated shaman Houshken. Bridges related that it was a clear, moonlit night when the snow on the ground helped to make the scene as bright as day. To begin the demonstration Houshken broke into a monotonous chant and then appeared to take out of his mouth a short strip of leather. This he began to shake loosely back and forth between his hands until it apparently grew to a length of eight feet. The shaman then caused the strip to shrink back to its original length, in what was probably a not very complex feat of sleight of hand. Bridges remarks that there were twenty or thirty people present, not all of whom were friendly to the shaman, and then continues:

Had they detected some simple trick, the great medicine man would have lost his influence; they would no longer have believed in any of his magic.

The demonstration was not yet over. Houshken stood up and resumed his robe. Once again he broke into a chant and seemed to go into a trance, possessed by some spirit not his own. Drawing himself up to his full height, he took a step towards me and let his robe, his only garment, fall to the ground. He put his hands to his mouth with a most impressive gesture and brought them away again with fists clenched and thumbs close together. He held them up to the height of my eyes, and when they were less than two feet from my face drew them slowly apart. I saw that there was now a small, almost opaque object between them. It was about an inch in diameter in the middle and tapered away into his hands. It might have been a piece of semi-transparent dough or elastic, but whatever it was, it seemed to be alive, revolving at great speed, while Houshken, apparently from muscular tension, was trembling violently.

The moonlight was bright enough to read by as I gazed at this strange object. Houshken brought his hands further apart and the object grew more and more transparent, until, when some three inches separated his hands, I realized that it was not there any more. It did not break or burst like a bubble; it simply disappeared, having been visible to me for less than five seconds. Houshken made no sudden movement, but slowly opened his hands and turned them over for my inspection. They looked clean and dry. He was stark naked and there was no confederate beside him. I glanced down at the snow, and, in spite of his stoicism, Houshken could not resist a chuckle, for nothing was to be seen there. (E. Lucas Bridges, *The Uttermost Part of the Earth*, p. 262)

Though Mr. Bridges is plainly skeptical of the supernatural nature of Houshken's performance, it is clear that he cannot explain how the trick was done and also that the shaman's fellow tribesmen were in great awe of his powers. In that respect they were no different from spiritualists of the nineteenth and twentieth centuries who witnessed the appearance in the séance room of the mysterious substance known as ectoplasm. Though there is little agreement on the nature and functions of ectoplasm, it is generally described as a semitransparent fluid that is emitted by the body of the medium and that can, under the right conditions, be caused to condense or "materialize" into spirit forms. It is usually whitish and either vaporous or thready in texture. It must always be reabsorbed into the body of the medium, they say, because it is part of the individual's vital energy or life force. (If this definition is unsatisfactorily vague it is because there is no precise meaning for terms like "life force.")

In other forms of shamanism, ectoplasm is not a feature. The spirits of dead relatives or heroes may appear to take over the shaman's body and "speak with his voice," as frequently happens among the Siberian Tungus. Still other tribes, such as the Samoyeds, expect their shamans to prove the supernatural nature of their powers by allowing themselves to be bound hand and foot during the séance. In a darkened tent the shaman summons the aid of the spirits, upon which the tent shakes and there are loud and frightening noises such as the growling of bears and the hissing of snakes. When the lights are relit the shaman is found to have been freed from his bonds, no matter how securely he may have been trussed. This same manifestation will be encountered again in the genteel drawing rooms of nineteenth-century Europe rather than on the Siberian tundra.

CHAPTER II

SAINTS AND SOMNAMBULES

We have now had a brief look at the ancient and primitive beginnings of the ideas and practices that were to appear in the spiritualist movement. (About the only popular phenomenon of the modern séance room that does *not* have roots in antiquity is spirit photography, for the very obvious reason that the ancients had no cameras.)

At this point it will be necessary for us to leapfrog over several centuries, making only a few brief stops to focus on developments that influenced the future course of spiritualism. In general the pattern set in ancient times continued to exist in western Europe. This may appear surprising, considering the fact that Christianity was to be the dominant religion in the area for close to two thousand years. But though the Catholic Church (for so long the *only* church) took a very negative attitude to all activities that had to do with raising the dead or foretelling the future, mediumism and other occult practices survived anyway, with or without the permission of the Church.

A primary source of knowledge about such phenomena

was of course the Bible itself, particularly the New Testament, which recounts a wide variety of what would now be called psychic manifestations. Without going into these in detail, since few are actually mediumistic, we might recall the prophetic dream that warned Joseph of the enmity of King Herod, St. Paul's falling into a trance and hearing a mysterious voice on the road to Damascus, and the visions of Jesus that came to the apostles after the crucifixion. That is not even to mention the many miracles of Jesus, which would have been called examples of psychic healing, prophecy, clairvoyance, apportation, and so on, had they been performed by an ordinary human being. For the Christian who could read the Bible or who heard the sermons of the preaching friars and saw their words illustrated in the wall paintings and carvings of the medieval churches, it would be plain that supernormal events might be rare but were by no means unheard-of.

In point of fact the writings of the Church Fathers (the saints and patriarchs of Christianity's first few centuries) make it clear that in the early churches events of this type were not even very rare and were looked upon with favor. Apparitions, clairvoyance, clairaudience (hearing voices), prophecy, healing, levitation (the floating of the body in the air) and speaking in tongues (the ability to converse in languages normally unknown to the speaker) were all referred to as Gifts of the Holy Spirit and were taken to be marks of grace. In the course of the Church's growth from a small and persecuted sect to the official religion of all Europe, such manifestations became more unusual and ceased to play a major part in religious life. Yet certain saints continued to have visions, to perform miracles (especially of healing), and to engage in prophecy or even levitation.

Attitudes to such things were not consistent in the medieval period, however. Jeanne d'Arc experienced clairaudience in which she received instructions from voices claiming to be those of St. Margaret, St. Catherine, and St. Michael. Yet she was burned as a witch and only declared a saint five hundred years after her death. For though the time has been called the Age of Faith, that faith extended to devils as well as to God and the angels. Woe to the person who spoke openly of strange experiences—who "saw" distant events in his mind's eye, foretold the future, or worst of all talked in voices not his own. Such a person was likely to be seen as a victim of demonic possession, as was anyone afflicted with epileptic "fits," delirium, or other types of sudden and violent behavior. The person "possessed" in these ways was often either locked up as a lunatic or beaten in order to drive out the supposed demon, so one can see why mediumism was largely a secret activity in this period.

At least part of the Church's objection to séances and other psychical manifestations was that they were too closely connected with some of the pre-Christian religions which still, in the early centuries, had not been entirely uprooted. So, perhaps as a result of this suppression, there was always a sort of religious underground in Christian Europe. Sometimes the purpose of this movement was simply to preserve the "Old Religion" of pagan times, with its gods and sacrifices. Sometimes it was directly opposed to Christianity, seeking to substitute the devil for God as the chief object of worship.

In either case, the Church recognized its danger and called the practice heresy or witchcraft, imposing the most severe punishments on those involved.

Having thus been rejected by the Church, mediumism and the other psychical abilities almost inevitably took refuge in the religious underworld. Naturally, little direct evidence survives to tell us just how the spirits of the dead were viewed at the time. Those who engaged in "witchcraft" did not publish minutes of their meetings. It is only occasionally that the documents of the time grant us a glimpse of that forbidden realm. Thus the records of the witchcraft trials that took place in Scotland during the sixteenth and seventeenth centuries tell us things that are both horrifying and informative. For example, among the "witches" burned in the year 1576 was a woman named Bessie Dunlop, who may or may not have been a follower of the witch religion but was very obviously a medium. The trial record states that Bessie was regularly "visited" by the spirit of one Thomas Reid, who claimed to have been killed at the Battle of Pinkie in 1547. With the help of this "spirit control" (a personality that takes control of the medium), Bessie had claimed to be able to cure illness and restore lost property—activities that seem harmless enough. Yet Bessie, and one can only guess how many other mediums, was condemned just the same.

The days of such persecutions were definitely coming to an end, however. True, the witch trials would continue and even increase for a time during the religious wars and upheavals of the seventeenth century. But the same forces that were at work in the terrible and (some would now say) pointless wars also contributed to a great change in the intellectual climate of Europe. Chief in importance for the future of spiritualist thought was the introduction of Protestantism. Whatever may have been the ultimate causes of the breakup of the Catholic religious monopoly, one of its central moving forces was an increased awareness of the importance of the individual. Almost all the early forms of Protestantism turned away from what they believed to be an undue emphasis on rituals and ceremonies and an insufficient regard for private religious experience. Accompanying this development was a conscious effort to go back to the more spontaneous spirit of the early days of Christianity. The Catholic Church had said that no one could be a priest without lengthy training, rigorous vows, and ceremonies of ordination. Many of the new sects drastically altered these requirements. Since spiritual experience, in their view, was a private affair, a man (or woman) might become a minister simply by beginning to preach the gospel and declaring that he had "heard the call." Forms of worship became less standardized and (often) more emotional. Under the influence of the new spirit of equality that characterized the eighteenth century, all worshipers were regarded as equal before the Lord with the result that all religious experiences were equally valid. Many of the new groups welcomed the occurrence of clairvoyance, clairaudience, trance speaking, prophesying, and so on. Thus by the nineteenth century psychic manifestations like mediumism were no longer under threat of universal religious condemnation, at least not among such groups as the Shakers, Primitive Baptists, Anabaptists, Seventh-day Adventists, Pentecostals, and Evangelicals, to name only a few.

Then, as perhaps at no time since the late Roman Empire, "anything went."

Along with increasing tolerance for all shades of religious and semireligious opinion, the eighteenth and nineteenth centuries saw a very rapid growth in the sciences. Of course this was not a sudden, isolated happening. Various great scientific discoveries and the birth of the scientific method can convincingly be traced back to the humanist scholars of the Renaissance, the medieval universities, the Islamic sciences that flourished during Europe's Dark Ages, the scientist-philosophers of ancient Greece, or even to the Egyptians, Chaldeans, and Babylonians, depending on the bias of the historian. Nevertheless, the period of which we are speaking was one when scientific methods of thought became familiar to large numbers of ordinary people as well as to the educated. For the first time it became possible, and even fashionable, to test ideas scientifically before accepting them on the authority of "the Church," or "the King," or "the ancient sages." A spirit of inquiry was about, and like some later Spirits it occasionally took its advocates down rather odd pathways.

In 1773 a German doctor named Friedrich Anton Mesmer announced that he had discovered a marvelous new method of healing, based on a force he christened animal magnetism. His cures were wrought by a number of bizarre devices, one example of which was a "magnetized" tree to which the patients tied themselves with ropes. Now while Mesmer was neither the first nor the last person to claim miraculous cures, the embarrassing thing to the medical profession was that in this instance some of the patients indisputably got better.

Scientists were upset and annoyed because they could find nothing to confirm the German doctor's explanation of *why* his cures worked.

Mesmer, inspired by the then recent discoveries concerning electricity and magnetism, believed he had found a hitherto unknown fluid that filled up "empty" space and transmitted the doctor's "influence" to his patients. If the notion sounds strange it is because later investigation has conclusively shown that no such magnetic fluid exists. Nevertheless, Mesmer's cures were a sensation. It was observed that some of his patients not only got well but in doing so exhibited an unusual relationship with the doctor, a heightened sensitivity to his feelings and wishes that was generally termed rapport. Some appeared to fall asleep while being treated, yet were still able to respond to commands and to speak, though, like the ancient mediums and shamans, they did not remember their words and actions when they "awoke." A commission appointed by the French government in 1784 published a report on his claims that pictures the mesmeric technique very vividly.

The sick persons, arranged in great numbers, and in several rows around the *baquet* [a large tub or bath filled with water and various "magnetic" substances] received the magnetism by means of the iron rods, which conveyed it to them from the *baquet* by the cords wound round their bodies, by the thumb which connected them with their neighbors, and by the sound of a pianoforte, or an agreeable voice diffusing magnetism in the air.

The patients were also directly magnetised by means of the finger and wand of the magnetiser, moved slowly before their faces, above or behind their heads, or on the diseased parts.

The magnetiser acts also by fixing his eyes on the subjects; by the application of his hands on the region of the solar plexus; an application which sometimes continues for hours.

Meanwhile the patients present a very varied picture. Some are calm, tranquil, and experience no effect. Others cough and spit, feel pains, heat, or perspiration. Others, again are convulsed.

As soon as one begins to be convulsed, it is remarkable that others are immediately affected. . . .

Nothing is more astonishing than the spectacle of these convulsions.

One who has not seen them can form no idea of them. The spectator is as much astonished at the profound repose of one portion of the patients as at the agitation of the rest. . . .

All are under the power of the magnetiser; it matters not what state of drowsiness they may be in, the sound of his voice, a look, a motion of his hands, spasmodically affects them.

> (quoted in Lewis Spence's *An Encyclopedia of Occultism*, pp. 218–19)

The opinion of the commission, which included Benjamin Franklin (then U.S. ambassador to France) and the chemist Lavoisier, was that the cures were entirely due to the patients' "imagination" and that the mysterious "animal magnetism" did not exist. This view was almost entirely correct if for "imagination" one substitutes some reference to the power of the mind over the body (psychosomatic mechanisms), a subject about which science still has much to learn.

Ironically, the commission's report had the effect of quashing public interest in mesmerism, as it had come to be called, for in those days to say something was due to "imagination" was to call it a fraud. Only a relative handful of mesmeric doctors continued to offer treatments, and it seemed that the furor was over.

Then came a revival of sorts. In 1823 a young French physician published a book entitled *Treatise on Somnambulism*. The author was Alexandre Bertrand, and he had had the wit to see that the most interesting thing about Mesmer's inexplicable cures was not his strange ideas and apparatus but the frequent occurrence in his patients of what was then called somnambulism (sleepwalking) but would now be classified as hypnotic trances. As the excerpt quoted above from the French report makes quite clear, those who did not enter this state of heightened subconscious awareness experienced no violent physical or emotional symptoms and also *were not among those cured*. Bertrand concluded that the explanation for the cures was to be found in somnambulism and his book had the effect of increasing public interest in mesmerism and trances in general.

However, the scientific and medical professions continued to be openly hostile. One probable reason (in addition to the general conviction that animal magnetism was not even a fact, much less a true explanation) was that many other phenomena besides cures had been reported to occur during the subjects' trances. Early mesmerists often claimed their patients were able to read their minds, to see with their eyes closed, to become insensible to pain, or to speak in voices not their own and display knowledge not known to their waking selves —in other words, to possess psychic powers. Such claims were universally rejected by conventional physicians, and many went so far as to suggest that mesmerism was not only a fraud but potentially dangerous. In some quarters it came to be believed that the influence of the mesmerist could be applied against the patient's will or even without his knowledge. (It is true that some experimenters had attempted to do those things, but their results were, to say the least, doubtful.)

Thus was born that sinister figure of nineteenth-century melodrama, the evil mesmerist who uses his mysterious powers to influence the actions of statesmen, force his victims to commit crimes for his benefit, and even (oh, horror!) to ravish innocent maidens who would otherwise prefer death to dishonor. The monk Rasputin and his supposed hypnotic (a later word for mesmeric) control of various members of the Russian imperial family is the best historical example of this sinister figure. The image must have added spice to the public interest in mesmerism, trance healing, and so on.

At this point we ought to make it clear that the procedure stumbled on by Dr. Mesmer was undoubtedly effective in certain cases. Specifically, there are several symptoms whose cause may be mental rather than physical. Given a strong enough unconscious motive, the mind can sometimes cause blindness, vomiting, pain, paralysis, dumbness, and skin rashes, among other maladies. There is nothing faked about the sufferings

of those with this type of disability. The pain or in-
capacity is absolutely real to them and quite beyond
the power of their conscious minds to control.

Yet hypnotism, which induces a state in which the
unconscious mind comes temporarily to the surface, can
cause miraculous disappearance of conditions whose
origins are mental, or psychosomatic. The power op-
erating here is the power of suggestion; the lame do
walk and the blind do see because the hypnotist tells
them they will. Sometimes a person who is not entranced can also be influenced by suggestion. However,
there is no proof that suggestion can affect a genuinely
physical ailment. Sight will not be restored if the optic
nerve is severed, nor will the polio victim regain the
use of his legs.

It was to be some decades before hypnosis was recognized as a legitimate medical tool, though one to be
applied with caution only by a trained practitioner.
Nevertheless, the genuine *effectiveness* of this type of
therapy was recognized as early as 1836 by a second
French commission appointed as a result of the revival
of interest sparked by Bertrand. The main importance
of the new commission's report was to certify that the
trance state was a genuine condition rather than a theatrical performance, as had been charged. It made little
contribution to knowledge concerning the causes of the
trance or the evaluation of the behavior of the entranced
subjects. But the acceptance of the reality of trances
was, one might say, one of the last missing pieces of the
puzzle that was to spell out SPIRITUALISM only
twelve years later.

The influence of mesmerism and hypnotism in pre-

paring the minds of the public for future developments
was undoubtedly great. Besides popularizing the idea of
the trance, it had introduced the concept of group partic-
ipation in a situation where certain individuals became
"possessed" or controlled by personalities not their own.
The circle of Mesmer's patients holding hands in order
to communicate the magnetic force or current was to
be imitated in the joined hands of the spiritualist séance.

Finally, there was the matter of the trance utterances
of mesmerized patients. In cases where the subject
seemed to speak with the voice of another person, the
idea of spirit control had already been suggested. For
example, a mesmerized somnambule in Stockholm in 1788
had spoken words she attributed, while in trance, to her
own dead child and another from the same town. Why
these early implications of spirit return did not catch
on at the time is impossible to determine. Perhaps in
Europe the subject was submerged by the controversy
over animal magnetism. In any case, it was in the United
States that spiritualism suddenly blossomed into an international craze.

Mesmerism and hypnotism had of course been known
in America almost since their beginnings. (Remember that
Benjamin Franklin was on the first commission to report
on Mesmer's methods.) Both foreign journals and visiting mesmeric doctors had further familiarized the American public with the trend. But there, as on the other
side of the Atlantic, mesmerism and its trances were
of direct concern to only two groups—patients and
doctors. It may be that spiritualism's coming success
was partly due to the fact that it became a game everyone could play.

CHAPTER III

MR. SPLITFOOT AND FRIENDS

The birth of spiritualism can be given an exact date. On Friday, March 31, 1848, in Hydesville, New York, two young girls named Margaret and Katherine Fox had the first of a series of "spirit conversations" that were to make the Fox family and the new spiritualist phenomenon the talk of two continents.

The famous "Hydesville rappings" took place in a small frame house not far from Rochester. After the event it was suggested that the house already had the reputation of being haunted when the Foxes moved into it in December 1847. Whether or not this was so, within two months of the arrival of Mr. and Mrs. John Fox and their daughters strange things began to occur in the house. Persistent knocks and rapping noises were heard at all hours and were especially noticeable when the children were present. It seems clear from later accounts of the disturbances that the parents were considerably more upset than were Kate and Margaret. This was particularly true of Mrs. Fox, who was a devout Methodist and feared that the rappings were the work of the devil.

Though frequent attempts were made to find the source of the noises that troubled the Foxes' rest, no one found an obvious explanation, such as a rattling shutter. The family even checked up on a shoemaker who lived nearby but the man replied (perhaps a little tartly) that it was not his habit to use his hammer in the middle of the night.

This was the situation on March 31, when the rappings were as loud and persistent as ever. The family had gone to bed early, but sleep was impossible. As the sounds showed no signs of stopping, one of the children (accounts differ as to which one) sat up in bed and pertly addressed a remark to the air. "Here, Mr. Splitfoot, do as I do!" she said, snapping her fingers. She was answered by a rap. She snapped again repeatedly and was answered by the corresponding number of raps. Next it developed that the entity that had thus been christened Mr. Splitfoot would also respond with raps if one merely held out a number of fingers. Obviously "Mr. Splitfoot" could see as well as hear.

Having made the exciting discovery that they could communicate with the thing that had been disturbing them, the Foxes continued to question the rapper. Mrs. Fox was correctly told the number and ages of her children, not all of whom lived at home. A code was then worked out so that the rapper could answer questions with yes and no as well as with numbers. In this fashion "Mr. Splitfoot" stated that he was not a man but a spirit, though he had been a man in his previous life. To a fascinated audience that now included some hastily summoned neighbors, he also revealed that he had been a traveling peddler, murdered in that very house, robbed of five hundred dollars, and buried in the cellar.

The effect of these events on Hydesville was of course tremendous. Word blew through the town like milkweed fluff, and in the days that followed the Fox house was constantly full of curious neighbors and strangers. Some came to scoff, but none succeeded in pinpointing a normal explanation for the raps.

Naturally attempts were made to confirm the tale of the murdered peddler. It is unfortunate that testimony as to what was or was not found under the dirt floor of the cellar is contradictory and that some of the most important points appear to rest solely on the word of the Foxes. Thus although it is clear that no body was actually dug up, some sources state that there were decomposed bones and quicklime, while others disagree. Perhaps more to the point is the fact that no one was ever able to identify the supposed victim, since no traveling peddler had been reported missing in the Hydesville area.

In spite of this lack of confirmatory evidence, however, many of those who continued to crowd into the Fox home were convinced that they were witnessing the dawn of a new era, one in which the barriers between the material and the spiritual worlds would at last be lowered so that mortal men could catch a glimpse of what lay in the "great beyond." As the excitement—and the rappings—continued, it was decided that Kate and Margaret should be sent away to stay with their older sister, Mrs. Leah Fox Fish (later Mrs. Underhill), in Rochester. This move probably had the opposite effect to that intended by the girls' parents, for the rappings were soon found to follow them to Rochester. There, in a much larger town, "the Fox girls" attracted even more attention and though Kate left shortly for Auburn, New York, Margaret was soon the center of a devoted "spirit circle."

Certain enthusiastic citizens of Rochester made it their custom to gather at Leah Fish's home to witness the wonderful revelations that came to Margaret via the "rapping telegraph." It was at this time that the financial possibilities of Margaret's talent became apparent to her sister Leah. Twenty-three years older than Margaret, Leah had been a music teacher but had lost some of her best pupils as a result of the sensational publicity surrounding Margaret's phenomena. Now, since Rochester seemed equally divided between rapture and denunciation, Leah cannily arranged a public lecture and demonstration. The event was to take place in Corinthian Hall, the city's largest auditorium, and admission was the then respectable sum of one dollar.

If the skeptics of Rochester expected to witness a public exposure of fraud in return for their dollar, they were disappointed. A committee of leading citizens reported itself completely unable to give a natural explanation for the rappings, which had been plainly heard by all. Disappointed, the doubters formed a second committee, which was instructed to report at a later date. However, when the time came, that group also declared it had been unable to detect any trick. A doctor had even listened to Margaret with a stethoscope in order to rule out ventriloquism, all to no effect.

Public opinion in the city was now becoming inflamed. A third committee was formed, and one of its members swore publicly that if he could not discover how the raps were made he would throw himself over Genesee Falls. It is to be hoped that this foolhardy gentleman's friends were able to dissuade him, because the third committee had little more luck than the first two. Though some of its members were privately certain that the raps were not produced by spirits, the third committee, like the others, was forced to admit that it couldn't tell how the trick was done, if a trick were indeed involved. On this occasion the audience in the hall became enraged. Amid angry shouts and the noise of firecrackers a squad of police arrived to break up the meeting and were forced to escort Margaret and Leah home in order to save them from the indignant mob.

But despite the fact that the majority of the spectators had shown they had little use for the spirit world, this series of meetings at Corinthian Hall was only the first ripple of a flood that soon spread far beyond Rochester. Not only Margaret and Kate Fox but also their shrewd sister Leah went on to lengthy careers as professional rapping mediums. In that capacity they toured the country, usually attracting large crowds to their public demonstrations and doing equally well by giving private sittings to those who could afford them. The younger girls, especially Margaret, did no harm to their careers by being both youthful and noticeably pretty. Among those who attended Margaret's sittings were such famous, intelligent, and influential figures as James Fenimore Cooper, Harriet Beecher Stowe, William Cullen Bryant, and the great New York editor Horace Greeley. In later years Kate Fox was to achieve the ultimate in mediumistic status by having one of her séances attended by Mary Todd Lincoln, who was attempting to communicate with the spirit of the assassinated President.

It is interesting to note that already in the Fox case, the foundation stone of the whole spiritualist movement, there are features that are to become characteristic of the problems and progress of spiritualism in general. First of all, there is the tricky, unsatisfactory, even slippery nature of the evidence. There is no agreement on such simple facts as the ages of Kate and Margaret, much less the knotty question of the bones in the cellar. One might think that as the Fox girls' powers attracted more and more attention the problems of evidence would be simplified, but that is not so. Lawyers and policemen are familiar with the fact that two witnesses to a crime or accident hardly ever give the same account of it. How much less accurate are people who are personally involved with what is going on, whose emotions are aroused, and who therefore have a very strong tendency *to see what they expect to see.* Everyone likes to make a good story, and everyone likes to be right. Thus it is very difficult to know what went on at the Fox sisters' sittings, even when those present were otherwise reliable citizens.

Another factor that was to play a growing role in the movement was the conflict over what, if any, relationship spiritualism should have to religion. By the simple choice of the name Mr. Splitfoot the Fox girls were reflecting the suspicion that such manifestations came not merely from the supernatural world but from the devil himself, with his cloven hoofs. And certainly this attitude of fear was the one that Mrs. Fox took from the beginning. Her Methodism taught her that the rappings must be evil, and she was by no means alone in her conviction. On the other hand, many people immediately saw in the spirit world a chance to support and confirm the teachings of the churches. The information obtained in the séance room was to replace faith as "the evidence of things not seen."

Significantly, the public meetings held by Margaret Fox in Rochester had originally been scheduled to take place in one of the local churches. However the spirits, when consulted through Margaret, had expressed a preference for Corinthian Hall. It would perhaps be unkind to suggest that Leah may also have preferred the hall since one could hardly charge admission to a church. In any case spiritualism was already, from its beginning, the focus of very mixed feelings—damned as a devil's tool and at the same time hailed as the dawn of a new age of devotion.

The third feature of spiritualism that soon became apparent, though not quite as immediately as the other two, was the fact that many people were determined to believe in it, no matter what, for the Hydesville knockings did not remain a mystery for longer than two years. In March of 1850 yet another committee was appointed to investigate the Fox sisters. It was not the last such assemblage of learned gentlemen, either for the Foxes or for spiritualism in general, but it was a good deal luckier or more capable than some of its successors. The members of this committee were all professors of medicine and they took their task seriously. Besides conducting the usual examinations, the three of them sat on the floor of a soundproof room for an hour while firmly holding Margaret Fox's legs. It was a rather undignified way for three gentlemen to pass time with a young and unmarried girl in those days, but they stuck to it gamely. And they were rewarded. For it was noted by all that the spirits only chose to make themselves heard when one or another of the investigators was forced to relax his hands a bit out of sheer fatigue.

The report of the committee of March 1850 stated that, in the opinion of the investigators, the spirit rappings were made by Margaret's knee joints. It was suggested that she had the ability to snap these joints in much the same way that some people crack their knuckles, but with no visible motion. This explanation, as will be seen, was so close to the truth that the gentlemen were certainly entitled to hearty thanks in the name of science. That is not what they got.

First they were the target of outraged denials from the Foxes, especially Leah, who asserted that there had been few rappings because "the friendly spirits had retired when they witnessed the harsh proceedings of the persecutors." Leah's sentiments were of course understandable, since she stood to lose her share of Margaret's earnings as a medium. More remarkable was the spirited way in which many prominent persons sprang to Margaret's defense. The accusations were untrue, they insisted, because they *could not* be true. After all, everyone knew that spirits existed, and so why would Margaret have to use her knee joints to imitate their rappings? It was a classic example of the argument that leads round in a circle. All it proved was that there were already some believers so deeply involved with spiritualism that their views on the subject could not be influenced by logic.

One of the members of the controversial committee had been Dr. Charles Alfred Lee. He became so disturbed at the fact that its findings were being ignored and the Fox girls were in more demand than ever that he decided to do something about it. Dr. Lee conducted a search among his friends and patients until he found a man who had the ability to produce joint raps that were even louder and less detectable than Margaret Fox's. Then, under the sponsorship of the University of Buffalo, he set out to put an end to that nonsense about spirit rappings once and for all. Accompanied by the man with noisy joints, Dr. Lee made a lecture tour of upper New York State, stopping here and there to give demonstrations and explain the nature of the fraud carried out by the Foxes. The results of the tour were unexpected. Instead of being warned away from the tricks of false mediums, many of those in Dr. Lee's audiences became *converted to spiritualism* by his earnest attempts to discredit it. The Fox sisters had apparently aroused a determination to believe that simply could not be undermined.

It was not until thirty-eight years later that the public was given confirmation of the findings of Dr. Lee's committee. On October 21, 1888, Margaret Fox gave a lecture and demonstration at New York's Academy of Music. The purpose of the occasion was to expose the hoax begun at Hydesville. The rappings, Margaret first explained and then demonstrated for all to see (and hear), were caused by the snapping of the joint of her big toe. "That I have been mainly instrumental in perpetrating the fraud of spiritualism, you already know," she was reported as saying in the next day's New York *Herald.* "It is the greatest sorrow of my life. I began the deception when I was too young to know right from wrong." The newspaper account continues:

> There was a dead silence; everybody in the hall knew they were looking upon the woman who is principally responsible for spiritualism. She stood upon a little pine table, with nothing on her feet but stockings. As she remained motionless, loud distinct rappings were heard, now in the flies, now behind the scenes, now in the gallery.

It was Margaret who made the raps but, as before, it was the acoustical properties of the room that helped give the audience the illusion that the sounds were coming from different locations.

If Margaret Fox's confession has been made within a year or two of the famous occurrences at Hydesville, it is possible (though perhaps not likely, considering the failure of Dr. Lee) that spiritualism might have died in its infancy. However, by 1888 it was already far too late for even so sensational a revelation to have much effect on the movement as a whole. No doubt a few spiritualists were disillusioned by Margaret's self-exposure, but many more rushed to defend her and the movement she had founded.

It was publicly argued by various individuals and groups that Margaret had been forced into a false confession by the churches or bribed by the newspapers.

It was also pointed out, a little more reasonably, that the existence of one fraudulent medium did not prove that others were not genuine. Some even claimed that Margaret did not know her own powers, that she was a true medium in spite of herself. This view was bolstered by the unfortunate but undeniable fact that Kate and Margaret Fox had at this time become victims of alcoholism. Within five years they had both died in relative poverty and obscurity. In the end the only one to profit from the doings of Mr. Splitfoot was the wily Leah, who kept herself in comfort through mediumship and two marriages and bitterly resented her sisters' confessions (Kate later having joined in Margaret's statement).

Leah must have been pleased a year or so later when the two withdrew their confessions and began to give séances once again, a fact that also added fuel to the arguments of the spiritualists. However, there is little reason to believe that Margaret was not speaking the exact truth as she knew it on that evening in 1888. The astonishing thing is that in a mere forty years the spiritualist movement had become so firmly rooted that even a confession of fraud by its acknowledged founders would have little lasting effect.

The years since 1848 had seen spiritualism grow and develop at a rate that can still impress us today. Perhaps the twentieth century, with its instant, worldwide communications by satellite, has a tendency to regard the age before radio as one in which the flow of information was a mere trickle. Nevertheless, the idea of "spirit circles" raced across the country in record time. The topic was in the air. Mesmerism and the phenomena of the religious revival meeting had made Americans familiar with the notion of strange powers, whether as natural talents or as gifts of God. Furthermore, many of those who had become disillusioned with the various established religious creeds still felt the age-old need to believe in something beyond the everyday world. Recent scientific findings about electricity had also captured the popular imagination. An invisible force that flowed through metal and also made the lightning—what could be more mysterious? Not the happenings in the séance room. So now there was spiritualism, a way in which everyone could take part in one of the most exciting developments of the times. It was as if, tomorrow, someone should advertise a game with the slogan, "You and Your Friends Can Split the Atom, Right in Your Own Home!"

For a while it seemed that even the most casual contact with the Fox sisters was enough to bring out hidden spiritual powers. Several who stayed at the same boarding house as Kate during her visit to Auburn, New York in 1848 discovered that they too could produce rappings under séance conditions. Visitors from other cities seemed to take the manifestations home with them. As early as 1850 a newspaper account of the movement mentioned well-established spirit circles in Rochester, Auburn, and Syracuse, New York, in Hartford and Bridgeport, Connecticut, and in Springfield, Massachusetts, as well as many in New Jersey and "some two hundred" in Ohio. Considering the fact that there were then just thirty-one states in the Union (it was the year of California's admission) and that much of the territory beyond the Mississippi River was still the wildest sort of frontier or wilderness, this list indicates a very rapid growth indeed, and there is every reason to suppose that the larger cities of the South were soon equally affected.

The growth of spiritualism was not only geographical. Séance-room procedures also changed, particularly in the development of table tipping, for which no medium was needed. The method for table tipping was both simple and effective. All that was necessary was for several people to sit or stand around a small table, each one resting his hands or fingertips lightly on the surface. Frequently it was found that the table would move beneath the hands of the participants, tilting or tipping first one way and then another. If someone meanwhile called out the alphabet letter by letter, the "spirits" could spell out messages by causing the table to tilt each time the appropriate letter was reached. The great attraction of this approach was that it was not essential that a medium be present, although many future mediums first became aware of their powers through finding that the table tipped more vigorously when they were present. Table tipping was also, of course, an agreeable social pastime, especially among groups whose religious beliefs forbade them to "gamble" by taking part in card games.

Those who enjoyed table tipping at home often progressed to the more serious forms of spiritualism by attending genuine séances. There, too, the simplicity of the Foxes' rappings was soon abandoned in favor of more complicated but much more interesting techniques. For the first time in Western society the classic form of trance mediumship, as practiced by shamans and oracles, became known to a fairly wide audience. Trance mediums of the period spoke "spirit messages" that ranged all the way from personal (and sometimes strikingly accurate) trivia to hours-long public trance-lectures on subjects of the deepest philosophical and religious import. However, much of the material that constituted these communications was of doubtful value in proving the existence of "discarnate entities"—souls that were supposed to have left their bodies and gone on to another life as pure spirits. The entranced medium's dialogue with a sitter might go along some such lines as these:

MEDIUM: Chief Redwood [a spirit control] tells me there is the spirit of a young woman here who wishes to talk to you.

SITTER (eagerly): Yes, yes, I know who it must be.

MEDIUM: I think he says she was your sister. [Not very unlikely in those days of large families and high rates of infant mortality.]

SITTER: Amelia! Are you there?

MEDIUM: She says there was great affection between you. [Who will admit to having disliked a dead relative?]

SITTER: Oh, you are so right.

MEDIUM: She wants you to know she has been watching over you in spirit since her untimely death. [After all, what person who is "young," as specified at the beginning, has not died untimely?]

SITTER: How wonderful! It is Amelia for sure. She died suddenly of brain fever when she was only sixteen.

MEDIUM: She wants to know whether you remember the doll she was so fond of. [What little girl hasn't had a favorite doll?]

SITTER (overjoyed): Oh, yes, yes! The wooden doll Uncle Will gave her for Christmas when she was six. And so on.

The thing to notice about the entirely fictional but typical exchange above is that the medium really says nothing to the sitter except some pleasant generalities. The sitter, however, expects miracles and may easily leave the session with marvelous tales of the great medium who "told me all about my sister Amelia and her doll and how she died of brain fever." Furthermore, the sitter is probably genuinely convinced that he has "spoken to" his sister, partly because he sincerely wishes to do so and partly because in the emotion-laden situation of the séance he has made no attempt to separate what the medium told him from what he told her.

On the other hand, even at this early period of the movement, when few accurate records were kept, there were certainly some level-headed and initially skeptical people who came away from the séance room convinced that they had been given straightforward and highly factual descriptions and information concerning members of their families—information that they had certainly *not* told the medium themselves and that in some cases was known only to them. Later, when scientific analysis and record-keeping became more accurate, it was possible to go into such cases in great detail. However, a constant and confusing feature of the development of the spiritualist movement is this same mixture of transparent (and not so transparent) fraud with happenings that are much harder to explain in terms of the known laws of communication.

As trance mediumship grew in popularity, it produced many new kinds of phenomena. Like the shamans, most mediums insisted that the spirits could only work in darkness, so that many manifestations had to do with "spirit lights" and glowing objects. Thin veils of vapor or ghostly fabric often appeared to hang luminously before the sitters. Sometimes shining hands or arms were seen or even felt, grasping the spectators in a grip that was either cold and clammy or warm and lifelike.

Music also became a common feature of séances. Chimes, trumpets, tambourines, mandolins, or accordions appeared to play tunes in midair, a startling effect in those days before recorded music. In some cases a trumpet or megaphone hung suspended before the sitters and spoke to them directly with the voices of the alleged spirits. More rarely small objects seemed to appear out of thin air and rain down on the séance table. These apports, as they were called, were said to be souvenirs from the spirit world that had been materialized by the spirits as gifts for the sitters.

Many mediums gave written as well as spoken messages, by means of the planchette or through automatic writing, in which the entranced medium wrote as if at the spirits' dictation and sometimes, it was claimed, in the handwriting of the deceased. A third sort of message was slate-writing. In this method the words of the spirits were found written on the inner surfaces of two slates locked together face to face, and the hand that wielded the ghostly chalk was believed to be that of the spirit itself. Slate writing could thus be termed direct writing because it did not require the help of the medium's hand, just as the direct voice came from a point some distance away from the medium and did not seem to come from his mouth.

A different class of phenomena had to do with the medium's physical appearance. Frequently reported from the 1850s to modern times has been the elongation of the body, sometimes up to several inches. The spiritualist explanation was that the material of the medium's body was being stretched by the spirits. However, the ability to change one's height is not necessarily supernormal. Some individuals like the circus performer Clarence E. Willard (who died in 1962) are recorded to have the ability to "grow" up to six inches at will by using the muscles to stretch apart the bones of the spine.

A manifestation that became increasingly popular after the 1870s was the production of ectoplasm. The name of this mysterious material comes from two Greek words meaning "a substance exteriorized or extruded," and the drawing out of ectoplasm from the medium's body is said to sap his strength so that he is in a vulnerable condition and must never be touched, disturbed, or exposed to direct light while the materialization is taking place. Although it is plausible that the temporary loss of whatever is meant by this "material fraction of the life force" would be hazardous for the medium, it is unfortunate that the idea has repeatedly been used as an excuse to avoid any scientific examination of the supposed nature and uses of ectoplasm.

CHAPTER IV

"CURIOUSER AND CURIOUSER"

Historians are fond of remarking that the United States has, throughout its relatively short history, been a nation of extremes. Whether for good or ill, it has often been host to strong passions and great enthusiasms, which range from the vicious hysteria of the lynch mob to the ecstasies of the religious revival meeting and the rip-roaring progress of "gold fever" among the Forty-niners. This tendency to go a bit overboard is as apparent in the history of spiritualism as elsewhere in America.

Although spirit rappings, table tipping, and trance speaking were frequently and seriously undertaken by a wide variety of thoroughly respectable people, what are we to think of houses built according to plans transmitted by the spirits, of an invention called the Super-ray, which rivaled anything in a modern comic book, of spirit-directed murders, and of the construction of something called "The New Motor," a machine that was supposed to use spirit power to supply the world with endless electricity? Ranging from the crankish to the criminal, these developments of spiritualism constitute a fascinating sidelight on the United States in the middle of the nineteenth century.

The first of the peculiar houses referred to above was built by a farmer named Jonathan Koons in Dover, Ohio in 1852. Koons constructed it especially for the holding of séances, according to the design laid down by the spirits. It was a free-standing log cabin about twelve feet by sixteen and was equipped with all sorts of spiritualist paraphernalia such as tables, trumpets, tambourines, and phosphorus paint.

The spirits who directed Koons to build this spirit room claimed to be those of 165 men who had lived before the time of Adam. They promised Koons that the spirit room, if correctly built, would help him and his eight children to develop their spirit gifts and become powerful mediums. Whether or not all of the eight young Koonses did in fact become mediums is uncertain, but their father achieved considerable local fame for his abilities, and the design of the spirit room was widely copied among spiritualists of the Midwest.

An even more exotic invention for the development of mediumistic gifts was the Super-ray, the cherished discovery of a Mr. N. Zwann in the early 1850s. It is not clear what, if any, actual rays were generated by the device built by Mr. Zwann, but it was claimed that the Super-rays had the ability to induce mediumship in susceptible individuals or even to substitute for the medium altogether in the production of physical phenomena such as levitation and apportation (the appearance in the séance room of objects seemingly materialized out of thin air). Zwann was the founder of an organization called The Spirit Electronic Communication Society, one of whose purposes was spiritual healing. At one time the Society had quite a number of adherents, and it was not until 1952 that the whole thing was definitively exposed as a fraud. It would probably have been a harmless fraud if it were not for the possible injury to those who sought medical treatment from the Super-rays rather than going to reputable physicians.

Very far from harmless, however, were the murders and other crimes committed, it was claimed, at the prompting of the spirits. For example, in October 1851, a girl of thirteen was brought to trial on a charge of having killed her infant brother. Almira Bezely had been one of the many who had been seized by the spiritualist craze and had become a rapping medium a few months before. According to the story told at the trial, the baby's death had been predicted by the spirits who spoke through Almira, and she had become convinced that she must make the prophecy come true. Aside from its shock value, Almira's case is interesting because it suggests an explanation of the girl's mediumship that has nothing to do with spirits.

Every reader of detective stories knows that the first question to be asked in a case of murder is, "Who benefits?" And, upsetting as the idea may be, the answer in this case could well be Almira herself. At this distance in time, of course, we cannot know the circumstances well enough to make a definite judgment, even if we were judge, jury, and clinical psychologists in one. But Almira would not be the first child to be jealous of the attention given a younger one. The strange thing here is not, perhaps, that Almira should have wished her brother dead, but that the prevailing climate of spiritualism allowed her to feed her fantasies to such an extent that she came to believe she was not responsible for her own actions because "the spirits command it." The situation belongs more properly in a casebook of insanity than in a history of spiritualism.

The same thing could be said of the remarkable story of the Wakemanites. The entire background of Mrs. Rhoda Wakeman, the founder of the sect, is too long to tell here, but its outlines are as follows. Before the day in December 1855 when she came to prominence via the courtroom, Mrs. Wakeman had lived for many years in New Haven, Connecticut. Her life had been full of unusual experiences, the very least of which had been the bearing of seventeen children. At one time a practicing medium, she had, she testified, been murdered by her husband at some unspecified time in the past. Presumably because of her relations with the spirit world, however, she had been resurrected after lying dead for seven hours. She was carried up to heaven, where she had personal interviews with both Jesus and God the Father. In the course of her stay in heaven Mrs. Wakeman learned that she was to be the savior of the world. She was then returned to earth alive and well—much to the surprise of her husband, one supposes.

Though Mr. Wakeman, her alleged murderer, died somewhat later of natural causes, the widow's troubles were not over. A few years later it was revealed to her by the spirits that a man named Amos Hunt had put an evil demon into a friend of hers by the name of Justus Matthews. The devilish purpose of this act was to force Matthews to poison the medium. If this were to happen, Mrs. Wakeman and her followers believed, the entire universe would immediately be destroyed. It was to save the world from such disaster that Matthews *volunteered* to allow himself to be murdered. So, at least, the group testified later. And so bizarre was the mental state of the Wakemanites that it seems possible Matthews did indeed offer to sacrifice himself for Rhoda Wakeman (and the universe).

In any case, all the evidence agreed that Justus Matthews had been beaten to death with a club made of witch hazel in the hands of Mrs. Wakeman's brother—a man with the sinister name of Samuel Sly. Though Sly later swore he "was influenced by a wrong spirit to go further than I had anticipated, or had any idea of," he certainly made very sure of his victim. Matthews had his throat cut "several times" and was also stabbed with a fork.

The trial of the Wakemanites, seven of whom were indicted on various charges, naturally caused quite a sensation. At the close of the trial Mrs. Wakeman added a dramatic climax by rising and warning the court that if any of her followers were convicted the world would come to an end forthwith. However, the jury refused to be quelled and convicted Samuel Sly of murder and another of the group as accessory. Mrs. Wakeman was detained in a state institution for the insane until her death in 1859. Apparently, the mere imprisonment of the medium was not sufficient to bring on the end of the world.

Even more eccentric than Rhoda Wakeman, and certainly more widely influential, was John Murray Spear. Originally an eminent preacher of the American Universalist Church, Spear became a convert to spiritualism in 1851. As a trance medium he produced immense (and immensely tedious) volumes of spiritualist sermons, but later became involved in more unusual activities. In 1853 a band of spirits calling themselves the Association of Beneficents made themselves manifest through his mediumship. This Association revealed the existence of six other similar groups. These were called, respectively but ungrammatically, the Electrizers, the Healthfulizers, the Educationizers, the Agriculturalizers, the Elementizers, and the Governmentizers.

It was the Association of Electrizers that eventually gave Spear the instructions for his great work. He was to construct, for the benefit of mankind, a New Motor. This invention would at the same time demonstrate the principle of a hitherto unknown power source and be, in Spear's term, "self-generative." It was explained that the device would work by feeding upon the endless magnetic life of Nature (whatever that meant). Especially to be noted is the fact that the New Motor was to be not only a sort of perpetual motion device but a living organism rather like those that appear in twentieth-century science fantasy.

Now, there is nothing in itself bizarre about the dreaming up and building of strange mechanisms, as could be testified by inventors from Aristotle to Wilbur and Orville Wright. But the New Motor was something special. Spear built it in a wooden shed at a place called High Rock near Lynn, Massachusetts. The complicated mass of zinc and copper then stood waiting for the ceremony that was to make it literally spring to life.

A disciple of Spear's who was probably Mrs. Semantha Mettler (though she was delicately referred to in subsequent newspaper accounts as Mrs. ___), had been notified in a vision that she was to become the spiritual "mother" of the New Motor. The lady took herself to High Rock, where she fell into a trance and appeared to all onlookers to be suffering from violent birth pangs. After two hours of convulsive labor on the part of the "mother," Spear's awed and reverential followers were rewarded by signs of movement from the machine, which then settled down to a steady pulsation. Thereafter, for the first few weeks of its "life," the Motor was treated with the care appropriate to a newborn child and hailed by its enthusiasts as "the Art of all Arts, the Science of all Sciences, the New Messiah, God's last Best Gift to Man."

Unfortunately, the Motor failed to fulfill its primary purpose, the supplying of endless electric power. It was therefore moved to Randolph, New York, a spot that was thought to be more favorably located with regard to natural electric currents. Spear and his disciples had not reckoned on the unfavorable nature of one other feature of Randolph, however. The determined if superstitious villagers refused to have anything to do with "God's last Best Gift to Man." One night a band of them broke into the shed that housed the Motor and smashed it to smithereens.

Thus perished the New Motor movement. Even among spiritualists, it was felt by many that J. M. Spear had gone a bit too far. Andrew Jackson Davis (a highly respected medium of whom we shall hear more in a later chapter) came to the conclusion that some of the less responsible inhabitants of the spirit world had been conducting an experiment at Spear's expense. If so, the expense involved was real as well as metaphorical. The construction of the Motor had cost Spear two thousand dollars, so that the "last Best Gift" could more logically be said to have been made by Spear to the spirits.

What has just been said of the more eccentric aspects of spiritualism will be helpful in understanding why the rapid rise of the movement was not made without opposition. The citizens of Randolph, New York, had merely been more violent than most in expressing their disapproval of the spirits in their midst. The attitude of many of the organized churches was no less unfavorable, and the 1850s saw the calling of public prayer meetings to beg for the disappearance of mediumism and other devilish manifestations. Then, as now, attacks on spiritualism were made from two principal points of view.

The more conservative religious groups held the the opinion that communion with the spirits was *possible* but that it was evil or at least dangerous to the welfare of one's soul, while the scientific realists believed that communication was *impossible* and that all spiritualists must be frauds or candidates for the asylum. To both groups, the so-called spiritualist murders such as those involving Almira Bezely and the Wakemanites appeared to confirm their conviction that spiritualism must in some way be morally damaging. All that need be said of this argument is that there has never been a group of people whose members were entirely free of crime, and the spiritualists were no exception. Whenever something new appears on the human scene, it seems that some people are frightened by it and try to blame it for all the world's troubles, whether "it" should be a change in women's fashions, a religious reform, a new kind of entertainment, or a scientific invention.

Still another objection to spiritualism was made on the grounds of its supposed association with the then revolutionary notion of "free love." It was true that at least one early group of spiritualists had come out in favor of disregarding the ties of marriage in their spiritual (and sexual) life, but the idea was by no means a genuine part of spiritualist belief. And though the ceremonies surrounding the birth of the New Motor were a little unusual, even by modern standards, they were certainly nothing like the prolonged orgy of perversion that was hinted at by the lip-licking sensationalist press of the period.

The third, and probably the most damaging objection to spiritualism was based on its attitude to the beliefs of the churches. Even those who did not hold that spiritualist practices were evil in themselves were disturbed by the thought that spiritualism might lead its adherents into heresy or unbelief. The religious claims of John Spear and Rhoda Wakeman were undoubtedly sacrilegious by most standards and there were many who feared that spiritualism would spell the end of religious (which in those days meant Christian) piety in the country.

The opponents of spiritualism were often as energetic as its advocates. In addition to denunciations in the press, public prayer meetings, and occasional acts of mob violence, they organized lecture tours at which to express their views. The lecture tour was a very popular entertainment in those premovie days, and speakers on controversial subjects often attracted large audiences. In 1857, there took place one such lecture that proved even more exciting than anticipated.

The speaker was the Reverend C. H. Harvey, a former spiritualist who had given up attending séances when he became convinced that he could not reconcile a belief in spirits with the teachings of his church. This course had not made him popular with the spiritualists, and his decision to attack their ideas in public had made him even less so.

On this evening Harvey was just reaching the climax of his speech when he suddenly collapsed upon the platform. A doctor in the audience rushed up, examined Harvey, and pronounced him dead. However, before the the startled watchers could take in the scene another man, a spiritualist, bent over the victim and succeeded in reviving him. The whole affair appeared even more astonishing when it was found that, although Harvey was certainly not dead, he had been struck dumb. Naturally, the public impression was that the hand of God, or at least of Providence, had smitten the former spiritualist in order to prevent him from slandering the spirits. Harvey himself, it is said, took the more sinister view that he had been the victim of a spirit attack.

Though a modern psychologist would probably explain Harvey's unconsciousness and subsequent inability to speak as a hysterical reaction to his conflicting feelings about the lecture, such a view of the event would not make it any less clear that the emotions of the time were running very high on the topic of spiritualism. In fact, the movement suffered a rather serious, though temporary, decline in the period approximately from 1856 to the end of the Civil War. In 1860, the State of Alabama went so far as to enact a law fining anyone who gave a public demonstration of spiritualism the rather hefty sum of five hundred dollars. And in the years immediately following, the country had too much on its mind to pay more than passing attention to spiritualism.

In the postwar period, however, the movement proved in some ways stronger than ever. The sad thing about any war is that at its end there are large numbers of bereaved wives and parents. For them, spiritualism seemed to hold out hope of direct communication with those who had died in the war, and persons of every economic and social level flocked to the séance parlors.

Several prominent advocates of spiritualism continued their support as strongly as ever, particularly New York Supreme Court Judge John Worth Edmonds. It was even rumored that President Lincoln had become interested in the movement before his assassination. But although it is certainly true that medium Charles E. Shockle gave a sitting for the Lincolns at the White House in April of 1863, there is no real evidence to indicate that the President himself was any more than a detached observer. He might have repeated on that occasion a wry comment he had made two years earlier after hearing a long dissertation on spiritualism. "Well," remarked Lincoln to the paper's distinguished author, Robert D. Owen, "for those who like that sort of thing I should think that is just about the sort of thing they would like." Nevertheless, Lincoln's name had become linked with spiritualism, if only by suggestion, a fact that surely did no harm to the movement's prestige.

In fact, by the late 1860s, spiritualism had already become quite firmly established as an international phenomenon. Introduced into England as early as 1852 by the American medium Mrs. W. B. Hayden, it had quickly spread to the rest of the British Isles and continental Europe. Mesmerism and various forms of magnetic healing had of course been popular in those areas for some time, but it was Mrs. Hayden's contribution to make believers in the power of the spirit world consider the possibility of communicating with the ones on "the other side," rather than simply using them for man's benefit.

As an introduction to spiritualist practices, Mrs. Hayden was a good deal less spectacular than the Fox sisters had been. She was the wife of a Boston newspaper editor, and her mediumship consisted of a limited sort of rapping that never became either as fluent or as complex as that of the Foxes or many other mediums. She made her historic trip to England in the company of a man named Stone, of whom little is known except that he called himself a lecturer on "electro-biology"—a technique of hypnotism that made use of metal disks. Mrs. Hayden soon outshone her mentor, drawing crowds to her sittings at half a guinea each.

However, most of the British press was quick to ridicule her supposed powers. It was claimed that her control spirit could not even spell out messages alphabetically unless she herself could see the alphabet as each letter was indicated. If true, this fact should have roused suspicions in even the most credulous, since all the more accomplished spirits of the time seemed quite independent of the medium in their ability to "see" the letters. Nevertheless, sitters sometimes claimed to have received information about their departed friends and relatives that could certainly not have been known to the medium through ordinary sources, and a number of influential people became convinced of the genuineness of her phenomena. Among them were Robert Owen (father of the Robert Dale Owen who was to read his paper on spiritualism to Lincoln) and Professor Augustus de Morgan, a well-known mathematician and logician. Mrs. Hayden and another American medium, Mrs. Roberts, who followed her to England, were undoubtedly the founders of the movement in Britain, even though both ladies shortly returned to the United States.

Among the developments that followed closely upon the visits of these first emissaries of spiritualism were the founding of the first Spiritualist Church in the town of Keighley (1853) and the publication of the *Yorkshire Spiritual Telegraph* (1854).

Already in these earliest days of British spiritualism, two tendencies had appeared that were to set off the movement in Britain from its more flamboyant American counterpart. The first, as indicated above, was toward organizations. For though there have been plenty of spiritualist churches, spiritualist papers, and spiritualist associations on the western side of the Atlantic, their British equivalents have usually been both more numerous, more stable, and more widely patronized.

A second trend that spiritualism encountered in the European sphere was much more important for the development of the movement as a whole. Scientific research before the turn of the century was very much farther advanced in the Old World than in the New, and although the situation in the United States improved steadily after the end of the Civil War, it would be many years before the spiritualist hypotheses and happenings could have been given such thorough testing at home as they were to receive at the hands of British and continental scientists.

The period of the great mediums and the equally great men of science who investigated them was at this time (roughly the first twenty years of the spiritualist movement) still in the future. However, the introduction of spiritualism into England had already led to one important scientific development by the middle of 1853. The man responsible was Michael Faraday, whose pioneering experiments with electricity are still mentioned in textbooks of physics. Faraday became upset by the unscientific attitudes of the majority of researchers into spiritualist phenomena and decided to make his own investigation. Since at that early date the most popular forms of spirit communication were by raps and table tipping, Faraday fixed on the latter for close examination. (Perhaps he felt that the rappings had already been accounted for by the report on the Fox sisters in 1850 and other, similar exposures of later date.)

At any rate, Faraday spent a good deal of time in the presence of tipping tables and then came up with a very ingenious device to apply to them. It was his hypothesis that the tables moved on account of the *unconscious* expectations of the sitters, which expressed themselves in muscular pressure. The flat boards and glass rollers of his measuring device clearly indicated that his guess was correct—it was almost impossible not to respond ever so slightly to the séance situation with tiny movements that were quite enough to move a light table.

The reaction that Faraday thus discovered is a somewhat cruder version of the principle that governs the modern "lie detector test," or polygraph. In the case of the polygraph, the subject's heart rate, skin tone, respiration rate, and other involuntary physical functions respond automatically to the subject's knowledge that he has told a lie. In the table tipping situation, the subject's muscles respond automatically to his unconscious expectations about what the supposed spirit will say. The tendency is for the unconscious mind of the person who is most strongly affected in this way to dominate the "message" that is produced at any one sitting.

A little consideration will show that Faraday's discovery also gives a good explanation of such ancient devices for producing automatic messages as the planchette and the ouija board. They all rely for their effect on the tiny movements of the members of the group using them. It is worth emphasizing, however, that those who participate may easily be quite unaware of what is going on and are thus completely honest in asserting that they have not affected the movement of the device in any way. It should also be pointed out that Faraday's experiments are not universally accepted in spiritualist circles. There are still some who believe that the touch of several hands acts as a focus for spiritual energy and that the messages received are produced by disembodied intelligences.

Of course, table tipping and planchette writing are only relatively minor aspects of spirit communication. They have nothing to do with the genuineness of trance mediumship, materialization, levitation, apports, and the host of other phenomena that flourished during the later history of the movement. They, too, were investigated by famous and indisputably competent scientists, with results both interesting and puzzling. But before proceeding to look at these later developments along the lines of scientific investigation, we should take some time to consider spiritualism's other major sphere of influence, that of religion and philosophy.

CHAPTER V

THE POUGHKEEPSIE SEER
IN SUMMER-LAND

In some respects, the middle decades of the nineteenth century in the United States must have been among the yeastiest and most volatile in the history of religion. Not only did many of the established Protestant sects produce their own splinter groups, but the continuously arriving stream of European immigrants included religious nonconformists of every shade of opinion from dozens of national backgrounds. The relations between these bodies were not always serene, by any means, especially in the less staid frontier regions. Nevertheless, dissent, within certain ill-defined limits, was met with more tolerance than was generally available anywhere else in the world at that time.

As we have seen, the happenings at Hydesville initiated a sort of spiritualist craze, so that in its early days it could as well have been called a popular pastime as a movement. The Fox sisters and the more adept trance mediums who followed them had established a technique for the (so to speak) practical side of spiritualism. But it was not until the events of the séance room were fitted

into theory or philosophy that spiritualism became a full-
fledged system of belief.

The most important insight into this branch of spiritualism in America is to be found in the work of a
remarkable man named Andrew Jackson Davis (1826–
1910). Born in Bloomington Grove, New York, Davis
was gifted with clairvoyance and began to hear voices
while still a child. His father was a poor and allegedly
drunken shoemaker, who provided his son with no education whatsoever up to the age of sixteen, when he was
apprenticed to a man named Armstrong, also a shoemaker.

The Davis family was living in Poughkeepsie, New
York, at that time, and young Andrew Jackson was
among those who went to hear a series of lectures on
mesmerism given in that city by a Dr. S. J. Grimes. The
lectures included demonstrations of mesmeric technique.
Davis volunteered himself as a subject, and though he
failed to go into a trance on the lecture platform, he
apparently became fascinated with mesmerism. After the
departure of Dr. Grimes, Davis persuaded a local tailor
named Livingston to make further attempts. These were
successful. Davis not only became entranced, but practiced clairvoyant medical diagnosis while in the trance
condition.

All this had occurred in 1843. The next year, Davis
had an experience which, like the similar crises of personalities from Buddha to St. Francis, was to change his
life. In a condition of semitrance, he wandered away
from Poughkeepsie and came to himself the next day to
find that he had traveled forty miles into the mountains.
There, he recalled, he had been visited by the spirits of

the great early Greek physician Galen and the Swedish mystical philosopher Emanuel Swedenborg (1688–1772).

Under the influence of this experience, Davis began to write and teach on spiritual subjects, especially magnetism. Soon he had attracted to himself a sort of retinue consisting of the Reverend William Fishbough and a Dr. Lyon. Fishbough was Davis' official recorder, while Lyon's function was to put the Poughkeepsie Seer, as he had come to be called, into trance when required. Thus attended, Davis embarked on the book that was to make his reputation. Its title was *The Principles of Nature, Her Divine Revelations, and a Voice to Mankind* and the manner of its composition was unusual. Davis, having been placed in trance by Dr. Lyon, would dictate to Lyon, who in turn repeated the words for transcription by Fishbough. This method would have had the advantage of allowing both attendants, who were men of education, to regularize Davis' prose before it reached final form, though it was later denied that any such editing had taken place. (Davis, as has been mentioned, had no formal schooling.)

It should be pointed out here that the type of trance that Davis exhibited cannot properly be called mediumistic. During part of his career he required the services of a mesmerist in order to enter the trance state. Further, Davis' own account of his trances makes it clear that he did not usually have the experience of conversing with the spirits of particular individuals. Instead, he said, "I possess the power of extending my vision throughout all space, can see through past, present, and to come. I have now arrived at the highest degree of knowledge which the human mind is capable of acquiring . . . I am master of the general sciences, can speak all languages," and so forth. His title of Poughkeepsie Seer was accurate, since his trance writings were the result of general inspiration and not of the individual communication later claimed by trance writing mediums.

After fifteen months of dictation, the *Principles, Revelations, and Voice* was published in the summer of 1847 and was an immediate success. This fact was due in some measure at least to the support of the Reverend George Bush, a highly respected professor of Hebrew at New York University. Bush not only vouched for the genuineness of Davis' trance, but praised the book itself in glowing terms. "Taken as a whole, the work is a profound and elaborate discussion of the philosophy of the universe, and for grandeur of conception, soundness of principle, clearness of illustration, order of arrangement, and encyclopedic range of subjects, I know no work of any single mind that will bear away from it the palm."

Elsewhere Bush added that the style was "easy, flowing, chaste, appropriate, and with a certain indescribable simplicity which operates like a charm on the reader." From such a description, one might suppose the work would achieve unanimous acceptance as a university text in philosophy.

It will be worthwhile for us to look at Davis' book more closely, for it was certainly remarkable, though perhaps not in the way Professor Bush suggested. Its nearly eight hundred pages are divided, as the complete title suggests, into three sections. The *Principles* is an outline of mystical philosophy, the *Revelations* reviews the religious history of mankind and the history of the universe, while the *Voice* contains semipractical prescriptions for man's future, developed along the lines of a primitive socialism. An idea of the style and contents of the book can be had from Davis' description of the origin of the universe.

> In the beginning the Univercoelum was one boundless, undefinable, and unimaginable ocean of liquid Fire! The most vigorous and ambitious imagination is not capable of forming an adequate conception of the depth and length and breadth thereof. There was one vast expanse of liquid substance. It was without bounds—inconceivable—and with qualities and essences incomprehensible. This was the original condition of matter. It was without forms, for it was but one Form. It had not motions, but was an eternity of Motion. It was without parts, for it was a Whole. Particles did not exist, but the whole was *one* Particle. There were not suns, but it was one Eternal Sun. It has no beginning, and it was without end. It had not length, for it was a Vortex of one Eternity. It had not circles, for it was one Infinite Circle. It had not disconnected power, but it was the very essence of all Power. Its inconceivable magnitude and constitution were such as not to develop forces, but Omnipotent Power. (Thirty-fourth American edition; Boston, 1875, pp. 121–22)

It is a temptation just to go on quoting this passage indefinitely. There is such a fine, sonorous tone to the prose that one is instantly reminded of the quality that Professor Bush thought operated "like a charm on the reader." The whole thing is reminiscent in style of that other great description of the same event, the first chapter of Genesis. And since everything is specified to be "undefinable," "unimaginable," "inconceivable," it is not very useful to argue with the author whether the universe really did originate in this fashion.

Later portions of Davis' exposition are not so immune to criticism. Even leaving out of consideration the changes that 120 years of subsequent research have made in the state of our scientific knowledge, Davis' spiritual sources reveal themselves as decidedly fallible.

> Chemistry will unfold the fact that *light*, when confined in a certain condition and condensed, will produce *water*, and that water thus formed, subjected to the vertical influence of light, will produce, by its internal motion and further condensation, a gelatinous substance of the composition of the spirifer, the motion of which indicates animal life. This again being decomposed and subjected to evaporation. The precipitated particles which still remain will produce putrified matter similar to earth, which will produce the plant known as the *fucoides*. It is on the results of this experiment (the truth of which, as above represented, can be universally ascertained) that rests the probability, though not the absolute certainty, of the truth of the description which I am about to give concerning the first form possessing life. (page 237)

It is hardly necessary to point out that since water is a compound of hydrogen and oxygen (a fact revealed by

Lavoisier more than fifty years before Davis began to write), the all-knowing spiritual influences that allegedly directed Davis in his trance should have been aware of the fact. And though the book does follow a broadly evolutionary view of life on this planet, its "scientific" passages are so packed with similar gobbledegook as to put it in a class with the most imaginative vintage science fantasy.

Other parts of the book attracted much more public attention. For example, attached to a discussion of life on other planets there is the following prophecy:

> It is a truth that spirits commune with one another while one is in the body and the other in the higher spheres . . . and this truth will ere long present itself in the form of a living demonstration. And the world will hail with delight the ushering-in of that era when the interiors of men will be opened, and the spiritual communion will be established such as is now being enjoyed by the inhabitants of Mars, Jupiter, and Saturn. (pages 675 and 676)

The day when the Fox family moved to Hydesville was only a few months away at the time of the book's publication. For this reason, many of his increasing number of followers later considered Davis to be something like the St. John the Baptist of spiritualism—the announcer of things to come. Others would have found the comparison blasphemous. The latter group would not have been pleased by Davis' views on the Bible either. A portion of the *Revelations* is devoted to a book-by-book examination of the Old and New Testaments, in which the author disputes their claim to be the exclusive source for the word of God and suggests that Jesus was no more than a great moral teacher with no claim to divinity.

Probably this last assertion was the reason why Professor Bush disavowed his support of the work soon after its appearance. In a small pamphlet entitled *Davis' Revelations Revealed*, he warned the public against accepting the book's errors, although he still maintained that Davis himself had been no more than misled by ill-educated and mischievous spirits. Apparently, the professor had not completely read the volume before praising it so enthusiastically a few months earlier.

By this time, however, it was much too late to halt the work's acceptance. In those days before best-seller lists, a book's success was best gauged by its printing history. *Principles, Etc.* came out in thirty-four editions in the space of its first thirty years and was widely read in Europe as well as in the United States.

But it was neither his visions of the history of the universe nor his implied attack on orthodox Christianity that formed Davis' most lasting contribution to spiritualist thought. It was his general view of various stages in the moral progress of the spirit. Both in the *Principles* and in some thirty volumes of his later work, Davis described his view of the afterlife in vast detail, calling his system as a whole The Great Harmonia. Its ever-elaborated complexity makes it extremely difficult to summarize, but there are certain central ideas that can be discerned. The soul is constantly progressing from a lower to a higher state. What we call the real world is in fact only a rather minor way-station on the path to truth, whereas the trance world is in actuality far more "real."

The universe is one great harmonious whole, in which the ruling principle is one of correspondences. Thus everything in this world has analogies both above and below in the spiritual scale. Angels are simply more advanced spirits, some of whom have been assigned to help those who are still "in the body" in their quest for enlightenment. Thus a few of the spirit controls who manifest themselves at séances are not the recently dead who seek to reassure the living of their continued existence, but are much more "advanced" beings who have almost forgotten their original identity as they become more and more absorbed in the universal wisdom.

Davis does not say so specifically in his account of the spirit system, but it was an easy deduction for later spiritualists that the "spirit teachers" who busied themselves with mankind in this way were performing something of a sacrifice. It was as if a group of great mathematical geniuses should spend their time teaching numbers to a kindergarten class.

Many famous mediums of later decades were controlled by spirits of this type, who gave themselves such names as White Eagle, Zodiac, and Imperator. Books of spiritual wisdom were dictated under their influence, although, like the spirit inspirers of Davis himself, they sometimes turned out to have been mistaken in matters of scientific fact. A further disadvantage of these higher spirits, from the point of view of the psychic investigator, was that they could not profitably be questioned about their past lives. Either they had lived incredibly long ago,

like the "predecessors of Adam" who instructed Mr.
Koons in the building of spirit rooms, or their past exist-
ences had become as dim to them as our first two or
three years of life generally are to us.

Returning to Davis' classification of spirits, we have
already seen that besides the recently dead and the
highly evolved spirit teachers, there is a third group
best described as mischievous. These spirits constituted
something of a problem for spiritualists, since to admit
that some spirits were positively evil would have been
to grant the truth of the view that conducting a séance
was akin to trafficking with the devil. Yet it could
hardly be denied that incidents like the building of the
New Motor were obvious failures in spite of the alleged
spirit guidance that accompanied them. Such events were
put down to the existence of spirits at a very low level
of enlightenment, not malicious but merely too un-
educated spiritually to comprehend the results of their
actions. They are like small children who poke at ants'
nests with sticks because they are genuinely curious to
see how the ants will react.

The world inhabited by all these types of spirits (who
are really the same, though at different stages in their
education) was christened by Davis the Summer-Land.
It is one of the most appealing aspects of his system
that there appear to be no permanent places of punishment in it. The various spheres he describes are all
heavenly to a greater or lesser degree, so that his view
of the afterlife is like that of the great poet Dante,
but with the inferno left out and only purgatory and
paradise remaining. Yet, though Davis' system lacks the
more horrifying aspects of the traditional hell, there is

no abandonment of the idea of reward and punishment in the afterlife. One's rank in the Summer-Land is rigorously determined by one's moral worth rather than by surface appearances. It is thus the individual's duty to seek enlightenment while on earth so that he may not have to spend eons in remedial education when he enters the spirit realm.

To acknowledge the reality of spirits and seek their advice is a sign of great wisdom. Similarly, to scoff at spiritualist beliefs or to investigate them with too skeptical an attitude is to demonstrate that one is at a low stage of development, not yet ready for higher things. Understandably, those who do not agree with spiritualist teachings have always found this last statement particularly irritating. In the latter part of the nineteenth century there appeared an alternate notion of the fate of skeptics. Those who had refused to believe while in this life, it was suggested, would remain unaware of the delights of the Summer-Land after death as well, perhaps by self-hypnosis. One can't help remarking that this constitutes a sort of spiritual blackmail: The deliberate unbeliever had better reconsider or he won't even be allowed to discover his error but will condemn himself to an eternity of blindness.

For most, however, death is only the gateway to further development. It is not precisely clear whether the Summer-Land is itself divided into several spheres or whether it is only one (the second) of a series that becomes ever more sublime. In different places Davis uses the term in different ways. Possibly he wanted to say that, though there are other spheres beyond the Summer-Land, not even the most educated souls in this

world are capable of receiving or comprehending information about them. One particular passage seems to
imply as much.

> What would you say if you should hear something
> concerning the third sphere, of the one beyond that,
> or of another and still higher? I have seen mediums
> who think they receive communications from in-
> numerable upper places! No. Many of them have
> not heard from the gifted in these Brotherhoods.
> Now and then some one of them says, "Oh, that
> is nothing! *I* get communications from the seventh
> heaven—way up out of sight!" That is all ecstatic
> inspiration without any analyzing judgment—no rev-
> elation to balance the mind in truth. Men and
> women get more humility when they get more
> wisdom. (*Death and the After-life*, page 75)

In any case, the idea of the different spheres has been
developed at vast (and often confused) length by later
writers. What is important is that after Davis the idea
of the spheres became a semipermanent part of the
spiritualist movement. And now we shall take a somewhat more detailed look at the Summer-Land and its
inhabitants, although space unfortunately allows us only
a ten-cent tour of that fascinating realm. The passages
quoted are taken from one of Davis' later books, a fairly
concise lecture entitled *Death and the After-life*, published in 1876.

> The Summer-Land is vastly more beautiful than
> the most beautiful landscape on earth. Celestial waters

are more limpid, the atmosphere more soft and genial, the streams are always musical, and the fertile islands there are ever full of meanings. The trees are not exotics. The birds are literally a part of the celestial clime, every one having its lesson of divine significance. (page 21)

On later pages Davis becomes even more lyrical about the scenes of Summer-Land.

In 1854, I had an opportunity, for the first time, to contemplate a celestial garden. It was unlike anything I had ever seen in this world. The Garden of the Hesperides, of which we dream, only vulgarly represents the beautiful fact. When I saw the immense landscape and the innumerable beauties that come up from the soil, and the labyrinth of leafage which gathered upon the vision to the right of the scene, I could not but ask, "Will some one not tell me the extent?" After a few moments a cerebro-tele-graphic dispatch came into the mind, whispering distinctly, "It would reach from here to Scotland —near four thousand miles in length—five hundred miles in width." It seemed to be a far-extending avenue of flowers and beautiful trees, and there seemed no limit to the number of persons that were walking leisurely, lovingly, arm-in-arm; and oh! the thousands of beautiful children that were at play through the devious labyrinths of that vast heavenly park! (page 39)

I saw celestial birds that excluded all rays except the *yellow*. They were singularly, wonderfully yellow —quite different from the hue of the canary. It

seemed as though composed of yellow crystalline
air. I could see the nervous systems of these birds
—their whole physical interior—they were so transparent. They were, I observed, swift in their flight.
I also saw a bird which excludes all rays save that
of *blue*, and that looked like a diamond cut out of
pure ethereal immensity. I never could have imagined
anything so expressive of pure, immense, heavenly
love! This particular bird was a representative, I saw,
of universal private affection. The yellow bird was
also a representative. It had a great meaning—the
mellower affection which comes from wisdom. (page
41)

The Summer-Land has a specific, as well as a general
geography, and this also is described in detail. Some of
its place names alone are enough to convey the atmosphere of the place. One of its chief islands is called
Akropanamede, on which there is a spring called Poril-
leum. Most of the island's inhabitants are occupied in
the education and cure of souls who have deluded themselves while on earth with the love of earthly objects.
Other islands are called Rosalia, Lonalia, Alium,
Poleski, and so on, each one being dedicated to a particular aspect of Summer-Landish existence. There are also
temples devoted to various purposes and bearing such
names as Hospitalia and Concilium. As for the actual
spatial location of the Summer-Land, Davis has this to
say:

It may seem to your imaginations that this spiritual
world is afar off—that it must be a vast and remote
existence, because astronomers have not peered into

it. But it is my belief that astronomers, with their physical instruments, will one of these fortunate future days, recognize the Summer-Land, and I believe, furthermore, that astronomers will see landscapes and physical scenes there more clearly than those vague images which are now revealed through telescopes, as existing upon the moon and different rolling stars. (page 36)

Since, in one of his earlier books, the distance of the Summer-Land from Earth had already been specified as fifty million miles, it seems that the Spirit Realm is not to be taken symbolically but is actually inside the solar system, either somewhere near the orbit of Mars (if it is farther from the sun than we) or between the orbits of Venus and Mercury (if it is nearer). Yet there is no suggestion that the Summer-Land is located *on* any of those bodies, since the spirits of Martians and Venusians are to be found in the Summer-Land along with those from Earth.

Those who live in the Summer-Land seem to spend much of their time either in self-education or in unspecified "philanthropic labors." Yet no one should make the mistake of supposing that life there is all work and no play. Not only are there music and feasting, described in sumptuous terms, but Davis' vision has even informed him about the style of dress among the spirits.

Those of both sexes . . . wear clothing of various appearance and wondrous fashions, different from anything you would or could imagine. I have never yet seen any silken gauze or gossamer fabrics to compare with the garments there used. Many wear a peculiar flowing dress, which, in a moment, can be either wound about the person in graceful folds or taken off. This garment, for either man or woman, is appropriate and beautiful beyond all imitation. (page 50)

Social life, too, is highly developed. There are numerous societies or associations in which gather those who have special interests, such as healing, or those who share particular beliefs. Catholics, Gnostics, Ancient Greeks, and the followers of Mohammed are only a few of those who come together in this manner. Furthermore, far from abolishing ties of love and kinship, as do some other views of the afterlife, Davis describes these relationships as even stronger there than in the Winter-Land (Earth). In the Summer-Land each person is united with his spiritual mate, whether or not the two were married, or even ever met one another in their lifetimes. Likewise the children of indifferent parents find their true spiritual mothers and fathers, and, of course, long-parted relatives are here reunited.

One has to admit that many of Davis' ideas are very attractive. The man was no narrow sectarian preaching salvation for a small group of followers. Neither was he a grim advocate of fasting and penitence, in either of the two worlds. Instead, he offered his followers a poetic (though high-flown and conventionalized) picture of things to come, coupled with assurances that almost no one who made the slightest effort to be worthy would be considered beyond saving. It was a compassionate and humane system, and it attained very wide circulation among spiritualists for more than a century.

It would of course be a mistake to imagine that Davis was the sole inventor of the ideas characterizing the Great Harmonia and the Summer-Land. He borrowed a good deal of his prose style from the translators of the King James version of the Bible, and, as we have noted, the general concept of a universe made up of many corresponding spheres had been popular in the medieval period and received its greatest expression in the works of Dante. Likewise, many of the basics of Davis' ideas about the afterlife had first appeared in the works of Emanuel Swedenborg. We will recall that Swedenborg's was one of the two apparitions who conversed with Davis during his early spiritual crisis in the mountains near Poughkeepsie. It would not have been necessary for Davis to have direct contact with Swedenborg's writings in order to have been influenced by them, since the Swedish mystic's works were not only widely discussed at the time, but had given rise to a religious sect calling itself the Church of the New Jerusalem, and a philosophical school of Swedenborgianism, both of which had introduced their teachings into the United States.

Davis had certainly exercised good taste in choosing his spiritual and intellectual model. Like Davis, Swedenborg had been a seer of great repute (though not a medium) and had also possessed extraordinary gifts of clairvoyance. He was, in fact, the central figure in one of the best attested cases of the kind on record, having "seen" in vivid and convincing detail the disastrous Stockholm fire of July 1759 while residing at Gothenburg, some three hundred miles away (obviously, well before the age of telegraph or radio). The incident was investigated by no less hardheaded a person than the philosopher Immanuel Kant, who spoke to many confirmatory witnesses and confessed himelf totally unable to explain away or discredit the story.

Swedenborg was also one of the most brilliant intellectuals of his time, expert in metallurgy, mining and military engineering, astronomy, political economy, and other sciences before he resigned his responsibilities in 1747 to devote himself to the spiritual revelations that were pressing themselves upon his mind. He, however, regarded his experiences as unique—statements of the Word received directly from God—and would surely have disapproved Davis' claim to be his (Swedenborg's) successor.

Yet it was just this difference between the two men that enabled Andrew Jackson Davis to become the trend-setting theoretician of spiritualism. Though Davis did indeed believe his own revelations to be infallible, he did not deny, especially after the events at Hydesville, that the spirit world might be manifesting itself with increasing frequency to increasing numbers of believers. It was in accordance with this outlook that Davis should have been the founder of what was certainly one of the first and may have been the very first periodical that set itself to report on topics of interest to spiritualists, such as dreams, clairvoyance, mesmerism, somnambulism, trance, and prophecy.

Mediumship and table tipping were not mentioned in the original prospectus for the *Univercoelum* (as Davis called it, after a phrase from Swedenborg) for the simple reason that its first issue appeared on December 4, 1847, several months before the debut of Mr. Splitfoot. Some words of the Reverend S. B. Brittan, a Universalist minister who was the paper's editor-in-chief, summed up its point of view very well. "The *Univercoelum* will, in its general tone and tendency, recognise the Great Supreme Intelligence as a Cause, Nature as the Effect, and the immortalized Human Spirit as the Ultimate Result, the three being united in the formation of one Grand Harmonious System."

Thus it was that Mr. Splitfoot and his colleagues had received the sort of advance billing that would be the envy of any actor. Davis himself had predicted the expansion of communication with the spirit world, and the spirits, when they appeared, seemed willing to conform to the roles expected of them.

None of the foregoing discussion is meant to imply that spiritualism was on its way to becoming a distinct religion. In spite of Davis' doubts about the divinity of Christ, spiritualism was always allied, sometimes very closely, to Christian doctrines of various degrees of orthodoxy, and spiritualists continued to include members of most of the established Protestant churches. Davis, indeed, expended much energy in trying to show that his system was not in basic conflict with that of Christianity. In that, judging by the growth of the movement, he was frequently successful.

Of the subsequent career of Andrew Jackson Davis there is not much more to be said, if only because it continued on very much the same lines. Though the *Univercoelum* was short-lived as an independent publication, there were by then several other spiritualist papers that set themselves to continue the work of proving the truth of spiritual philosophy through spiritual phenomena. For eleven years after July 1849, which saw the last issue of *The Christian Rationalist* (a paper that had earlier absorbed the *Univercoelum*), it was the *Spirit Messenger* that served as the main forum for Davis and his followers.

Then, in 1860, Davis started a new weekly paper called the *Herald of Progress,* which later absorbed another called *Spiritual Telegraph.* He remained an active force in all aspects of spiritualism for decades and in his later years ran a small bookshop in Boston, from which he dispensed herbal remedies in accordance with his clairvoyantly obtained medical opinions. If the Seer dosed himself as he dosed his patients, his remedies must have been effective ones, for he lingered in the Winter-Land until the age of ninety-four. He thus survived all but one of the four great mediums who are considered the pillars of modern spiritualism, and of whom we shall speak next.

CHAPTER VI

MR. HOME OR MR. SLUDGE?

In the history of spiritualism the period from 1855 to 1917 might be called the Age of Phenomena. That is to say that at no time before or since has mediumism been attended by such a variety of startling and puzzling physical happenings. Research in mental mediumship is concerned with information; one asks questions of the spirits with a view to proving that they are identical with the persons they say they once were, or to obtain from them facts that could not be known to anyone living. Physical mediumship, on the other hand, produces visible, audible, tactile, or sometimes even scentable happenings that are taken to be the efforts of the spirits to demonstrate their existence for the confounding of the skeptical and the admiration of the enlightened. It was this latter type of event that came to dominate the spiritual scene to an unequaled degree. And the unequaled master of physical mediumship was Daniel Dunglas Home (1833–86).

The story of Home's early life is as mysterious and romantic as that of any folk hero, a fact that Home can hardly be blamed for playing on in his later life. He was born near Edinburgh, Scotland, the son of William Home, who was himself the illegitimate son of Alexander, tenth Earl of Home. It was for this reason that the medium always followed the custom of the noble family from which he claimed descent by pronouncing the name "Hume."

It is not at all clear why Daniel was adopted by his mother's sister while he was still a young child, but it is known that he emigrated with her and her husband to the United States when he was about nine years old. By his own account and that in the biography of him written by his second wife, he was a very delicate and sickly child, fond of nature and books, though he was sometimes so ill that he was not expected to live. His first psychic experience supposedly took place when he was thirteen, when a boyhood friend who died in Greeneville, Connecticut, appeared in a vision to Home in Troy, New York, three days later. As Troy is some three hundred miles from Greeneville, the means of communication of the period could not have brought the news to Home in that time even if someone had thought to inform him.

As Daniel grew older he had other strange experiences with increasing frequency. His mother and father had followed their son to America and were living not far from Daniel and his aunt and uncle, who had in the interim returned to Greeneville. This odd arrangement does not seem to have meant that the young man was prevented from seeing his parents, for his mother (who also came of a Scottish family and was said to have "second sight") reportedly told Daniel of a dream she had had predicting her own death. Three months later the prediction was fulfilled to the day, and the fact of her death was announced to her son in a similar dream.

Sometime around 1850, raps similar to those of Hydesville began to occur in Daniel's presence. His aunt was both angry and frightened at this development and even went to the length of calling in three ministers of different denominations to pray over her nephew. Far from discouraging the mysterious sounds, however, the praying seemed to have the effect of bringing them on. In the wake of this incident the aunt apparently concluded that the young man was possessed by the devil. She turned him out of her house in the best tradition of melodrama, leaving it up to an imaginative and delicate youth of seventeen to make his own way in the world.

For the next four years, Home resided with various generous persons who became interested in his abilities. Much has been made of the fact that neither then nor later did he accept direct payment for his mediumistic services, a fact that certainly appears to be true as far as it goes. Yet, while, from the point of view of the serious psychic investigator, any medium who charges fees is already convicted of having a fine motive for fraud, it is only fair to point out that there are other kinds of payments and other kinds of motives. Throughout his life Home was taken care of by "kind friends" who would probably never even have heard of him if it had not been for his abilities. He ate at the tables of the rich; he hobnobbed with the noble, the brilliant, and the powerful. In short, he did very well for a poor young man who happened to be the illegitimate grandson of an earl, and no sensible conclusion about his abilities can be reached without taking his background into account.

During this early period of his mediumship, Home exhibited almost all of the main types of phenomena that marked his later career. Objects and pieces of furniture became almost spritely during a Home séance. Tables not only tipped, but wallowed, waltzed, shuddered, and floated, while bric-a-brac maneuvered itself about the room like in a game of musical vases. As an accompaniment accordions played and bells rang, apparently without the touch of human hands, while armless "spirit hands" hung glowing in the air of the darkened séance room, only to melt away when touched.

One phenomenon that Home first displayed at this time has, in the opinion of most investigators, never been duplicated. Levitation is generally considered the province of Hindu fakirs, Tibetan monks, and other remote mystics on the one hand or of professional stage magicians on the other. But in Home's presence it was not only objects but individuals who were lifted. The most frequent subject of the levitation was of course the medium himself, but occasionally a sitter also was seen to float, if "seeing" is the correct word for an event taking place in almost total darkness. A similar phenomenon was the elongation of the medium's body, thought to result from the stretching of the body's substance by the spirits.

Home's demonstrations of such phenomena had not failed to attract attention. Among the eminent Americans who attended his trance sessions were the poet William Cullen Bryant, New York State Supreme Court Justice John Worth Edmonds, and the same eminent

Professor George Bush, who had been so influential in vouching for A. J. Davis a few years previously. Home's second wife's biography of him asserts, in fact, that it was due to his overgenerous taxing of his strength during the numerous sittings he gave at this time that he again became seriously ill and was advised to visit England for a rest and change of scene. Whatever the reason, Home did sail for England in the spring of 1855. His arrival was ideally timed to benefit from the interest already aroused by the American mediums Mrs. Hayden, Mrs. Roberts, and others. That Home's mediumship was superior to theirs in every way there is no doubt. His demonstrations were more impressive than theirs to the same degree that a symphony of Beethoven is more impressive than the tunes of a penny-whistle.

In England, as previously in America, Home spent most of his time as the guest of one or another of his admirers. In return for their hospitality, he was always very willing to give demonstrations and soon found himself in the midst of a raging journalistic dispute over the merits of spiritualism. Among those who at first testified to the genuineness of Home's phenomena were Lord Brougham, Sir David Brewster, Sir Edward Bulwer-Lytton, and T. A. Trollope (father of the novelist Anthony Trollope). Unfortunately, Brewster disavowed his support of Home as soon as it was reported in print, though it must be noted that Sir David had his reputation as a scientist to consider. He was known for his researches into the polarization of light and for the invention of the kaleidoscope, so that his denial might have been motivated by fear of ridicule. It became clear in the course of the ensuing controversy that Sir David had at the very least changed his mind sharply sometime after he recorded his first impressions of Home. It was not until 1869 that Brewster's daughter included in her published collection of his papers Sir David's indisputably authentic impression of his first session with Home. It is worth quoting if only because it is typical of the many similar accounts that appeared at the time.

> Last of all, I went with Lord Brougham to a *séance* of the new spirit-rapper, Mr. Home, a lad of twenty. . . . Mr. Home lives in Coxe's Hotel, Jermyn Street, and Mr. Coxe, who knows Lord Brougham, wished him to have a *séance*, and his lordship invited me to accompany him in order to assist in finding out the trick. We four sat down at a moderately-sized table, the structure of which we were invited to examine. In a short time the table shuddered, and a tremulous motion ran up all our arms; at our bidding these motions ceased and returned. The most unaccountable rappings were produced in various parts of the table; and the table actually rose from the ground when no hand was upon it. A larger table was produced and exhibited similar movements. A small hand-bell was then laid down with its mouth on the carpet: and, after lying for some time, it actually rang when nothing could have touched it. The bell was then placed on the other side, still upon the carpet, and it came over to me and placed itself in my hand. It did the same to Lord Brougham. These were the principal experiments. We could give no explanation of them and could not conjecture how they could be produced by any kind of mechanism. (quoted by Mme. D. D. Home in *D. D. Home, His Life and Mission*, p. 27)

The researcher is left to wonder what moved Sir David to such a decisive change of heart that after making this entry in his diary he not only described himself as unconvinced but asserted that all Home's effects could have been obtained by the adroit use of the medium's feet and similar tricks. (The séance room was, of course, dark.)

Other incidents of this first stay in London give us the impression that Home was the sort of person who almost always inspired strong feelings, whether favorable or unfavorable, in those who met him. His partisans were nothing if not warm in his defense and, on the whole, they seem to have outnumbered his detractors. The general picture one receives of him from contemporary accounts is of an affectionate, generous, volatile young man with the manners of a gentleman and probably some inclination to vanity. He could certainly be very attractive to women, though most observers agreed that he was not conventionally handsome. Instead, he was probably what the times would have termed "poetic" looking, an effect that would have been enhanced by his ill health. (He had that most romantic of nineteenth-century diseases, "consumption," or tuberculosis.)

One of his earliest American friends, a Miss Ely, described him thus: "tall for his age, fair complexion, hair neither red, brown, nor auburn, but a complete mixture of the three—like a three-coloured changeable silk—rather inclined to curl: a large, broad forehead, well-developed, lively grey eyes, nose not remarkable, and a handsome mouth and teeth; easy manners; very intelligent for his age, perfectly artless and very affectionate." He was also an accomplished parlor pianist and had a definite talent for the dramatic recitations that were then almost as popular in genteel society as spiritualism. All in all, it seems surprising that he ever made an enemy.

Yet, Home assuredly did make at least one enemy during his first few months in England—one who was in a position to do him considerable harm. The poet Robert Browning (1812–89) and his wife Elizabeth had been among the earliest visitors to the spirit circle that gathered around the young medium in 1855, and at first it seemed they were as much impressed as any of Home's new English acquaintances. At one session a garland of clematis was brought by a "spirit hand" and placed on Mrs. Browning's head, a pretty gesture of favor from the unseen.

There seems little doubt that Mrs. Browning, who had always been more ready to accept spiritualism than had Robert, enjoyed herself very much on the occasion, as is revealed in her description of it in a letter to her sister. "We were touched by the invisible," she said, "heard the music and raps, saw the table moved, and had sight of the hands. . . . Robert and I did not touch the hands. Mr. Lytton and Sir Edward *both did.* The feel was warm and human—rather warmer in fact than is common with a man's hand. The music was beautiful." However, only a day or so after this séance Robert Browning threatened to throw Home out of the house when the medium came to pay a social call.

Neither then nor later did Browning make a specific accusation of fraud or any other wrongdoing against Home, and the matter would no doubt have ended there if Browning had not shortly afterward written a

satirical poem entitled "Mr. Sludge, 'The Medium.'"
Since Browning's aversion to Home was by now well
known in literary circles, it was widely supposed that
the poem referred to him personally. Using the form
of the dramatic monologue, for which he was so justly
famous, Browning presents Mr. Sludge as a thoroughly
despicable character, not only fraudulent in his mediumship, but a liar, a false friend, a self-seeker, a leech, a
drinker, a braggart, and a toady. The first few lines
make an excellent introduction to what is to follow.

> Now, don't, sir! Don't expose me! Just this once!
> This was the first and only time, I'll swear,—
> Look at me,—see, I kneel,—the only time,
> I swear, I ever cheated,—yes, by the soul
> Of Her who hears—(your sainted mother, sir!)
> All, except this last accident, was truth—
> This little kind of slip!—and even this,
> It was your own wine, sir, the good champagne,
> (I took it for Catawba, you're so kind)
> Which put the folly in my head!

The poem would probably have done Home considerably more harm than it actually did if it had not been
so very long (about two thousand lines) and occasionally so murky and repetitive. As poetry it is decidedly
not among Browning's better pieces, being so choked
with outrage that it sometimes becomes almost incoher-
ent. One might even think that Browning's indignation
is out of all proportion to the subject, since Home
was only one among many mediums on whom the poet
might have chosen to vent his wrath, nor was he at

this time so extremely famous as to make him the one
obvious target for an attack on spiritualism in general.

Recently, Eric J. Dingwall, one of the most perceptive
of modern psychical researchers and historians, wrote a
piece suggesting that Browning's disillusionment with
Home might have sprung not from a conviction that
his mediumship was a fraud but from the suspicion that
Home was a homosexual. Such an idea was of course
very scandalous a hundred years ago, when it would
certainly have brought ruin to anyone so accused in
public. And whether or not Dr. Dingwall is correct in
his assessment of Browning's motive, he has certainly
shown that there were rumors of some "mystery of
iniquity" in Home's private life, rumors that were referred to here and there in whispers throughout the
medium's career. There is certainly no absolute proof
either way, and since the topic is quite irrelevant to an
evaluation of Home's mediumistic powers, there would
be no point in raising it here if it were not that it may
throw some light on Browning's attack and suggest that,
whatever the degree of his skepticism, he did not detect
Home in any specific fraud.

Browning, however, was too acute an observer of
human nature not to have put something into "Mr.
Sludge" besides a personal attack. In the course of
Sludge's long-winded, whining self-justification, the character touches repeatedly on a topic that makes the
study of séance phenomena the exasperating and fascinating thing it is: the psychology of the audience.
Something has already been said of this in Chapter III,
and we have by no means heard the last of it. In fact,
Mr. Sludge will become almost a recurrent character in

these pages, acting as a commentator on the methods and psychology of mediumship in general. Whether or not his personality was that of D. D. Home, Sludge made some observations that spiritualists would have done well to remember.

Home himself, meanwhile, had not stayed long in London. In early fall of 1855, he went to Italy to visit Mr. and Mrs. T. A. Trollope. It must have been a rather trying period in his life. Browning's attack on his reputation in London was followed by an attack on his life in Florence. Apparently the superstitious peasants of the area had heard that Home was one who conversed with the dead, and they came to the conclusion that he must therefore be a sorcerer. It was even rumored that he was in the habit of feeding the Holy Sacrament to toads in order to raise up evil spirits. Late one night, Home was ambushed in the street by a man with a dagger; fortunately, Home was only slightly injured. Whether there was a connection with the local attitude to his activities is unknown, for the attacker was never caught.

Even more upsetting must have been a spirit message Home received at about this time, warning him that his powers would desert him for a year. It was one spirit prediction that was entirely accurate. For exactly a year Home held no séances, heard no voices, and produced no raps. As his wife says, "clouds darkened the natural sunshine of his spirit; a veil had suddenly dropped between him and the world beyond, and all counsel and comfort from it was withdrawn."

The promised return of Home's abilities found him in Paris in February 1857. As soon as the good news got around, the medium was summoned to the Tuileries in order to give a demonstration for Napoleon III (1808–73) and the Empress Eugénie. This was an honor indeed; Home's previous acquaintance had risen no higher than a few lords and Prince Luigi of Naples. No reliable records were made of the sittings Home gave for Their Imperial Highnesses, but like the vast majority of those who sat with him, the royal pair appear to have been highly satisfied. The Empress was said at one point to have been convinced she held the hand of her dead father in hers, declaring she would know it anywhere because of a scar or deformity on one of the fingers. In general, however, not a great deal is known of this series of sessions, which probably accounts for the fact that Home was the subject of all sorts of imaginative and lurid rumors in Paris that year.

In spite, or perhaps because of this circumstance, the medium's status remained very high, and in the following year Home visited Russia in order to display his powers before Czar Alexander II (1818–81). While there, he married "a Russian lady of means," Alexandrina De Kroll, whom he had met in Rome. Despite his vaunted refusal to accept payment for his séances, Home must have been doing well financially at this period, having access now to his wife's fortune and having also received gifts or "mementos" from the Russian court. One of these was a valuable ring, a wedding present from the Czar, and though the second Mrs. Home does not describe it in detail, she does mention an emerald set with diamonds that Home received from Alexander on the occasion of the birth of Home's son a year later, and "a sapphire of great size surrounded with diamonds" that arrived from the same source when she herself married the medium some years later.

Between 1859 and 1862, the events of Home's career followed much the same pattern. Dividing his time between England and the continent, he continued to number the rich and prominent among his sitters. One of those who came to Home's circle at this time was the poet Alexis Tolstoy (1817–75), not to be confused with his distant cousin Leo, the novelist. After describing the usual manifestations in a letter to his wife, Tolstoy concluded, "What would have, above all, convinced me, were I a sceptic, are the hands I have felt, which were placed in mine and melted when I tried to retain them. A cold wind passed around the circle very distinctly, and perfumes were wafted to us."

A more important convert, from the scientific point of view, was Robert Chambers, a prominent writer and publisher who had previously been among spiritualism's most vocal opponents. Though Chambers insisted in remaining anonymous for the sake of his public reputation, his change of heart was well known in spiritualist circles and contributed greatly to Home's prestige.

Following the death of his wife, in 1862, Home found himself in financial straits. His first book, *Incidents in My Life*, had done well and entered a second edition, but was not by itself sufficient to support him. For a while he considered taking up some other career. He visited the Papal States of Italy with a view to becoming a sculptor, but was ordered to leave within three days on the grounds that he had been practicing sorcery. His next project took him back to the United States, where he gave some quite successful stage performances as a dramatic reader. Returning to London, he began combining his readings with public lectures on spiritualism, but found that his health would not stand the strain. It was at this point, in 1866, that a group of concerned friends founded the Spiritual Atheneum and offered Home the post of residential secretary. The Atheneum was to be a sort of headquarters for spiritualists, and the job, which didn't involve any very arduous duties, was certainly a godsend for the ailing medium. Among other benefits, it enabled him to continue giving private sittings at no charge.

It was during the years 1867 to 1869 that Home was the central figure in a series of séances one of which has probably become the most analyzed single session on record. The principal sitters were two young men prominent in London society, the Master of Lindsay (later the Earl of Crawford) and Viscount Adare (later the Earl of Dunraven). At the time of Home's most famous feat, the Ashley Place levitation, the two men had been acquainted with the medium for a number of years and Adare, in fact, was one of his closest friends. The fourth person present was Captain Charles Wynne, a cousin of Adare's. The date was either the thirteenth or the sixteenth of December 1868, the discrepancy in various accounts being only one of the factors that later gave doubters reason to discredit the eyewitness testimony that follows. Lord Adare wrote:

> Wynne and I went over to Ashley House after dinner. There we found Home and the Master of Lindsay. Home proposed a sitting. We accordingly sat round a table in the small room. There was no light

in the room, but the light from the window was sufficient for us to distinguish each other and to see the different articles of furniture. Home went into a trance. . . .

Lindsay suddenly said: "Oh, good heavens! I know what he is going to do; it is too fearful."

Adare: "What is it?"

Lindsay: "I cannot tell you; it is too horrible.— Adah [the spirit of an American actress who often spoke at these sessions] says that I must tell you. He is going out of the window in the other room, and coming in at this window."

We heard Home go into the next room, heard the window thrown up, and presently Home appeared standing upright outside our window. He opened the window and walked in quite coolly. "Ah," he said, "you were good this time," referring to our having sat still and not wished to prevent him. . . . "Adare, shut the window in the next room." (quoted by Mme. Home in *D. D. Home, His Life Mission*, p. 301)

Here is Lord Lindsay's version of the same event.

I was sitting with Mr. Home and Lord Adare and a cousin of his. During the sitting Mr. Home went into a trance, and in that state was carried out of the window in the room next to where we were, and was brought in at our window. The distance between the windows was about seven feet six inches, and there was not the slightest foothold be-

tween them, nor was there more than a twelve-inch
projection to each window, which served as a
ledge to put flowers on. We heard the window in
the next room lifted up, and almost immediately
after we saw Home floating in the air outside
our window. The moon was shining full into the
room; my back was to the light, and I saw the
shadow on the wall of the window-sill, and Home's
feet about six inches above it. He remained in this
position for a few seconds, then raised the window
and glided into the room feet foremost and sat
down. (from a letter dated July 14, 1871)

Among the many persons, both believers and critics,
who have commented on this episode, probably none
are more helpful and thought-provoking than Frank Podmore and Trevor Hall. Podmore (1856–1910) was one
of the earliest of a generation of pyschical researchers
(as distinguished from spiritualist believers), and was the
respected "skeptic-in-chief" of the London Society for
Psychical Research. Mr. Hall is one of the most astute
of modern investigators, combining twentieth-century
scientific techniques with a cheerful and readable writing style in his many books.

In examining the above accounts of the happenings at
Ashley Place, there are one or two objections that
can be—and were—made immediately. Thus, Podmore
pointed out that a glance at an almanac for the year 1868
reveals that the night of the séance, whether the thirteenth or the sixteenth, was within a day or two of the
new moon and thus could hardly have been bright
enough to produce Lord Lindsay's "shadow on the wall

of the window-sill, and Home's feet about six inches above it."

Further, there is the question of Home's precise position in the air during the occurrence. Adare describes him as upright, while Lindsay specifies that the medium glided into the room feet foremost. To add to the complications, Adare recounts in a later section of his testimony that following the levitation he had gone into the other room to shut the window as requested and had returned to remark that he couldn't see how Home had gone through it, since it was "not raised a foot." Home returned with him to the next room and asked Adare to reopen the window. "He then went through the space, head first, quite rapidly, his body being nearly horizontal and apparently rigid. He came in again, feet foremost, and we returned to the other room." Thus, to make the three accounts consistent with each other, we must imagine the spirits to have been flipping the medium about in midair in an apparently pointless (not to say dangerous) manner.

Yet, beyond such questionings of details of the occurrence, or of the accuracy of the reporting, the fact remains that three witnesses (Wynne confirmed the testimony of the other two) were agreed, to put the matter at its very simplest, that they had seen Home leave the room by a door and come back in through the window, with the strong suggestion that the medium had left the building via the window of an adjoining room. (We must note that none of the witnesses actually claimed to have *seen* Home's exit, only his supposed return.) If, for the sake of argument, we suppose that the levitation was not a genuinely supernormal event, what *did* happen at Ashley Place on that December night over one hundred years ago?

For many decades, it was probably Frank Podmore's conclusion that was most popular among skeptics. After giving the closest attention to all the available evidence, he suggested that Home had used a rather elementary trick, a combination of suggestion and adroit sneaking. A letter written by H. D. Jencken (who was, as it happens, Kate Fox's husband and another regular attender of Home's séances) records that the following incident had occurred a few days earlier. In the presence of Lindsay and Adare, Home had opened the same window and stepped out onto the ledge, looking down into the street some eighty feet below. In Podmore's view, this scene was a sort of dress rehearsal for the levitation, serving to implant the image of the medium outside the window firmly in his subjects' minds. On the night in question he had only to walk into the other room, audibly raise the window, slip back into the séance room under cover of darkness, and then mount the windowsill in order to silhouette himself against the window *from the inside*. Alternatively, Podmore proposes, Home may simply have reappeared from behind the window curtains.

This explanation is highly ingenious and certainly cannot be ruled out as impossible. As has already been said, the room was very dimly lit by a mere sliver of moon, the sitters were all convinced of Home's powers, their minds had been prepared for what was to come, and they were in an excited state owing to Lord Lindsay's alarm at the danger of the feat. None of these circumstances is helpful in maintaining a cool and objective frame of mind.

On the other hand, even the disbeliever in psychical phenomena might balk at the notion that three young men whose sight and hearing were (presumably) at least average could have failed to hear, if not see, Home returning by the same door through which he had left.

A more psychological version of Podmore's solution was proposed by Trevor Hall in 1965. Hall discusses in detail the personal relationship of Home with the participants, particularly Lord Adare. He points out that Adare's own writings show him to have been greatly dependent on Home in many ways. They had traveled together, lived together, even shared the same bed, and Home had several times used his powers to cure his friend of various illnesses. It is not necessary (though it may be useful) to invoke Dr. Dingwall's view of Home as a homosexual in order to say that he exerted an exceedingly strong influence upon Adare. The same was true to a slightly lesser extent of Lord Lindsay and Wynne. It is Hall's contention that the three could as properly be called Home's disciples or devotees as his friends, that the medium had so dominated their minds that they were nearly incapable of doubting him.

We must be careful at this point not to let the shadow of the Evil Mesmerist loom between us and reality. Mr. Hall is not suggesting that Home dangled golden disks before the eyes of his sitters while muttering, "Sleep, sleep," in an appropriately sinister manner. On the contrary, as the actor, the psychologist, the politician, and the salesman know, the most effective ways of influencing one's audience are much simpler and less spectacular. We probably can never know for certain precisely what went on at Ashley Place, but there is no question at all that, given the right conditions, it is possible to produce the sort of mental state to which Mr. Hall is referring. Our minds are peculiarly likely to see what they expect to see, with or without the help of our eyes. When the expectation is high enough and emotion clouds the judgment, no one—except possibly the man who has carefully arranged these conditions—can predict the result.

The Ashley Place levitation stands as one of the great landmarks among spiritualist phenomena. Some investigators have gone so far as to state that the movement itself can stand or fall on this one incident. Before considering the final years of Home's career, it need only be noted that in a diary entry for May 6, 1920, the great stage magician Houdini noted that he had "offered to do the D. D. Home levitation stunt at the same place that Home did it in 1868." Apparently, however, Houdini's assistant became frightened of the danger involved and refused to take part, thus quashing the project permanently. Our curiosity may prompt us to wish that the assistant had been made of sterner stuff.

During the period of the Adare-Lindsay sittings, Home continued to have financial problems. In 1868, London society was atwitter with the news that a rich widow, Mrs. Jane Lyon, was suing Home for the recovery of a total of thirty thousand pounds that she said she had been persuaded to settle on him in return for Home's becoming her adopted son and changing his name to Lyon-Home. The judgment went against Home, to the extent that he was instructed to return the money. At the same time, the court was forced to remark that the plaintiff had made "misstatements so perversely untrue that they have embarrassed the court to a great degree." All in all, the episode appears to have been that of an old woman who changed her mind (and who may at first have hoped to profit from her adopted son's social connections). Home, who had given up his post with the Spiritual Atheneum at the time of Mrs. Lyon's original settlement, was left, once again, to the kindness of friends.

Beginning in 1871, Home engaged in what was probably his most important series of sittings, scientifically speaking. He became the first major subject of the investigations of Sir William Crookes, whom we shall encounter again in later chapters. Crookes (1832–1919) was one of the most eminent physicists of his day—discoverer of the element thallium, inventor of the radiometer and spinthariscope, founder of the *Chemical News*, and at various times president of the Chemical Society, the Institution of Electrical Engineers, and the Royal Society. When Crookes spoke, the scientific world was forced to listen.

For this reason, Sir William's announcement that he intended to launch a full-scale scientific probe of spiritualist phenomena was greeted with delight by opponents of the movement, particularly the press. There seemed every reason to believe that Crookes would fulfill his published intention to "drive the worthless residuum of spiritualism hence to the unknown limbo of magic and necromancy."

The rationalists, realists, and other scoffers were disappointed. In a long series of experiments using weights, balances, and other apparatus to test and register changes in the weight of objects under the medium's hand (such

as usually occur in levitation or table tipping), Crookes
became convinced that he was in the presence of a
physical force previously unknown but as real and meas-
urable as electricity or gravity. His published report to
that effect stirred up a tremendous controversy, which
is to some extent as lively today as ever.

Crookes' conclusions were criticized from many angles,
both at the time and afterward. Few ventured to ac-
cuse the great man of collusion or outright fraud in the
matter, but several felt there was some fault in the construction of the apparatus. Even his critics, however,
admitted that Crookes had shown himself more than willing to make any changes in his equipment that might
increase its sensitivity or decrease the possibility of interference by the medium. A second school of opinion
held that while it was certainly impossible to cause a
recording mechanism to have a hallucination, the same
was by no means true of the investigators themselves,
who were just as susceptible to the conjurer's trick as
any other audience.

The most telling points against the Crookes experiment may be those made by Frank Podmore, though
one must remember that, having come to the conclusion
that all physical phenomena of the séance room were
the result of fraud or mistaken observation, Podmore is
reasoning from a position of bias. He *assumes* that by the
time Home encountered Crookes, he was already an
accomplished conjurer and psychological manipulator.
Nevertheless, Podmore is quite right in asserting that
Crookes had admitted to violating one of his own (and
the scientific world's) most inflexible requirements. To
be valid, an experiment must be repeatable—whenever

the conditions are the same, they must produce identical results.

Instead, Crookes said that "the experiments have been very numerous, but owing to our imperfect knowledge of the conditions which favor or oppose the manifestations of this force, to the apparently capricious manner in which it is exerted, and to the fact that Mr. Home himself is subject to unaccountable ebbs and flows of the force, it has but seldom happened that a result obtained on one occasion could be subsequently confirmed and tested with apparatus specially contrived for the purpose." This meant, simply, that Home was able to dictate the experimental conditions, such as the degree of illumination and the relative positions of the experimenters (part of whose job was to insure that the medium used neither his hands nor his feet to interfere with the apparatus). Whenever the setup was not to his liking Home had only to declare that the spirits were absent or the power was weak.

It is in a sense irrelevant to this discussion whether or not *we* are convinced by the Crookes experiments, in the light of the fact that at the time many former skeptics *were*. Crookes' report was tremendously influential and launched him on a second career that was only a little less important and considerably more colorful than his role as establishment scientist.

By contrast, these sittings were more or less the last ones of note that were conducted by Home. He had married again in October of 1871. His second wife was also an aristocratic Russian lady of wealth, Mlle. Julie de Gloumeline. Although she wrote a useful biography of her husband entitled *D. D. Home, His Life and Mis-*

sion, Julie seems to have discouraged him from giving séances, perhaps partly for the sake of her social position.

After about 1876, Home lived in semiretirement, his health having seriously given way. He died on June 21, 1886, in Paris after a nearly lifelong battle with tuberculosis. His tombstone at St. Germain carries the words, "To another discerning of spirits," referring to God's bestowing of spiritual gifts as enumerated by St. Paul in I Corinthians. Perhaps a better epitaph would have been found in the words of Frank Podmore, who did his best to discredit Home's phenomena but summed up the great medium's career with his accustomed fairness: "Home was never publicly exposed as an impostor; there is no evidence of any weight that he was even privately detected in trickery." The "skeptic-in-chief" made no such admissions about other physical mediums.

CHAPTER VII

TOO MANY COOKS AND PROFESSOR CROOKES

If D. D. Home, in his time, was the undisputed master of levitation and moving furniture, it was other developments in the séance room that captured the attention of the public soon after. Spirit hands, as we have said, had long been a feature of the work of all but the least advanced mediums. In the 1860s, this materialization was taken several steps farther. First faces, then entire human figures invaded the séance room, strolling about, delivering messages from the next world, bestowing "spirit gifts" and occasionally touching or being touched by the sitters. Mrs. Leah Fish (now Mrs. Underhill), the older sister of Kate and Margaret Fox, was one of the first to produce the so-called full-form materialization. Like other such developments, it spread rapidly across the Atlantic to find an immediate success in England.

One accompaniment of the new interest in materialization was a change in the furniture of the séance room. To the usual tables, chairs, slates, and musical instruments was now added a structure referred to as a cabinet, though as often as not it was formed simply by hanging a curtain across one corner of the room. Without exception, mediums of the period claimed that materializations could only be performed inside the cabinet, which of course had the effect of preventing the sitters from seeing what went on until the fully formed spirit was ready to appear.

Opponents of spiritualism have not been slow to remark that this is like ordering your meat from a butcher who does his cutting and weighing behind closed doors at the back of the shop. In response to the criticism, it was asserted that the enclosed space of the cabinet makes possible the concentration of psychic energy that is required for the difficult feat of materialization. The cabinet thus acted like a power battery for the medium, who was also said to be in a highly vulnerable state at such times. It was dangerous either to upset the medium before she entered the cabinet or to touch her or the materialized figure during the course of the sitting without express permission. Such interference was especially to be avoided, since it might result in the medium's failing to reabsorb the ectoplasm that had been used in the materialization, thus seriously affecting her health.

It was against this background that there emerged in the early 1870s spiritualism's most accomplished practitioner of full-form materialization, Florence Cook (1856–1904). The importance of Miss Cook's phenomena for the history of spiritualism is indisputably great. Not only was she celebrated in her own time, receiving the unequivocal endorsement of one of the age's leading scientists, but later historians of the movement have continued to cite her case as one that should put the skeptics to shame. Mr. B. Abdy Collins, an eminent English writer on spiritualist topics, wrote in the widely circulated *Psychic News* for May 8, 1948, "I felt that the materialization of complete figures which behave like ordinary persons in every way stands or falls by this one case." Mr. Collins joined many others in suggesting that the mediumship of Florence Cook went a long way toward giving proof of the literal truth of Christ's resurrection, thus making it of the greatest religious, as well as scientific interest.

The exact date of Florence Cook's birth may never be known. Most sources give it as 1856, based on a statement by Florence in 1872, that she was sixteen. Oddly enough, however, her birth was not legally registered in that year, or indeed in any year from 1849 to 1858, making her age a matter of the Cook family's unsupported word. Any doubts on the subject would be trivial were it not that Florence's youth was frequently used in defense of her mediumship. How could an innocent child of fifteen have been guilty of any sort of fraud, demanded the upright Victorians who came to her defense. Today we may not be so wholly convinced of the automatic innocence of youth, but it is clear that at the time a reduction of her age by two or three years might have been quite convenient.

Florence's mediumship officially began in 1871, although she had reported seeing spirits and hearing voices throughout her childhood. As with so many others, however, it was table tipping that enabled her to discover her gift. The event took place at a tea party, and we may hope the table used was not the one holding the tea things, for Florence proved so gifted that the table became uncontrollable. At other sessions held soon after,

levitation and automatic writing were added to her manifestations. Unfortunately, the identities of the sitters at
these early séances, except for Florence's mother, were
never revealed, so there is little means of inquiring into
them further.

Soon a small group of spiritualists began to gather
regularly at the Cook house on Eleanor Road in Hackney. No more levitations occurred, for by this time
Florence had turned her attention to the materializations
that were to make her famous. The first such manifestations were not especially spectacular. There was in the
house an old wooden corner cabinet of the type that
has an opening in the upper part of its doors. In this
cabinet Florence would sit, tied to her chair (a customary precaution against fraud that most mediums accepted). On some occasions the spirits even performed
the tying themselves as proof of their cooperation.

Meanwhile, messages received while Florence was in
trance had directed the family to seek out the Dalston
Association, a nearby spiritualist organization. The leading members of the Association were much impressed
with the young and pretty medium. Their newspaper
The Spiritualist began to carry accounts of her sittings,
thus spreading her fame in spiritualist circles.

The Dalston Association probably did Florence the additional favor of introducing her to the notice of Mr.
Charles Blackburn. Blackburn was a wealthy gentleman from Manchester who made regular contributions
toward the cost of publishing *The Spiritualist*. By 1873,
Blackburn had become interested in Florence's career
and had generously offered to pay the Cook family a
stipend so that their talented daughter would not be

forced to accept fees for her sittings. The Cooks were
naturally grateful, for they were by no means well off,
and the gentleman from Manchester soon became a
personal friend and an important influence in all decisions
relating to Florence's career.

It was at this same time, or a little earlier, that Florence
became associated with another medium, a man named
Frank Herne. Herne and his partner Charles Williams
were then enjoying considerable success in the spiritualist world and were certainly much better known than
Florence, a relative novice. Thus it was kind of Herne
to give his time to the new medium's "development,"
as it was called.

In later years, however, defenders of Florence's performance might well have wished that Mr. Herne had
been less generous, as he was repeatedly denounced and
exposed in fraudulent materializations. Herne's accusers
included not only critics of the movement but convinced spiritualists such as W. H. Harrison, editor of the
influential *Spiritualist*, and later one of Florence's foremost supporters. There is little doubt that Herne was
thoroughly discredited, and that there were many "tricks
of the trade" that the older medium could have taught
Florence, had he (or she) been so inclined.

It was during this period of working with Herne that
the spirit control "Katie King" first began to make herself known through Florence. "Katie" in fact claimed to
be the daughter of Herne's principal control, the former
pirate Henry Morgan, whose "spirit name" was John
King. Florence (and "Katie") soon gained enough assurance to leave Herne's circle and set up on her (or
their) own. The manifestations at this time were gener-

ally limited to the showing of the spirit face in the
opening of the cabinet. One such session was amusingly,
but fairly, described by the Reverend C. Maurice Davies,
a member of the Council of the British National Association of Spiritualists, in a book that appeared in
1875.

Now, I do not purpose going through the details
of the séance, which was considerably irksome, being
protracted by endless psalm singing. What I want
to do—with Miss Cook's permission—is to calculate
the chances of her being sufficiently athletic to perform the tricks herself, without the aid of spirits.
Does she not underrate her unaided powers in assigning a supernatural cause for the effects produced?

Well, then, this lithe little lady is arrayed in the
ordinary garb of the nineteenth century with what
is technically termed a "pannier," and large open
sleeves, each of which, I fear, she must have found
considerably in the way, as also the sundry lockets
and other nick-nacks suspended from her neck. However, there they were. We put her in a cupboard,
which had a single Windsor chair in it, and laid a
stoutish new cord on her lap. Then came singing,
which may or may not have been intended to drown
any noise in the cupboard; but, after some delay,
she was found tied around the waist, neck, and two
wrists, and the ends of the cord fastened to the back
of the chair. These knots we sealed, and consigned
her to the cupboard again. Shortly after there ap-
apeared at an aperture in the upper portion of the
cupboard a face which looked utterly unspiritual and
precisely like that of the medium, only with some
white drapery thrown over the head. The aperture
was just the height that would have allowed Miss

Cook to stand on the chair and peep out. I do not say she did; I am only calculating the height. The face remained some minutes in a strong light; then descended. We opened the cupboard and found the little lady tied as before with the seals unbroken. Spiritual, or material, it was clever.

After a pause, the same process was gone through again; only this time stout tape was substituted for rope. The cord cut the girl's wrists; and tape was almost more satisfactory. Again she was bound, and we sealed the knots; and again a face appeared —this time quite black, and not like the medium at all. I noticed that the drapery ran right around the face, and cut if off at a straight line on the lower part. This gave the idea of a mask. I am not saying it was a mask. I am only throwing out a hint that, if the "spirits" wish to convince people they should let the neck be well seen. I am bound to say it bore a strong light for several minutes; and some people say they saw eyelids. I did not. I do not say they were not there. I know how impossible it is to prove a negative, and only say I did not see them. (quoted by Trevor H. Hall in *The Spiritualist*, pp. 13–14)

Davies' remarks about the resemblance of the spirit face to that of the medium, and in fact many other features of his account, were frequently echoed by other observers. Either the face in the aperture was mobile, lifelike, and very like Florence's, or it was exotic, unfamiliar, and rather stiff. Skeptics then and now have assumed that the explanations so carefully "not suggested" by Davies were largely correct—that is that under cover of darkness and the noise of singing the medium succeeded in freeing herself at least sufficiently to stand on her chair and present her veiled or masked face for the amazement of the sitters. In spite of the justification for the use of the closed cabinet given earlier, it must be noted that neither Florence nor any other well-known medium of the time gave the sitters an opportunity to *see* what went on in the cabinet and that the advantages of this arrangement (for the medium) are clear.

If Florence Cook had continued to produce such relatively simple phenomena, she would merely have joined the dozens of minor mediums whose doings served to fill up the back pages of spiritualist papers. However, by the spring of 1873, the appearances of "Katie King" had entered a new phase, both much more impressive and more difficult to explain. While the medium was, as usual, tied up and entranced inside the cabinet, the full-length figure of "Katie" would appear, first in the doorway of the cabinet and later completely outside it. The effect on Florence's sitters was electrifying. Here at last was the proof of what many of them had so long taken on faith: that there is literally "no death," that the spirit not only continues to perceive and communicate but can, under the right conditions, resume a replica of its original body and can walk, touch, talk, and breathe like those who are still "in life."

The procedure for these remarkable séances was usually as follows. The sitters were the invited guests of the Cook family (all of whom, parents and children, were now actively engaged in the development of Florence's career). Before the actual start of the session, Florence would be searched by some of the ladies who were to be present in order to insure that she carried nothing with her into the cabinet that could be used in disguising herself or in freeing herself from the ropes. The doors of the cabinet were opened, but curtained off with shawls, and the dim light of a candle or small lamp was provided in the séance room. After the medium was tied inside the cabinet and had become entranced, the by then familiar figure of "Katie" would appear, walking among the guests, conversing of her former life, and even shaking hands with some of the sitters. On several occasions, photographs of "Katie" were made, using a magnesium flash. The significance of the fact that "Katie" could be photographed was of course very great, as it showed that the sitters were not experiencing any sort of joint hallucination. Whatever else may be said of "Katie," there is little doubt that her name was attached to a genuine material body.

The "Katie" of this period is described as charming and attractive, though some observers remarked that she resembled Florence Cook. However, "Katie" generally appeared with bare arms and feet, and dressed in flowing white, while Florence wore a modest dark dress with the long sleeves and wide skirts of the times. At the end of each séance the white-clad "Katie" would return to the cabinet, which, when opened after a suitable interval, invariably revealed the medium in her original dress with all the knots and seals in place as before. Most of the guests found it impossible not to conclude that "Katie" had indeed faded into thin air, or rather into thin ectoplasm, precisely as the spiritualists claimed.

This smooth and convincing sequence of events at

"Katie's" appearances was seriously interrupted only once. In December 1873, a Mr. William Volckman, one of the guests, seized hold of the apparition and refused to let go. Volckman declared loudly that he believed that "Katie" was in fact Florence Cook, and invited the company to examine her more closely. However, it was not an examination but a scuffle that followed. Two men, one of them Florence's future husband Edward Elgie Corner, rushed to the assistance of the spirit, forcing Volckman to release his hold. Some bruises were received on both sides, "Katie" retired hastily to the cabinet, and the rest of the group made loud protests at Volckman's "ungentlemanly" behavior. Five minutes later, when the spirit voices gave permission for the opening of the cabinet, the medium was discovered to be both disheveled and distressed but securely fastened.

Reaction to this incident among spiritualists was immediate and violent. Mr. Volckman, though an active and influential spiritualist of several years' standing, was angrily condemned and his behavior labeled a "Gross Outrage" in the pages of *The Spiritualist*. The whole affair is of interest because it raises a number of points concerning the attitude of sitters at such private séances. Though it has been truly remarked that the taking of money from each sitter gives the medium a very compelling motive for fraud, it is equally true that sitters who are the nonpaying guests of the medium may often feel diffident about criticizing the proceedings or voicing suspicions of trickery. At least half of the outrage occasioned by Mr. Volckman's escapade was directed at his supposed breach of good manners (in taking hold of a lady and impugning the reliability of his hosts) rather than at the actual truth or falsity of his charges. The figure of Browning's Mr. Sludge may well appear in our mind's eye at this point, asking:

> . . . And for the fools, the folk
> Who came to see, the guests, (observe that word!)
> Pray do you find guests criticize your wine,
> Your furniture, your grammar, or your nose?
> Then, why your "medium"? What's the difference?

Little information is available as to Florence Cook's own reaction to Mr. Volckman's charges. Since she was only (officially) seventeen at the time, she appears to have taken the wise and maidenly course of letting her defense come from her supporters.

In any case, the past was soon to be overshadowed by one of the century's most complete and extended scientific examinations of spiritualist claims—an investigation whose results were to place Florence Cook in an almost unassailable position among physical mediums.

The principal figure in this next stage of Florence Cook's career (after Florence herself, of course) was the same eminent Sir William Crookes whose favorable report on D. D. Home had caused such excitement in spiritualist and scientific circles only two years before. Now Crookes, a vigorous and productive scientist in his early forties, decided to turn his attention to the phenomena associated with the materialization of "Katie King."

Crookes apparently began his investigation sometime in December 1873, and issued a preliminary report in February 1874. In it he made the very sensible point that no amount of tying and searching the medium could ever provide adequate proof that she and the materialized spirit were not the same; only their simultaneous appearance—one entranced in the cabinet, one moving about the room—would provide *proof* of the kind acceptable to science. At this stage of his researches, Crookes stated that he had decided to narrow the focus of his work to this one point and that he had already had some encouraging indications. In particular, Crookes testified that he had clearly heard the entranced Florence "moaning and sobbing" behind the cabinet curtain, at the same time as "Katie" stood before him in the room. Now, having thus become convinced that Florence was genuine, Crookes had arranged that Florence should devote herself exclusively to a series of experimental séances that would form the basis of a more comprehensive report.

The new investigations were to take place at Crookes' home in order both to give the scientist free access to his own apparatus and to prevent the medium from concealing anything in the séance room beforehand. The cabinet in this case was a separate room, the library, which opened off the séance room. The library also had a second door, which Crookes would personally lock before the session. All lights were then turned out in the library (the cabinet). Florence retired through the curtained doorway, and the witnesses waited in the lighted séance room.

According to Crookes' subsequent reports, the waiting

was not in vain. "Katie" made regular and lengthy appearances, unhindered by difficulties with the health of the medium, the absence of the "power," the attitude of the sitters, or any of the other factors that had allegedly been responsible for disappointments in the past. And there was more. Over forty photographs were taken, showing "Katie" to be as real and material as ever. Crookes was also allowed, on several occasions, to draw aside the curtain in the doorway of the cabinet/library, revealing the dark figure of the entranced medium lying on a sofa while "Katie" remained in the room with the sitters.

At other times, Crookes, and later other witnesses, were even invited by "Katie" to enter the cabinet and examine the two together by the light of a bottle of phosphorescent oil. Not only was Crookes utterly convinced that both Florence and "Katie" were living presences, but he even noted significant differences between them, such as a blister on Florence's neck and the fact that Florence had pierced ears while "Katie" did not.

This, very briefly summarized, is the evidence on which a large part of the case for materialization continues to rest even today. It rests on the word of an undeniably distinguished man of science, and to discount it is to believe that Crookes was either genuinely deceived or a collaborator in a stunning hoax. Outlandish as such suspicions may appear, there are circumstances that make them worth pursuing.

One might begin by remarking that the Crookes who experimented on Florence Cook seems a much different scientist from the one who tested D. D. Home so painstakingly with spring and balance. Where now were the admirable standards for this type of research that Crookes himself had set down in 1870 before his session with Home?

> The spiritualist tells of tapping sounds which are produced in different parts of a room when two or more persons sit quietly around a table.
>
> The scientific experimenter is entitled to ask that these taps shall be produced on the stretched membrane of his phonautograph.
>
> The spiritualist tells of rooms and houses being shaken, even to injury, by superhuman power. The man of science merely asks for a pendulum to be set vibrating when it is in a glass case and supported on solid masonry.
>
> The spiritualist tells of heavy articles of furniture moving from one room to another without human agency. But the man of science has made instruments which will divide an inch into a million parts; and he is justified in doubting the accuracy of the former observations, if the same force is powerless to move the index of his instrument one poor degree.
>
> The spiritualist tells of flowers with the fresh dew on them, of fruit, and living objects being carried through closed windows, and even solid brick-walls. The scientific investigator naturally asks that an additional weight (if it be only the 1000th part of a grain) be deposited on one pan of his balance when the case is locked. (*Quarterly Journal of Science*, July 1870)

As has been shown, the procedures used by Crookes in testing Florence Cook bore little resemblance to those outlined in the above quotation. It is true that many photographs were taken, but none, at least of those that survive today, actually shows the *faces* of both the medium and the apparition. Most are of "Katie" alone, while of the few showing the two together, Florence's face is always obscured, either by clothing, by bad lighting, or by "Katie" herself.

This raises a further point about the "proof" obtained by the sitters' frequent viewings of "Katie" and Florence. There is nothing in any of the reports to rule out the possibility that what was seen inside the cabinet amounted to nothing but the medium's discarded clothing and boots supported by sofa pillows, a trick as old as the first child who wanted to leave the house after his official bedtime. It is notable that the medium's head was always wrapped in a shawl at these times, supposedly because exposure to direct light was harmful. And as for the boots on the sofa, we may once again be grateful to the canny Frank Podmore for reminding us that "Katie" customarily went barefoot.

Perhaps it could also be considered odd that Crookes, who had been so willing to modify his equipment to satisfy fellow scientists during his work with Home, now constantly refused even the most elementary and harmless suggestions. One such was made by Edward Cox, a man who was not only widely known in spiritualist circles, but who had assisted Crookes in some of his former investigations. Cox's idea was that putting a drop of India ink on the medium's forehead would quickly settle the question of who came out from behind the curtain, but no such action was ever taken.

Yet, the "dummy" theory, though it would have allowed Florence Cook to be in two places at once, will not clear up all the mystery attending the "Katie" séances of the winter and spring of 1874. What, for example, is to be said of the times when not only Crookes, but others such as Florence's patron Charles Blackburn were allowed to enter the cabinet and verify *by touch*, as well as by sight, that the medium and the apparition were equally solid and alive? Even Mr. Podmore states that "there can be no reasonable doubt that on these two occasions, at any rate, the figure of 'Katie' seen, heard, and touched by Mr. Crookes and most of those present, was not that of Miss Cook masquerading as a spirit, but was a separate entity of some kind." Whether carelessly or charitably, Podmore does not pursue this point further, only footnoting the fact that the spiritualist press itself expressed the view that these sessions were not conducted under proper test conditions.

In what way, then, did the conditions differ from those of the previous experiments in which no one at all had been allowed actually to enter the cabinet? Rather startlingly, the records show that for no very apparent reason, the later sessions were held at the Cook family home in Hackney rather than at Professor Crookes' house on Mornington Road. Moreover, the proceedings no longer took place in the breakfast room with its now familiar wooden corner cabinet, which had been the scene of so many of Florence's earlier materializations. Instead, they had been moved to an upper floor, where there were two rooms arranged very much like the two rooms at Mornington Road. That is, there was a parlor with a table at which sat the guests, while the cabinet was actually Florence's own bedroom, which communicated with the parlor by a pair of folding doors.

As before, the doors were curtained off in order to keep the cabinet/bedroom dark. And as before, the bedroom had a second door that led into a hallway and so to the rest of the house. *But,* decidedly not as before, there is no mention made in the case of these Hackney sittings of Professor Crookes' or anyone else's locking this second door. Nor, even if the door had been locked, would it rule out the possibility that other keys to the door of her own bedroom were available to Florence Cook.

The circumstance is bound to sound significant even to the least suspicious person when we recall that in these two rooms, *and only in these two rooms,* was face-to-face confrontation among the medium, the materialization, and any third parties allowed to take place. There could hardly have been much difficulty in introducing an assistant conspirator into the bedroom through the hall door (locked or unlocked) at Hackney, whereas the matter would have been much more complex at Mornington Road, since the uninvited visitor would have had to avoid being noticed either by the household servants or by Mrs. Crookes (who was in residence there at the time but who did not attend the séances).

Assuming for a moment that there was a confederate employed in the Hackney appearances of "Katie," assuming therefore that Florence Cook was then and thereafter a fraud, it must seem equally inconceivable that a man of Sir William Crookes' stature in the scientific world could have been deceived by such goings-on and that he would have lent his immense prestige to any kind of fakery.

A possible solution to this dilemma has been suggested by the same Trevor H. Hall whose researches into the psychological background of the D. D. Home levitation were mentioned in the previous chapter. Making use of a considerable amount of evidence that was not available to earlier investigators such as Podmore, Hall reconstructed a story of the relationship between Florence Cook and Sir William Crookes that is none the less fascinating for having nothing to do with apparitions.

Florence, as we have said, was receiving money from the wealthy spiritualist Charles Blackburn, and it went without saying that Blackburn's generosity would cease if his pretty little protégée were to be unmasked as a fraud. Then came the incident of the presumptuous Mr. Volckman, who, in the face of the outcry by Florence's supporters, continued to maintain publicly that "Katie King" was none other than Florence Cook in a white shift and headdress. Moreover, Blackburn himself had been present at that disastrous sitting, and, though no correspondence on the subject survives, it is reasonable to assume that his suspicions would have been aroused. Like many spiritualists of the time, Blackburn exhibited "faith, but not blind faith," and as a successful man of business he surely had a due regard for the principle of "value for money."

In any case, the Cook family must have felt its livelihood threatened. It is impossible to know when or to whom the idea of seeking justification from Professor Crookes first presented itself. Perhaps it was to Florence's mother Emma, who showed herself then and later a shrewd manager of her daughters' careers (for Florence's younger sister Kate also became a medium).

In any case, it was in the same month as the Volckman incident that Florence went, as she said, "to offer myself upon the altar of science," that is, to propose that Crookes study her mediumship. By that time Florence had met Crookes at least once. Perhaps she knew or suspected that the scientist found her attractive; perhaps she was merely confident that he could be deceived as easily as other investigators. But the event exceeded the expectation, for there seems little doubt that the forty-two-year-old Crookes and the (possibly) seventeen-year-old Florence were soon involved in a love affair.

There, if we choose to accept Mr. Hall's conclusion, is the missing piece of the puzzle—a man approaching middle age, so infatuated with a young girl that he almost begs to be deceived by her and in the end will even endanger his career and his principles for her sake. Florence *had* to be certified as genuine or she would lose her patron. Very well, Crookes would do so—and quickly, judging from the fact that the preliminary report came out only six weeks after he began his study. Then followed the Mornington Road sessions and finally those at Hackney, where Blackburn was himself allowed to establish the existence of the medium and the materialization together.

The Cooks were now safe. Is it any surprise then that "Katie" announced in May 1874 that she would no longer visit her "dear Florrie"? The danger of exposure was ever present, and at this point it must have seemed better for Florence to return to less risky manifestations. There was a touching farewell scene at which many of the sitters wept and "Katie" distributed locks of her hair as mementos. Her final act before disappearing forever was to commend her medium to the care and protection of Sir William Crookes.

The affair with Crookes was not to continue much longer, however. Perhaps Florence broke it off in the knowledge that, after the publication of his highly favorable report in June, Crookes was of no further use to her. On the other hand, it may have been the announcement later in June of her secret marriage in April to Edward Elgie Corner that was responsible for both the break with Crookes and her ultimate fall from favor with Charles Blackburn. By late autumn Crookes had returned to his laboratory and Blackburn had finally and definitively withdrawn his financial support of Florence, whose subsequent story is one of an unhappy marriage, failing fortunes, and second-rate mediumship resting on past laurels.

Greed, deception, and philandering such as these would undoubtedly have created a monumental scandal had they become public knowledge in the 1870s. It was not until 1922, however, that the story actually came to light. A gentleman named Francis G. H. Anderson approached the Society for Psychical Research in London with the information that he had been involved in a love affair with Florence Cook Corner in 1893 (when she was at least thirty-seven and he twenty-three). In the course of their relationship, said Mr. Anderson, Florence had told him of her previous affair with Sir William Crookes and had confessed that her mediumship was fraudulent. The séances at Mornington Road had been devised in order to allay the suspicions of Mrs. Crookes, Edward Corner, and Charles Blackburn (the last of whom would certainly have dropped Florence if her name had become associated with scandal).

There seems little reason to doubt Anderson's sincerity in making his statement, which he later repeated in writing at much greater length, and which certainly stood to bring him nothing but trouble since he was a married man at the time. If corroboration is desired, it may be found in a statement by Mrs. Eileen Garrett, then president of the Parapsychology Foundation of New York, concerning a similar confession made by Florence to the French poet and dramatist M. H. A. Jules Bois and later revealed to Mrs. Garrett by Mr. Bois. Florence apparently regarded the success of her "Katie" deception with some pride and was in the habit of talking about it with her various lovers. It seems that her powers of attraction were stronger and more enduring than her powers of materialization, though neither brought her much lasting happiness. She died without possessions in London on April 22, 1904.

As a final footnote to the career of Florence Cook, we might note that her sister Kate, at least, seems to have profited from Florence's mistakes. At about the same time that Florence was dropped by Charles Blackburn, Kate began to develop mediumistic gifts so similar to Florence's that her séances were almost line-for-line copies. Blackburn was thus offered a new protégée, whom he happily accepted. This time there were no scientific tests or outside observers to disrupt the proceedings. Blackburn not only transferred his patronage to Kate, he eventually remembered the entire family (with the exception of Florence) in his will, transferring to them a substantial income and two imposing houses.

The story of Florence Cook and her "constant spiritual companion" Katie King was once described (in a wholly admiring manner) as a "fairy tale" by the widely read modern follower of psychic events, Nandor Fodor. It was indeed a fairy tale, in the sense that it had little to do with fact, though the happy ending was reserved for the heroine's relatives.

CHAPTER VIII

MANY PHENOMENA, ONLY ONE PALLADINO

Although, for a variety of reasons, the careers of D. D. Home and Florence Cook are those that attract the most interest among modern spiritualists, they were only two of the many famous, flamboyant, and fascinating practitioners of the art in England and America.

Notable on both sides of the Atlantic were the Davenport brothers, Ira Erastus (1839–77) and William Henry (1841–1911). Brought up in Buffalo, New York, the Davenports showed their mediumistic talents as early as 1850. By 1857, they were "on the road" together in the traditional theatrical sense, giving public performances from the stage and enduring alternate hardships and triumphs. In 1864, the Davenports followed the footsteps of Mrs. Hayden, D. D. Home, and many others to England accompanied by another medium, a theatrical manager, and the well-known revivalist preacher J. B. Ferguson.

The Davenports introduced into their séances a novel variation on the tying of the medium to prevent fraud. It was their custom to challenge members of the audience to tie them in such a way that the spirits could not release them. Almost invariably the most intricate knots in the heaviest cords were neatly and invisibly untied as soon as the lights were turned out. Sometimes the ropes were also found draped around the necks of the challengers, showing that the spirit world was not without a sense of humor.

Throughout their career, the Davenports contented themselves mainly with this phenomenon of release by the spirits, accompanied by spectacular raps and knocks and the playing of numerous airborne musical instruments, which whizzed through the audience with such vigor that, on one occasion at least, blood was drawn in a collision with a spectator. Though no doubt very entertaining (except to the man who was struck by the flying guitar), these manifestations had nothing about them that in itself suggested the presence of spirits. In fact, they were more like the peformances of professional conjurers, a fact that leading magicians of the day were not slow to notice. Several of them offered to duplicate the Davenports' feats in public and some were judged to have succeeded, though it must in fairness be admitted that other challengers were not as skillful as they had boasted.

The final undoing of the Davenports came in the city of Liverpool, where two gentlemen in the audience volunteered to tie the mediums with the famous and supposedly secret Tom Fool's knot. The brothers at first consented but then protested that the knots were unfairly and painfully tight. A doctor from the audience declared the knots were not hindering the circulation, whereupon the mediums refused to proceed. This created a furor, which reached the proportions of a riot the following night.

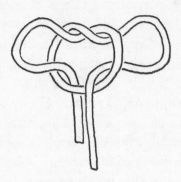

Tom Fool's Knot

In the wake of this incident, the two were forced to flee the city, and eventually the country, though it is interesting to note that they continued to attract admiring audiences elsewhere. The faith of some of the Davenports' supporters was so unshakable that they insisted that the professional conjurers who had imitated their feat were themselves spirit mediums without knowing it.

Of a totally different mold was another major medium of the period, William Stainton Moses (1839–92). It would be exceedingly difficult to find a man whose day-to-day life was more respectable, not to say humdrum, than Moses'. Son of the headmaster of Lincolnshire Grammar School, he was a graduate of Exeter College, Oxford, and became a minister in 1863, at the age of twenty-four. However, he was forced to give up his curacy on account of a form of throat trouble that prevented his preaching, and moved to London to become tutor to the young son of Mr. and Mrs. Stanhope Speer. Shortly afterward he became an English master at the University College School of London, a post he continued to hold until three years before his death in 1892. Clergyman, schoolmaster, and private tutor, he led an upright and sober life, apparently held in high regard by all who knew him.

Yet from 1872 on, William Stainton Moses was a trance medium of considerable reputation. In his presence, tables moved, raps and harplike sounds were heard, lights hung motionless in the air, spirit messages were found on supposedly blank papers, and sitters were showered with perfume. Moses also produced levitation, automatic writing, and the direct voice as well as the rarer phenomena of teleportation (moving of objects from outside the séance room, apparently through the walls).

However, Moses never gave a public demonstration, or indeed sat for anyone outside his own circle of friends and fellow spiritualists, and his phenomena, while very impressive, represented nothing unique as such things go. These circumstances, and the fact that he was never tied, restrained, or tested in any way has prevented serious investigators of physical mediumship from taking this aspect of his work very seriously. His importance for the spiritualist movement today rests rather on his character, his writing, and his activities outside the séance room. First in importance was Moses' utterly unimpeachable private life. The Speers, who were his friends, employers, and chief sponsors (and had after all chosen to entrust to him the education of their son) were only the first of a long line of commentators to insist that any suspicion of fraud in such a man was unthinkable.

Second was the influence of "Imperator," Moses' chief spirit control, who produced through Moses' direct writing several volumes of religious and spiritual teaching of the same sort as Davis' Great Harmonia but in a tone that was a good deal more scholarly. The words of "Imperator" were widely read among spiritualists and were taken to be a further indication of the high moral character of Moses and his associates.

Finally, Moses' position in the spiritualist community in general led him to play a major role in the founding of the British National Association of Spiritualists, to serve on the councils of the Psychological Society and the Society for Psychical Research, and to hold the office of president of the London Spiritual Alliance. Thus, as a pillar of organized spiritualism he became a sort of living monument to the integrity of the movement.

Oddly enough, the fact that these decades, the later seventies and eighties, saw the rise of several such spiritualist organizations such as those with which Stainton Moses was associated was partially responsible for a relative decline in the sort of mediumship practiced in their different ways by the Fox sisters, Home, Florence Cook and the Davenports. The reason was that the spiritualists undertook in their own defense to examine the claims of outstanding mediums and did so with such thoroughness that the threat of public exposure forced both mediums and potential audiences to act with caution. This is not to say that physical mediumship began to disappear from the scene, but that the emphasis seemed to shift at this time from tipping tables and tooting trumpets to a more serious attempt to examine those proofs of spirit existence that took the form of messages and information. Commercial mediumship suffered a temporary eclipse.

And then came Eusapia.

It seems safe to say that this Italian peasant woman was almost single-handedly responsible for restoring the prestige of physical mediumship and is today the single most famous medium of her own or any other period.

Eusapia Palladino (1854–1918) was born near Bari in southern Italy. Her mother died shortly after the child's birth and her father was murdered by brigands in 1866, leaving Eusapia an orphan at twelve. Even at that age, so it was later declared, she had experienced many strange things such as raps in the furniture, glaring eyes in the dark, and invisible hands that stripped off her bedclothes.

Friends and relatives now sent little Eusapia to Naples, hoping that she would find a position as a nursemaid. The experiment was not a success, however. Not only did disturbing things continue to happen in the child's presence, she also showed herself most unwilling to adapt to city ways. Neither then nor later was Eusapia going to be a docile person. She had strength of character, which showed itself at this time in a refusal to take baths, comb her hair, or learn to read. So Eusapia was dismissed. But wherever she went the phenomena continued.

The family with whom she had taken shelter after her dismissal became fascinated with her abilities and would have liked her to stay on indefinitely to entertain their friends. However, with typical independence, Eusapia declined and began to work as a laundress, although she continued to give séances. Then, like a movie star of today, she was "discovered" by a rich and influential spiritualist couple named Damiani in 1872. The Damianis also attempted to "civilize" Eusapia, but she showed herself at eighteen no more interested in acquiring an education and social polish than she had been at twelve. There was also the upsetting fact that a sort of reverse apportation seemed to occur at Eusapia's séances. Small, valuable objects and even items of clothing that sitters had *brought into* the séance room could not be found when the lights went on at the end of the session, and some persons voiced doubts as to the honesty of the medium—or perhaps of her spirit control. All in all, the Damianis' efforts to develop and study Eusapia's powers proved thankless, and she relapsed into a life of ordinary professional mediumship, virtually unknown outside a small circle in Naples.

In this way Eusapia would probably have ended her life if it had not been for the intervention of Ercole Chiaia, a doctor and student of occultism who became interested in her around 1886. Acting in a capacity almost like that of manager, Chiaia took it upon himself to print, in August of 1888, an open letter to the famous Italian psychiatrist and criminologist Cesare Lombroso (1836–1909). In it, under the guise of describing a patient, Dr. Chiaia gave a summary of Eusapia's powers as they appeared in the séance room and urgently requested Lombroso's aid in confirming or denying the existence of a new physical force. It was an excellent piece of what today would be called press-agentry because, although the eminent Signore Lombroso ignored

Chiaia's request at the time, Eusapia's career received an immediate boost. Certainly one can understand why Chiaia's description of the case of Eusapia Palladino captured the attention of so many who read it. Here is the most relevant part of his description:

She is nearly thirty years old and very ignorant; her appearance is neither fascinating nor endowed with the power which modern criminologists call irresistible; but when she wishes, be it by day or by night, she can divert a curious group for an hour or so with the most surprising phenomena. Either bound to a seat or firmly held by the hands of the curious, she attracts to her the articles of furniture which surround her, lifts them up, holds them suspended in the air like Mahomet's coffin, and makes them come down again with undulatory movements, as if they were obeying her will. She increases their height or lessens it according to her pleasure. She raps or taps upon the walls, the ceiling, the floor, with fine rhythm and cadence. In response to the requests of the spectators something like flashes of electricity shoots forth from her body, and envelops her or enwraps the spectators of these marvellous scenes. She draws upon cards that you hold out, everything that you want—figures, signatures, numbers, sentences—by just stretching out her hand toward the indicated place.

If you place in the corner of the room a vessel containing a layer of soft clay, you find after some moments the imprint in it of a small or large hand, the image of a face (front view or profile) from which a plaster cast can be taken. In this way portraits of a face at different angles have been preserved, and those who desire so can thus make serious and important studies.

This woman rises in the air, no matter what bands tie her down. She seems to lie upon the empty air, as on a couch, contrary to all the laws of gravity; she plays on musical instruments—organs, bells, tambourines—as if they had been touched by her hands or moved by the breath of invisible gnomes. This woman at times can increase her stature by more than four inches.

She is like an India rubber doll, like an automaton of a new kind; she takes strange forms. How many legs and arms has she? We do not know. While her limbs are being held by incredulous spectators, we see other limbs coming into view, without her knowing where they come from. Her shoes are too small to fit these witch-feet of hers, and this particular circumstance gives rise to the suspicion of the intervention of mysterious power. (quoted by Nandor Fodor in his *Encyclopedia of Psychic Science*, p. 271)

As with every other aspect of Eusapia's career, we may note in this description a mixture of the simplest and most common occurrences of the séance room with others that are much rarer and more difficult to explain. What, for example, is to be said of the making of impressions in a bowl of clay that the spectators are convinced the medium could not possibly have reached without leaving the chair to which they are equally convinced she was firmly tied? And what are these "witch-feet" and phantom limbs that are so eerily observed? Nearly the entire history of Eusapia's next thirty years is devoted to accounts of the commissions, committees, and learned investigators who sought to answer these and dozens of other questions about her.

Of the major researchers who sought out Eusapia, the first was the same Cesare Lombroso who had ignored Chiaia's invitation only two years previously. Lombroso came to Naples in 1890, and arranged to hold private séances with Eusapia at his hotel. Most of the results were below Eusapia's usual level of impressiveness, with this exception. At the close of one session the lights had been turned up and the observers were discussing their impressions, but the medium was still tied to her chair about eighteen inches in front of the curtain that formed her cabinet. Suddenly sounds were heard from inside the alcove, the curtains began to billow about, and a small table emerged and began to move slowly toward the medium. Lombroso and his associates rushed into the cabinet, convinced that Eusapia must somehow have hidden a confederate inside, but it was empty of all except the usual equipment, such as musical instruments. The observers were stupefied and Lombroso withdrew his previous doubts, saying that he was in a state of mental confusion and could in no way explain what had taken place.

Lombroso's announcement was greeted with a furor much like that aroused by Crookes' report on D. D. Home in England two decades earlier. As a direct result, Eusapia was asked to sit for a scientific committee in Milan during October 1892. Among its five members were Lombroso himself and Professor Charles Richet (1850–1935), a noted student of psychic phenomena and winner in 1913 of the Nobel Prize in Physiology and Medicine.

The sittings of the Milan committee were the first of which there are relatively reliable records, and they do not ignore a fact that can be read between the lines of all accounts of Eusapia's manifestations, both earlier and later: *Eusapia cheated*. There is no question whatever, even among most of her ardent supporters, that "The Queen of the Cabinet," as she has been called, took advantage of every lapse of attention or muscular relaxation on the part of those who were supposed to "control" her movements, in order to produce touches, raps, or movement of objects in places where they should have been impossible. Sometimes her tricks were clumsy and obvious; sometimes they were subtle. It made no difference to her that she might have been exposed in these activities, as she was repeatedly. Given the slightest opportunity, Eusapia cheated.

One of her commonest ruses was to convince the two persons assigned to control her arms that each had continued to keep contact with a separate limb, whereas in fact one of them had transferred his hand to her other arm. This was possible because Eusapia commonly moved about restlessly while in trance. In the course of her head-tossing and arm-waving it took great skill on the part of the controllers to be sure that they were not both controlling the same hand. This was the more true as the controllers were usually allowed only to *follow* the medium's hands by touch, never to restrain her movements. Nor was it much easier to be certain that Eusapia's feet were where they were supposed to be.

Yet there were other features of the Milan sittings that did not seem attributable to trickery on Eusapia's part. During sessions held by a dim red light, members of the audience were able to see and feel what were apparently a number of hands that groped outward from behind the cabinet curtains while the medium remained wholly visible in front of them. Given the certainty that Eusapia was not above faking her effects, was it *possible* for anyone (let alone a semiliterate peasant woman with no knowledge of applied mechanics) to bring about these phenomena through normal means? That, in essence, is the exasperating problem that haunted Europe's scientific minds at the time and haunts us still today.

Eusapia continued to baffle the learned. She sat for the Russian zoologist N. P. Wagner in Naples in January 1893, and again later in Rome. She sat for the Polish psychologist Julijan Ochorowicz in Warsaw at the end of that year and the beginning of the next. In all cases the results were mixed. Some effects were plainly the result of cheating. Some *could* have been produced by cheating, although witnesses were prepared to assert that no cheating had taken place. And some effects were judged inexplicable in terms of any of the methods of cheating Eusapia had so far been known to use, or possibly inexplicable in any normal way whatever. So much depended on the reliability of the observer and the completeness of the record, matters which are now beyond our verification.

A more revealing series of sittings was held in 1894 by Professor Richet (the same who had served on the Milan committee) at his home in France. Almost every member of this group of sitters was a major name in the history of psychical research, a field that had begun to produce investigators as formidable in personality as the mediums they investigated. In addition to Richet himself, the above-mentioned Dr. Ochorowicz, and the German researcher Baron von Schrenck-Notzing, there were four highly influential English spiritualists. They were physicist Sir (then Professor) Oliver Lodge, Professor and Mrs. Henry Sidgwick, and F. W. H. Myers, the last three of whom had been among the founders of the Society for Psychical Research in 1882.

These people were perfectly aware of the medium's reputation of freeing herself from control and of the consequent increased necessity for suspicious watchfulness. Yet curtains billowed when there was no breeze, the sitters experienced repeated "spirit touches" at times when all were certain Eusapia could not have been responsible, and, most striking of all, objects moved themselves about the room under the sitters' noses. One of these objects was a stalkless melon weighing over seven kilograms (about 15½ pounds), which was moved from a chair behind the medium to the séance table itself.

Even if Eusapia had managed to free a limb on this occasion, it is difficult to know how she could merely have *grasped* so large and smooth an object with one hand (or foot?), let alone moved it the required distance without rising from her chair. Alternative theories such as (a) that the observers were simultaneously and totally hallucinated as to the motion of the melon or (b) that one or more of them was in league with the medium seem equally untenable when one considers the great variety of sitters who dealt with Eusapia in the course of her career. In this case there can be no question of the detailed long-term preparation of those to be hallucinated, as in the Home levitation, or of overreliance on the unimpeachable character of one authority, as in the affair of Florence Cook.

What these French sittings did serve to indicate, as Dr. E. J. Dingwall and others have pointed out, was that there existed a crying need for the more extensive use of recording devices and photographs so that the control of the medium and the occurrence of the phenomena should not be subject to errors in human perception. Unfortunately, such improved methods of investigation were not used with Eusapia until a much later period, and even then were not as thoroughly applied as perhaps they could have been.

After the French sittings, her next important series of sessions took place in England, but these were generally rated a disaster. Of the four English participants in the investigations of Professor Richet, only Sir Oliver Lodge had found himself completely satisfied that Eusapia's phenomena were in part supernormal. The others, F. W. H. Myers and the Sidgwicks, apparently felt that they wanted further trials before reaching firm opinions. They invited Eusapia to sit for them at Mr. Myers' home in Cambridge, where she went in the late summer of 1895. Also among those present was Dr. Richard Hodgson, who was at that time an officer of the American Society for Psychical Research (A.S.P.R.) and who had written a criticism of procedures at the recently concluded French sittings.

It is extremely regrettable that the detailed record of the Cambridge sittings has never been published by the S.P.R. We therefore have no way of knowing precisely what led up to the conclusions reached by the sitters. We must be content with the fact that in October 1895, Professor Sidgwick, as president of the S.P.R., announced to the society's general meeting that nothing had been witnessed at Cambridge that could not be put down to trickery. He then went on to withdraw his previous limited support of Eusapia, based on the French sittings, and to state that he had come to believe all the manifestations were fraudulent. Sidgwick was joined by Myers in rejecting the Cambridge phenomena, although Myers chose to reserve judgment on what he had seen in France, which was admitted to have been far more impressive.

Denunciation before the S.P.R. was bound to be a serious blow to Eusapia. No matter how often she had been caught in petty cheating, no major investigation had ever been able to account for everything that went on in her presence. Now suddenly she was "beyond the pale" as far as the S.P.R. was concerned.

Whatever one may think of the truth or falsity of the conclusions reached after the Cambridge sittings, it is clear there were things about Eusapia that would probably have offended the Sidgwicks and their friends regardless of the quality of her mediumship. In fact, had it not been for her mediumship, it is highly unlikely that these cultivated English people would ever have met such a person as Eusapia. "Queen of the Cabinet" though she was, she did not at all fit into the mold established by previous major mediums. She had none of the social graces and charm of Home, none of the winning ways of Florence Cook, and certainly none of the sober and upright character of Stainton Moses. Instead, she was almost everything that her Cambridge hosts were not—ill-educated, coarse, emotional, stubborn, earthy, loud, crafty, and quite uninhibited about her interest in the opposite sex. These same qualities may have worked in her favor in France or Italy, but could only have served to irritate and upset all concerned when the setting was Cambridge. And it was in just these circumstances that Eusapia had been known to cheat most readily. For whatever reason, mediums frequently share the "temperament" usually attributed to actors and musicians. When they are unhappy or nervous, the performance, the concert, or the séance does not go well. (Actors and musicians, too, have their methods of "cheating," the little tricks that disguise the fact that this time they are not giving their best.)

There was another factor at work in the S.P.R.'s attitude to Eusapia. The society had been founded with the object of bringing spiritualism and other psychic manifestations out of the sensational press and obtaining for them a fair hearing among the educated. Though many members of the S.P.R. were convinced of the existence of the spirit world, they had been among the most zealous exposers of fraudulent mediums. From their point of view, therefore, Eusapia Palladino could only succeed in giving spiritualism a bad name by her acknowledged cheating, *whether or not* she also produced genuine phenomena. Perhaps typical of the era was the sort of reasoning that led many persons to believe that because Stainton Moses had a reputation for general honesty his phenomena could not be fraudulent, while because Eusapia was known to cheat when she could her phenomena could not be genuine. The ideas of subsequent decades cast doubt on both conclusions, as we shall see in a later chapter.

In the meantime, Eusapia's career was far from over, much to the displeasure of the S.P.R. She returned to the continent, where she had always felt more at home, and presided over numerous séances in private homes. The sitters were apparently more than satisfied, for she continued to be in great demand. It was not until November 1898 that Eusapia consented to exhibit her powers for another learned committee. This time the place was Paris and the organizer was Camille Flammarion, an eminent astronomer and student of the psychic (a term he himself had coined). One of his chief assistants was Professor Richet.

These Paris sittings produced a number of familiar manifestations and a few that were decidedly unfamiliar. One seemed almost like the early stages of a materialization, with the exception that the medium was not hidden in a cabinet as was the custom when materialization was the principal object of the séance. The medium was seated at one end of a table and controlled in the usual way when the sitters were riveted by the sight of a series of semitransparent female half-figures or busts that seemed to glide out of her body and down the length of the table between the rows of sitters.

Richet apparently felt the Paris sittings were so interesting that they ought to be extended, and when the series sponsored by Flammarion was ended (and Flammarion had declared himself satisfied that trickery could not account for what had occurred), Eusapia agreed to continue sitting for Richet. Richet also invited the attendance of F. W. H. Myers, as a private individual rather than as a representative of the S.P.R. These further sessions were truly spectacular, if the reaction of the participants is any guide. But as with the Cambridge sittings, it is unfortunate (and rather mysterious) that this individual reaction was the only official information regarding what went on.

Whatever it was, it led the formerly skeptical or positively hostile Myers to declare before the S.P.R.'s general meeting of December 1899 that he was now utterly convinced of Eusapia's genuineness and that what he had just witnessed was "far more striking" even than the séances of Eusapia's that he had attended in 1894. However, neither Myers nor Richet ever published any notes on these sittings, though in the case of Myers the continuing negative attitude of the S.P.R. leadership was apparently responsible for the omission. The only surviving account comes to us from the unofficial notes of Professor T. Flournoy (d. 1921) of the Faculty of Sciences at the University of Geneva, who was also present at some of the sessions.

Flournoy was an experienced observer of the mediumistic scene, and though he does not go into sufficient detail to permit a strict analysis of what was observed (that task having been left to Myers and Richet), there is no reason to doubt his over-all description of the conditions of the séances. Thus it is interesting to note that this time Eusapia not only agreed to produce her phenomena in a light that was dim but quite sufficient so that her movements could be seen by the sitters, but she also allowed her wrists and ankles to be firmly held rather than merely followed about.

Under these conditions, far more satisfactory for sci-

entific observation than those the medium usually au-
thorized, the manifestations that occurred were of familiar kinds but can hardly be called boring when so many
have been at a loss to explain them. The curtains of
the cabinet billowed as if in a strong breeze, although
in the closed séance room the air was naturally quite
still. A zither that lay on the floor of the cabinet, well
out of the medium's supposed reach, was first heard to
repeat one note several times and then to thump on the
floor. Finally, the instrument was observed to leave the
cabinet and land on the table between the sitters. During these and similar happenings, the sitters constantly
felt themselves pushed, tugged, pinched, patted, and
even struck by what was specified to be "a large hand,"
even though all were agreed that Eusapia's own hands
were clearly visible and were also firmly held.

In spite of the nonappearance of the scientific records
of these sittings, the results were well publicized in
other ways, and Eusapia's fame increased accordingly.
Judging from the fact that she had allowed test conditions to be so much stricter than was her habit, she
must have seen the Paris sittings as an opportunity to
recover the ground she had lost when the S.P.R. withdrew its support. If so, she had succeeded very well.
Even in England the Cambridge disaster was largely forgotten, and it sometimes seemed that every scientist in
Europe was anxious to sit with the great Palladino.

Her next major series of séances was held in Genoa
in 1901, under the sponsorship of a society called the
Minerva Scientific Circle. This time careful records were
kept and published. However, since the phenomena witnessed were neither more startling, less puzzling, nor

better documented than previously, we may as well save ourselves the trouble of considering them in detail. It is perhaps sufficient to note that the group's leading investigator, Professor Enrico Morselli, though fully aware of Eusapia's continued cheating, calculated that at least 75 percent of what took place was genuinely supernormal.

During the next few years, Eusapia seems to have sat for one commission after another, much as she had done for fifteen years. But there was this difference: The Queen of the Cabinet was growing old. Her strong face took on a look of suffering and also of bitterness. Sometimes the phenomena would not come, and sometimes she found herself so exhausted after a séance that she could hardly walk. This is understandable, whatever one thinks of her mediumship. The amount of thrashing about Eusapia did while in trance must in itself have constituted a stiff workout, not to mention the drain on her energies which, according to the spiritualist theory, was necessary for materialization and moving of objects. On the other hand, if all her phenomena were fraudulent, every séance must have had the status of a major stage performance that required extraordinary muscular coordination and powers of contortion.

And in either case, she was constantly aware of being put to the test and constantly under threat of exposure in the minor tricks that she seems to have been psychologically unable to abandon. No wonder that she was tired and no wonder that she began to betray a certain contempt for her sitters. Sensation seekers and scientists, the rich and the curious vied for the privilege of sitting around a table with her in the dark—and paid well for it, too. With nothing but her wits and her "powers," she had sent them all away converted or baffled, physicists and fools alike.

Yet now she knew she could not stop. The séance room was her profession and she had no other way to make a living. She had to keep on, even though the names and purposes of the various commissions may well have become as confusing and repetitive to her as they are to us.

So she was studied by Professor Bottazzi of the Physiological Institute of the University of Naples in 1907 and by Mr. Jules Courtier of the Paris General Psychological Institute at intervals from 1905 to 1908. In all instances the same problems were evident. It was Eusapia who made the rules as to what kind of control of her movements would be allowed. Any attempt to overstep her regulations resulted simply in an absence of phenomena. On the other hand, the kind of control she permitted was simply not foolproof. She was not only adept at the substitution of hands described previously, she could sometimes slip a foot out of its shoe without giving the controller the slightest hint that the shoe was not still occupied. And, as the Davenport brothers had shown, no amount of tying *by itself* is proof that the medium is immobilized. (So far as is known, no one ever offered to try the Tom Fool's knot on Eusapia.)

The one innovation associated with the tests conducted by Courtier was the fairly extensive use of simple recording devices during the séance. Measurements were taken of the temperature, humidity, barometric pressure, and electrical conditions of the room, of the medium's pulse and respiration rate, and of the increase and decrease in weight of various objects levitated. Nothing astonishing was shown by these tests, but they did serve to establish that on this occasion at least the phenomena were entirely real and not merely the hallucinations of the observers. Of course such methods revealed nothing about what *caused* the manifestations, whether it was Eusapia or an "unknown physical force." On that score the investigators were as much in the dark as ever. In fact, it is almost incredible that from such vast volumes of material, collected over a period of two decades, it appeared to be impossible to settle the questions raised by Eusapia's mediumship. Science was to make one last assault on the mystery.

In 1908, Eusapia sat in Naples for a three-man committee that was in some respects the most formidable she had ever encountered. One was Mr. Hereward Carrington, a highly skeptical American researcher who, though only twenty-seven at the time, had already been actively engaged in exposing fraudulent mediums for eight years and had written a comprehensive book on their methods entitled *The Physical Phenomena of Spiritualism*. Carrington had persuaded the British S.P.R. (despite its continuing misgivings) to send with him its honorary secretary, the Honorable Everard Feilding, a man slightly less experienced in the séance room than his colleagues, but in no way less difficult to convince. The third member was Mr. W. W. Baggally, who had behind him thirty years of psychical investigation in which, he had said, he doubted he had ever met a genuine physical medium. Baggally was also an accomplished amateur conjurer who used to amuse his friends by duplicating the tricks of fraudulent mediums.

In the hands of these three there was at least no flaw to be found in the séance records, which were taken by a shorthand stenographer and appear in their fullest form in Feilding's book *Sittings with Eusapia Palladino & other Studies*. These records have been cited repeatedly as models of their kind and established something of a standard for future investigators. In addition to the minute-by-minute picture of the impressions of the observers, the account gives extensive descriptions of the séance room and its furnishings, complete with diagrams and measurements, and carefully notes each change in the lighting arrangement as it occurred. The phenomena witnessed were not only noted but were classified and discussed one by one in a separate section, and finally each investigator was given ample space to note any disagreements he might have and to state his individual conclusions.

Since the proceedings occupy over 250 pages of text, it is obviously impracticable to attempt to give here a complete account of them. However, a list of the kinds of things that went on (or, as the experimenters themselves would surely have phrased it, appeared to go on) will give the general picture. They were (as abstracted from the report, pages 41–50): (1) movements and levitations of the séance table; (2) movements of curtains; (3) bulgings of the medium's dress; (4) raps; (5) bangs on the séance table; (6) noises inside the cabinet; (7) plucking of the guitar; (8) transportations of the small table from the cabinet onto the séance table, and movements and levitations of it outside the curtain; (9) transportation of other objects from the cabinet; (10) touches by invisible or unseen fingertips outside the curtain; (11) touches and grasps by a hand through the curtain; (12) appearance of hands outside the curtain; (13) appearance of heads and objects more or less like heads; (14) appearance of other undefinable objects; (15) transportation of objects outside the curtain by a visible hand; (16) movements of objects outside the curtain; (17) lights; (18) sensation of a cold breeze issuing from a scar on the medium's brow; and (19) untying of knots.

As for the conclusions that the three investigators reached concerning their eleven exciting and irritating sessions, it is perhaps as well to let them speak for themselves. The excerpts below are taken from the section entitled "General Account: Conclusions," which appears on pages 50–54 of the report above cited.

The evidence for the foregoing phenomena varies considerably both in quantity and quality, and we are of the opinion that any analysis dividing them into classes for which the evidence may be regarded as sufficient or insufficient would be of purely academic interest and of no real value.

It was only through constant repetition of the same phenomenon, in a good light and at moments when its occurrence was expected, and after finding that none of the precautions which we took had any influence on impeding it, that we gradually reached the conviction that some force was in play which was beyond the reach of ordinary control, and beyond the skill of the most skilful conjuror.

The question therefore seems reduced to a choice between two improbabilities. Either we were constantly thrown into a state of hallucination by means of a mysterious suggestive influence exercised by Eusapia, for the existence of which, either in her or in anybody else, there is otherwise, in our view, no evidence whatever; or, on the other hand, the ordinarily recognized laws of dynamics have to be enlarged by the assumption that there does actually exist some hitherto unascertained force liberated in her presence and for the existence of which, both in her and in certain other persons, the body of evidence is, we think, not inconsiderable.

With great intellectual reluctance, though without much personal doubt as to its justice, we adopt the latter alternative. Making, then, a reservation for the possibility of some form of hallucinatory influence of such a kind as fundamentally to invalidate the trustworthiness of all evidence and for the existence of which we believe there is neither warrant nor parallel, we are of the opinion that we have witnessed in the presence of Eusapia Palladino the action of some telekinetic force, the nature and origin of which we cannot attempt to specify, through which, without the introduction of accomplices, apparatus, or mere manual dexterity, she is able to produce movements of, and percussive and other sounds in, objects at a distance from her and unconnected with her in any apparent physical manner, and also to produce matter, or the appearance of matter, without any determinable source of supply.

Viewed from any angle, the report was a tremendous victory for Eusapia. And there was more. In an introductory note the council of the S.P.R. specifically withdrew its ban on Eusapia and reasserted her place among mediums meriting serious investigation, in spite of her trickery. The society had no wish, it was stated, to maintain "an obstinate attitude of incredulity" in the face of the fact that Eusapia "has been observed by probably a larger number of scientific men than any other medium." The Queen of the Cabinet had her revenge.

It is to be hoped that Eusapia enjoyed her triumph, for the rest of her story is sad. In spite of the success of the Naples sittings, it was clear that her health was breaking down and with it her power to produce phenomena. Naturally, Mr. Carrington was anxious to have her visit the United States without delay, so that his American colleagues might have the opportunity to witness her performances for themselves. The trip lasted from November 1909 to June 1910, a period during which almost nothing went right for Eusapia.

In her younger days she might have responded to the American scene as a challenge, and even enjoyed its vigor, impatience, and bravado. Now, however, she was tired and she was used to being taken seriously. That exuberant institution, the American press, treated her not as a visiting celebrity nor even as a scientific enigma, but rather as a traveling sideshow—the Fat Woman, the Juggler, and the Snake Charmer all rolled into one. She received many requests for her time, but more were from music-hall managers than from learned committees. Even though the large eastern cities she visited had always had their share and more of fraudulent mediums, the prevailing attitude seemed to be one of hostility: American ingenuity would succeed in exposing this foreign phenomenon where the best brains of Europe had failed.

Anyone who knew Eusapia could have guessed what would happen. Feeling herself undervalued, she became irritable. She recognized immediately that most of the sitters who came to her were completely inexperienced; the phenomena were slow in coming, and when they did come, Eusapia cheated. She was caught repeatedly (for not all of the American sitters were incompetent), and each time the discovery of a trick was labeled Exposure in the press, as if a single trick could account for all the manifestations the medium had ever produced.

In the absence of any competent records of the American sittings, it is impossible for us to judge whether Eusapia had come to rely entirely on her more usual tricks or whether there were still present any of the phenomena that Lombroso, Richet, Myers, Carrington, Baggally, Feilding, and the rest had labeled "genuine" or at least "unexplained." Dr. Dingwall is of the opinion that she continued to the end her pattern of producing a mixture of the false and the baffling, though the point does not seem very much worth debating. Whatever we may conclude as to Eusapia's case as a whole, the American "exposures" certainly added nothing new to what was known of her methods.

The time for additions to the world's knowledge about Eusapia Palladino had run out. When she left the United States it was to go into retirement, a sick and exhausted middle-aged woman with a stubborn jaw who had spent most of her life in foreign lands amid strangers.

Eusapia Palladino died on May 16, 1918, and left to the scientific world an exasperating legacy. It is possible that the questions raised by her mediumship simply cannot be finally answered on the basis of the data available.

As the Feilding-Carrington-Baggally report said, with praiseworthy moderation, what we are left with is "a choice between two improbabilities." Either *some* of Eusapia's phenomena were genuine, or human testimony in such cases is virtually valueless. There is no experiment that was done with her of which it has not been objected that other methods of recording or of control would have been surer, or that other sitters might have been better qualified to judge the results. Yet it seems no one can agree on precisely what, within the technical limits of the times, the experimenters should have done that they did not.

Naturally, the most serious indictment of Eusapia is her admitted cheating. Her supporters maintain that she used trickery only when the phenomena were slow in coming or that she did so to save herself from the exhaustion and illness that many mediums have testified often follows a successful séance.

Although Browning created him over forty years before Eusapia's heyday, the inimitable Mr. Sludge might have spoken for her when he asked slyly:

> Why, when I cheat
> *Mean to cheat, do cheat, and am caught in the act,*
> *Are you, or, rather, am I sure o' the fact? . . .*
> Well then I'm not sure! I may be, perhaps,
> Free as a babe from cheating: how it began,
> My gift,—no matter; what 'tis got to be
> In the end now, that's the question; answer that!

(1)   The Egyptian pyramids were one of ancient man's most elaborate (and most futile) devices for protecting the goods he provided for the spirits of the dead.

(2)   Mummification involved the use of bitumen and various preservative herbs, but probably succeeded more because of the dry climate than because of the substances used. Such careful attention to the body implies that the spirit was somehow dependent on it or might re-enter it.

(3) An early nineteenth-century portrait of some shamans of the Yakut tribe with various pieces of magical equipment and a reindeer-drawn sled in which they were believed to be able to fly through the air.

(4) Mesmer's therapeutic bath or *baquet,* showing the metal rods that reputedly conducted the "animal magnetism" to the patients.

(5) The farmhouse at Hydesville, New York in which "Mr. Splitfoot" first made his presence known to Kate and Margaret Fox in 1848. The house has since been moved to the spiritualist camp at Lily Dale, New York.

(6, 7, 8)   The famous Fox sisters: Margaret, Kate, and Leah, as they appeared some years after the beginning of their careers as mediums.

(9) Andrew Jackson Davis (1826–1910). A self-taught medium and journalist known as the Poughkeepsie Seer, whose adaptations of the philosophy of Emanuel Swedenborg widely influenced the development of spiritualism.

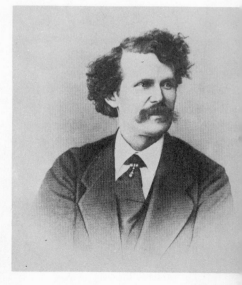

(10) Daniel Dunglas Home (1833–86) The famous Scottish-American medium included a czar and an emperor among his sitters and was reputedly the model for Browning's satire on "Mr. Sludge," but is generally admitted never to have been exposed in fraud.

(11) Ira and William Davenport (1839–77 and 1841–1911). American brothers whose spiritualist "road show" featured the untying of the mediums while shut inside a cabinet. The untying was supposedly done by the spirits as proof of their existence.

(12) William Stainton Moses (1839–92). A highly respected educator, founder of several spiritualist organizations, and private medium, Moses achieved his reputation before much was known of the possibilities of unconscious fraud in the séance room.

(13) The supposed materialization of the spirit entity "Katie King," as photographed by Sir William Crookes in 1874. Spiritualists still argue hotly over whether "Katie" was in fact the medium Florence Cook disguised.

(14) Sir William Crookes (1832–1919) The eminent physicist's declaratio that he had established scientifi proof of the medium Florence Cook' materializations is often cited as cornerstone of the evidence for spiri survival. However, a recent suggestio that Crookes and the medium wer involved in a love affair throws different light on the matter.

(15)   Eusapia Palladino (1854–1918) seated at the séance table, as she appeared around 1909. She was probably the greatest and most puzzling physical medium of all time.

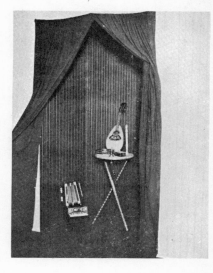

(16)   Eusapia's cabinet, arranged for a typical séance. Note the mandolin, accordion, bell, recorder, and tambourine—instruments on which the "spirits" were accustomed to make their presence heard.

(17)   Title page of the original edition of *Revelations of a Spirit Medium* (1891), a book that was speedily bought up and destroyed by outraged spiritualists. In it the author explains (along with much else) several fraudulent methods of producing "spirit hands" such as those appearing to the sitters in the drawing.

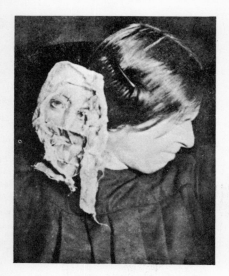

(18) Eva C. or Marthe Béraud produces a supposed ectoplasmic face from her ear during a séance. Many of Eva's "faces" were shown to have been cut out of a Paris newspaper. The picture was taken by Baron Schrenck-Notzing in 1912.

(19) Bishop James A. Pike (1913–69). A bishop of the Episcopal Church, Dr. Pike caused a sensation in 1967 by declaring on a Canadian television program that he believed he had received authentic spirit messages from his deceased son Jim. It was certainly the most widely publicized spiritualist case of the past thirty years.

CHAPTER IX

SPIRITUALISTS GET TOGETHER

As we saw in the previous chapter, in the opening years of the twentieth century spiritualism had become a movement of organizations as well as of individuals. In other pursuits splinter groups form new corporations, new churches, new sports teams, new professions, new scientific departments, and sometimes even new nations. Spiritualism too produced its own institutions.

Since the beginning there had been two sides to spiritualism: the religious and the semiscientific. It was natural that spiritualist organizations should also be of two main kinds. Of course the two were never entirely separate; history is rarely so neat. Questions of philosophy, for example, were of great interest to all groups and were much debated inside the movement. Nevertheless, almost all the founding members of spiritualist organizations shared the conviction that the individual human spirit survives after death and can communicate with the living by various means.

Another shared conviction was that the movement was being treated unfairly by the press and the scientists. Whether they hoped to perform mass conversions in the manner of the early Christian missionaries or merely to win an unbiased hearing for spiritualist beliefs, the majority of these organizations not only provided gathering places for those who shared their views but also attempted to influence public opinion through research, public demonstrations, publishing programs, or religious evangelism. It may be partly for this reason that the history of the movement after 1900 is so closely linked with that of the various spiritualist societies and churches.

Happily, it is neither necessary nor possible for us to go into great detail on this subject. However, the titles, purposes, and mutual relations of many of the spiritualist and semispiritualist groups are so important for later developments, and at the same time so confusing, that it is probably better to get them straight from the start.

Among the organizations concerned mainly with scientific research and public education, by far the most important was the Society for Psychical Research (the British S.P.R.), founded in 1882. It is necessary to emphasize that the S.P.R. is not now and never was an organization *of* spiritualists, though its leaders have at times leaned heavily toward acceptance of spiritualist doctrine. The distinction is well shown in the society's first council, which was made up of five spiritualists and five nonspiritualists. The reason is that many psychic phenomena do not necessarily have any connection with mediumism or disembodied spirits. It is possible to believe in the reality of such occurrences as levitation, telepathy, teleportation, apparitions, prophecy, psychometry, and clairvoyance (all sometimes lumped under the heading ESP) without in any sense being a spiritualist.

The spiritualists, by and large, believe in the phenomena

and attribute them to the intervention of spirits, whereas others may also believe in the phenomena but think the causes lie elsewhere. It has never been the policy of the S.P.R. to require that its members go on record as believing in any supernormal happenings at all. The society exists strictly to promote fair and unbiased research into psychic events and to inform the public of the results.

Its uncommitted attitude has given the S.P.R. a position like that of mediator between believers and skeptics. On the one hand, the society has often won the confidence of the scientific world by being the first and severest critic of all kinds of psychic fraud and trickery. In its publications it has always required high standards of evidence, so that the American psychologist-philosopher William James (1842–1910) once wrote, "In fact, were I asked to point to a scientific journal where hard-headedness and never-sleeping suspicion of sources of error might be seen in their full bloom, I think I should have to fall back on the Proceedings of the Society for Psychical Research."

This same refusal to take things on faith has sometimes brought the society into conflict with its own most famous members, however. A notable case was the resignation in 1930 of Sir Arthur Conan Doyle (1859–1930) in protest over the S.P.R.'s exposure of a spirit photographer named Hope. The case caused a good deal of comment because the famous creator of Sherlock Holmes had become a worldwide advocate of spiritualism since the beginning of his interest in the topic around 1885.

(However, Conan Doyle was by no means as careful about the rules of evidence as his fictional detective. In spiritualist matters the author more closely resembled the gullible Dr. Watson, believing without question in even such dubious propositions as the existence of fairies.)

Among the society's earliest members and most faithful supporters were many whose attitudes to psychical research was a good deal more level-headed. We have already mentioned Frank Podmore, Sir Oliver Lodge, F. W. H. Myers, Professor and Mrs. Henry Sidgwick, and Richard Hodgson. We shall hear much more of their contributions, particularly in connection with the S.P.R. cross-correspondences, the famous cases that took place at a period when some of the alleged participants were "in the spirit" rather than "in the flesh."

An equivalent of the S.P.R. was established in the United States in 1885. The American Society for Psychical Research (A.S.P.R.) was first located in Boston but later moved to New York City. Always similar in aims and structure, the two societies were formally affiliated from 1889 to 1906, or roughly the period during which Dr. Hodgson served as research officer of the A.S.P.R. Afterward the American group returned to its independent status, carrying out its own programs of publication and research. Like the British Society, its attitude is uncommitted. A current membership folder of the A.S.P.R. asserts, "Membership does not imply acceptance either of the factuality of paranormal phenomena or of any particular explanation of such phenomena."

By no means all the organizations that number spiritualists among their members have been so conservative. The London Spiritualist Alliance, organized in 1884 by William Stainton Moses from a previous group known as the British National Association of Spiritualists, was wholly committed to spiritualist belief, as the name implies. However, like the S.P.R. and the A.S.P.R., the L.S.A. undertook research projects and examination of mediums, giving its seal of approval to those it found to be free of fraud. On one occasion, in 1928, the secretary of the L.S.A., Miss Mercy Phillimore, was arrested together with Mrs. Claire Cantlon, a medium approved by the society. The two ladies were charged with telling fortunes under an English law known as the Vagrancy Act of 1824. The ensuing trial caused a considerable stir and served to point up the fact that spiritualism then found itself in a very doubtful legal position. Most European nations and the United States had laws against fortune-telling for money, and some even had statutes forbidding "sorcery and the calling up of spirits," a leftover from the infamous witchcraft trials of previous centuries. Now an official of a spiritualist organization and a medium were being tried on the testimony of three policewomen who alleged that at a séance the medium had not only failed to produce any true information, but had transmitted supposed messages from persons the sitter herself had invented.

A complete account of the sitting also revealed that the medium's chief spirit control had regularly broken off the proceedings whenever mealtimes approached, a curious habit for a bodiless entity presumably immune to the pangs of hunger. The judge found both ladies guilty, respectively of fortune-telling without a license and of abetting in fortune-telling. The L.S.A. was fined eight hundred pounds in costs and the defendants were dismissed with suspended sentences and the judge's comment that he "should strongly advise Mrs. Cantlon to get rid of a disembodied spirit who wants to know the time when the hour of lunch or tea approaches."

The Phillimore-Cantlon trial gave spiritualists some cause to feel that they were being subjected to persecution. Many were increasingly convinced that the skepticism of the rest of the world was like the blind, unreasoning obstinacy of the unconverted heathen who "refused to see the light."

Another result of the trial was more constructive. It helped bring about a concerted campaign for revision of the law, led by such prominent spiritualists as Sir Arthur Conan Doyle, who had also testified for the defense at the trial itself. Only six days before his death in 1930 Doyle was part of a deputation to Britain's Home Secretary urging modification of the law concerning mediumship. Unfortunately, it was to be another twenty years before any change was actually brought about.

From the late nineteenth century on, some of the conflict of spiritualism with the law was an echo of a conflict among spiritualists themselves. The question was, should spiritualism be considered a religion? and if so, was it a branch of Christianity? Legally, the acceptance of spiritualism as either a Christian or a non-Christian sect would have solved many difficulties, since in most Western nations such a status would have guaranteed to spiritualists complete freedom from prosecution for practicing their religion.

To this solution there were several sources of opposition. One came from outside the movement, particularly from the Catholic Church and certain Protestant groups that had religious objections to the practice of spiritualism. The movement had never been free of attackers since the first days in Hydesville, and time had by no means lessened their hostility. Every new outbreak of spiritualist enthusiasm was met with new denunciations. This was especially true during World War I, when mediums experienced a tragic increase in the number of their clients, as parents and sweethearts tried to communicate with those who had been killed in battle.

For some reason 1917 was a year particularly full of antispiritualist rhetoric. An English Wesleyan paper printed an article asserting that "New York is said to have one asylum devoted solely to people who lose their reason through trafficking in Spiritualism," while the influential *Strand* magazine carried a piece by a gentleman named Edward Clodd, whose least offensive comment was to describe the beliefs of spiritualists as "nauseating, frivolous, mischievous, spurious drivel." Groups and individuals with opinions such as these were not likely to sit tamely by while spiritualism won recognition as a religion.

Opposition of a very different sort came from those spiritualists who already felt themselves committed to an existing religious group, usually one of the more liberal Protestant churches. These people generally felt that there was no conflict between spiritualism and the churches and would have been dismayed at having to choose one or the other. Indeed, many felt that the whole meaning of Christianity had been illuminated for them in the séance room, deepening their faith and giving meaning to their lives. They wanted no change.

There were also some spiritualists, though perhaps a minority, who held that what they believed in was indeed a separate religion, one preaching universal love and tolerance, and that it should not be regarded as a Christian denomination at all. Finally, there were those in the movement who viewed spiritualism more as a science than as a religion and wished to approach it solely through research rather than worship.

Yet in spite of these internal divisions, it is indisputable that many people had in fact been practicing spiritualism as a sect of Christianity for some years. Though it is probably impossible to pin down the date of the first truly religious Spiritualist meetings, Sunday services had become a regular of the program of many spiritualist societies in England by the 1870s and perhaps somewhat earlier in the United States. Especially outside the larger cities, where the movement continued to emphasize proof more heavily than prayer, the tendency was for the local societies to transform themselves gradually into churches. The very large majority had a decidedly Christian outlook, the views of A. J. Davis about the divinity of Christ notwithstanding.

Services included hymn singing, prayers, Bible reading, and sermons that hardly differed from those heard elsewhere except perhaps that they spoke more often of heavenly joys and guardian angels than of sin and punishment. The climax of the occasion might be a recounting of spiritual experiences by members of the congregation, a lecture (often delivered while in trance) by a prominent spiritualist, or a sitting with a visiting medium, who would deliver "spirit messages" from the pulpit. Although of course these communications were not obtained under scientific conditions and were seldom evidential (that is, were seldom the sort of information the medium could not have discovered by normal means), the worshipers were often ready to testify that they had sensed the presence of the "spirit friends" and were convinced that their words were authentic.

Following the pattern of many Christian sects, Spiritualist religious organizations were often made up of member churches rather than of individual members. In the early days in England such church groups came and went like fireflies, changing their names and principles almost yearly. One of the more permanent was the Spiritualist National Federation, which was founded in 1891 at the suggestion of Mrs. Emma Hardinge Britten (1823–99), a very energetic medium and Spiritualist lecturer. Mrs. Britten traveled all over the English-speaking world in her zeal for the movement and had thus come in contact with such groups as the Society for the Diffusion of Spiritual Knowledge, an American organization that dated back to 1854. After 1901, having changed its name only twice, the Spiritualist National Federation settled down as the Spiritualist National Union, and by 1914 had 145 affiliated churches and societies. By 1919 the number had swelled to 309, under the influence of the war.

Another large factor in the strong growth of spiritualism during the first two decades of this century was the public conversion of Sir Arthur Conan Doyle and the eminent scientist Sir Oliver Lodge (1851–1940). Lodge was widely known for his contributions to the development of wireless telegraphy and his research on electrons and the ether and had long been interested in psychical phenomena as well. His change from investigator to believer occurred after he had received what he was convinced were authentic spirit messages from his son Raymond, killed in the war. His published account of his experiences had a tremendous effect on many of those who were similarly bereaved.

In the beginning, the Spiritualists' National Union (S.N.U.) had made no attempt to impose uniformity on its members. Forms of worship, methods of governance, and even basic beliefs differed considerably. However, there gradually emerged over the course of years a policy that was later formulated as the Seven Principles of Spiritualism, in its religious aspect. They were:

1. The fatherhood of God.
2. The brotherhood of man.
3. The communion of Spirits and Ministry of Angels.
4. The continuous existence of the human soul.
5. Personal responsibility.
6. Compensation and retribution hereafter for all the good or evil deeds done on earth.
7. Eternal progress open to every human soul.

Today the Seven Principles have also been adopted by some other organizations of Spiritualist churches.

As a branch of Christianity, Spiritualism probably belongs with those groups that have tried to recapture the spirit of the first few centuries after Christ. As we remarked in Chapter II, the "Gifts of the Holy Spirit" played a larger part in the worship of the early Christians than at any later time until the emergence of Spiritualism and other forms of "primitive Christianity." This fact was recognized by the Spiritualists and was sometimes used as an argument against the foundation of organizations such as the S.N.U. The reason was that some felt overorganization had led the established churches away from the true meaning of Christianity

and feared that the same fate might await Spiritualism.
Nevertheless, the centralists prevailed, as we have seen.

The American scene was somewhat calmer, perhaps
because the laws regulating mediumism were less strict.
One of the earliest and most lasting of all spiritualist
groups had been founded by A. J. Davis in 1863. It was
called the Lyceum Movement and was concerned with
the spiritual education of children. At a lecture in New
York City Davis had given such a moving description
of the education of the young in the Summer-Land that
several members of the audience were persuaded to put
his ideas into practice on earth. Davis' views were quite
progressive for the times. In the Lyceums there was to
be no learning by rote and no punishment for errors.
Instead the children would assemble once a week with
an adult called the Leader for discussion of such topics
as the nature of life after death, the customs of the
Summer-Land, and the universal law of love. Music
and exercise were also included, as Davis had borrowed
from the Greeks the idea that those activities were essential for spiritual development.

In two ways, at least, the Lyceums went beyond our
time as well as their own. The Leader and his pupils
were considered equal because they were all seeking
spiritual understanding. Thus everyone was free to question or doubt, and answers were not classified as right
or wrong. It was therefore logical that the Lyceums
were conducted on a democratic basis. Each member
over twelve years old had one vote, including the Leader
(since apparently not even Davis thought of extending
self-government to six-year-olds).

The Lyceum movement is still in operation today,

though like that of many spiritualist organizations its membership has decreased since 1930. It occupies much the same place among spiritualists as that held by religious or Sunday schools in Christian and Jewish congregations.

Not all spiritualist groups were concerned either with religion or research. There was, for example, the short-lived but interesting Julia's Bureau. Founded in 1909 by the British editor and publicist W. T. Stead, the bureau was a public institution that employed a staff of mediums to provide free communication with the spirit world. Stead himself was an ardent spiritualist who possessed the faculty of automatic writing. The suggestion for the bureau was said to have come to him in an automatic script from the spirit of a friend, Julia A. Ames, whence the bureau's name. Between 1909 and 1912 the bureau gave about thirteen hundred sittings to members of the British public. Each client was allowed to sit successively with three different mediums in order to provide confirmation of the information received. Those who lived too far away to come in person could send an object associated with the individual about whom news was desired. The "absent sitting" would then proceed by means of psychometry. Shorthand records were kept of all cases, and Julia's Bureau apparently had many satisfied customers. Unfortunately, the public-spirited Mr. Stead was unable to sustain his project after 1912, perhaps because the reported costs were fifteen hundred pounds a year.

Some spiritualist organizations were founded by individual mediums for the purpose of spreading the doctrine of an especially inspiring spirit guide. A notable example was "Zodiac," the principal control of an English medium named Winifred Moyes. "Zodiac" first announced his presence in Miss Moyes' home circle in 1921. He said that he had been a rabbi at the Temple in Jerusalem during the lifetime of Christ and that he had been the scribe mentioned by St. Mark as having asked Jesus which was the first commandment.

Unfortunately, "Zodiac" never revealed the name he had used during his lifetime, thus wiping out whatever slight chance there might have been of confirming his identity by searching the records of the time. However, his deeply religious addresses, given through the entranced Miss Moyes, had a profound effect on their audiences. The result was the foundation in 1931 of the Greater World Spiritualist League and its newspaper *The Greater World*.

Somewhat similar in origin, though not in doctrine, was the White Eagle Lodge, originated in 1936 by the medium Grace Cook in Kensington, England. The spirit control in this instance was "White Eagle," supposedly a deceased American Indian chief. Perhaps because he had not been a follower of Christ, however, "White Eagle's" messages were very different from those of "Zodiac." Members of the White Eagle Lodge adhere to the following six principles:

1. The Father-Motherhood of God.
2. That Christ, the Son of the Father-Mother God, is the Light that shines through Wisdom and Love in the human heart; and that by reason of this Divine Sonship all are brothers and sisters regardless of race, class, or creed; and that this brotherhood and sisterhood embraces life, visible and invisible.

3. The expression of these principles in daily life through service.

4. The awareness of the invisible world, which bridges separation and death and reveals the eternal unity of life.

5. That life is governed by five cosmic laws: Reincarnation; Cause and Effect; Opportunity; Correspondence (as above, so below); Equilibrium (the law of Compensation).

6. That the ultimate goal of mankind is the blooming of the Rose at the Heart of the Cross; the realization of the Christ-consciousness as exemplified by the Master; the reunion of the Holy Family.

Obviously, these six principles (particularly nos. 1 and 5) would hardly be acceptable to traditional Christianity or Judaism. There is besides, in no. 6, unmistakable evidence of the influence of Rosicrucianism. The Rosicrucians, or Brothers of the Rosy Cross, are a mysterious and mystical society that claims to date from the time of ancient Egypt and whose semisecret teachings emphasize the symbolic meaning of the Rose and the Cross. The appearance of some of their ideas in the works of "White Eagle" is an example of the sort of direction taken by spiritualism's more occult and less Christian branches.

There is one form of spiritualist organization that appears to have been typically American. Perhaps following the pattern of the "camp meetings" so popular among religious revivalists, certain rural areas became hosts to spiritualist camps where, during the summer months, healthful country atmosphere was combined with a wide variety of mediumistic activities. One of the best known of these centers was at Lily Dale, New York, a town about sixty miles south of Buffalo. The camp, as it was pictured around the turn of the century, must have been much like an informal country resort or children's camp of today. Its main feature was a large, raftered auditorium hung with banners and filled with straight wooden chairs for the audiences of its numerous lectures and guest appearances by famous mediums. The grounds also contained a number of small houses and cabins that housed not only spiritualists and mediums but also fortune tellers, astrologers, spirit photographers, and other professionals who offered their services to guests.

In August 1907, the camp was visited by Hereward Carrington (the future investigator of Eusapia Palladino) on behalf of the American Society for Psychical Research. Carrington had been asked to investigate the various forms of mediumship at Lily Dale, which included materializations, slate writing, and trumpet speaking. His account of his stay makes amusing reading, since he was able to discover a number of extraordinarily brazen frauds. His conclusion was that with regard to the physical manifestations (he was less critical of the mental phenomena witnessed), Lily Dale was nothing more than a charitable institution for the support of incompetent mediums and a pleasant summer resort for spiritualists who liked a little mystification with their fresh air and country scenery.

The increasingly energetic investigations of the A.S.P.R. and other research organizations probably helped to bring about a considerable decrease in the popularity of spiritualist camps during the next few decades.

There is one last organization without mention of which this chapter could not be complete, yet which poses grave problems for the historian. We do not know the name of this organization, or the date of its founding, or the location of its central office, if it had one. It held no public meetings, conducted no research, and listed no spiritualists among its members, yet it exerted a tremendous influence on the growth of spiritualism in the United States, as did its presumed sister organizations in other countries. Before we say more about this mysterious body, a little background material may be in order.

Even the briefest survey of mediumship makes it clear that séance-room phenomena run in cycles, like other human activities. It can almost be said that new phenomena seem to be contagious, as was shown by those who "caught" the ability to produce raps from the Fox sisters. Later it was table tipping, followed by trance speaking, spirit photography, apports, cabinet materialization, and ectoplasm, each in its turn. Some of this was no doubt due to the fact that practicing mediums sometimes kindly gave their time to "developing" promising new talents, as we have seen in the case of the disreputable Herne and Florence Cook. But there is evidence to show that, at least on the more commercial level of the profession, mutual cooperation was at one time far more widespread than even the skeptic might have supposed.

As early as 1891 there appeared in the United States a most informative book entitled *Revelations of a Spirit Medium*. From the author's description of himself, he seems to have been an otherwise unremarkable public medium with a sense of humor about his profession. (His true name is a matter of some controversy since, for obvious reasons, he chose to use a pseudonym.) "Charles F. Pidgeon," as he called himself, started his career at the very bottom of the mediumistic ladder, which is of course the proverbial method of "really getting to know the business."

The main fascination of Mr. Pidgeon's account of his mediumship—from his first hesitant rap through eighteen years of unmixed flummery—is in the degree of co-operation he received from other mediums. This spirit of brotherhood not only extended to the exchange of techniques for achieving a particular faked manifestation, but had actually taken the form of an organization devoted to compiling useful information about leading spiritualists in various cities. Each individual name was followed by descriptions, names, dates of death, anecdotes, and so forth concerning the subject's family and friends who were "in the spirit."

The list was apparently improved and updated from time to time in a manner that would have done credit to an international spy ring. Thus no one who made it a regular habit to attend public séances could long escape finding himself on that list, along with a neat notation of nearly every revelation he had ever made concerning his spirit friends. An idea of the scope of the list may be had from the fact that the entries for the city of Cincinnati alone occupied sixty-three pages. And all this information was available to any member of the organization who happened to conduct a séance in the city, though he might, as mediums often claimed in defense of their genuineness, "never have been there before and know none of the audience." No wonder Mr. Pidgeon was moved to remark wryly that "it was an excellent organization to belong to."

As might have been expected, the reaction of other mediums to Mr. Pidgeon's revelation of their trade secrets was not friendly. More surprising, at least to those unacquainted with the history of the movement, was the response of many spiritualists. They not only denied the existence of any such "Mediums' Benevolent Society" as the author described, but they also went to considerable trouble to buy up and destroy copies of his book. Within a relatively short time after its publication *Revelations of a Spirit Medium* had almost disappeared from the bookstores, and it is only by good fortune that a few copies survive.

CHAPTER X

THE DECLINE OF MEDIUMSHIP, OR HOW TO FAKE A SÉANCE

The history of science is filled with examples of the fact that the experiment that fails is often much more interesting than the one that succeeds. Likewise in the history of spiritualism the more ambitious and far-reaching frauds may give us information that is of great help in understanding the nature of mediumism in general.

Nothing could be more remarkable than the story of Catherine Elise Muller, who achieved fame under the name of Hélène Smith. As a child in Geneva, Catherine, or, as we may as well call her, Hélène, was exceedingly dreamy and imaginative. The family lived in what are described as "humble circumstances," and the child used her fantasies to escape into a more colorful world. At one time she startled her parents by demanding to know whether she was really their child, imagining that like Snow White or Cinderella her rightful place was amid rank and riches.

In the winter of 1891–92, when she was thirty years old, Hélène was introduced to spiritualism by a group of friends. Like so many others before her, she was excited to discover that tables moved under her touch and that she had the faculty of automatic writing. In short, Hélène was a medium. Her talent followed a normal but rapid course of development, and by April 1892 she wrote under the spirit control of an entity claiming to be the great writer Victor Hugo. Soon after, another spirit control took over, calling himself Leopold, and Hélène began to achieve the true mediumistic trance. So far, so typical. Nor was there anything particularly unusual about the other phenomena that now began to appear during her séances. There were apports and moving objects, clairvoyant and clairaudient messages, raps, and so on. The one feature perhaps foreshadowing future developments was that Hélène's trances were sometimes accompanied by symbolic visions of great vividness whose meaning was later explained to her by the spirit controls.

In the winter of 1894 something new was introduced into the sessions. For some time "Leopold" had been telling the sitters that his former identity was that of Giuseppe Balsamo, alias Count Cagliostro, the eighteenth-century adventurer, magician, courtier, and world traveler. Now "Leopold-Cagliostro" announced that his medium was the reincarnation of Queen Marie-Antoinette (with whom the real Cagliostro had been acquainted). For a period of about ten months Hélène's circle was principally occupied in listening to the supposed voices of the different royal and noble personages who now began to manifest themselves through her. Two of the sitters were also identified as reincarnations of famous historical characters, namely Louis-Philippe d'Orléans and the Marquis de Mirabeau. The sessions must have been like live performances of a historical romance by the elder Dumas.

However, this phase of Hélène's mediumship, later called its Royal Cycle, disappeared abruptly. Now the séance personalities revolved around another supposed incarnation of the medium, "Simandini," the daughter of a sixth-century Arab sheikh.

At this point, Hélène was brought to the attention of Theodore Flournoy, professor of psychology at the University of Geneva. It was he who chose the name Hélène Smith in order to protect the medium's privacy in his projected report on the case. From the winter of 1894–95 onward, Flournoy was a constant member of the circle and witness to the startling developments that began in November 1894. The romance of Simandini (the Oriental Cycle) gave way to a third major series of characters and narrative—one that was literally out of this world. In her trances now Hélène Smith believed she was transported to the planet Mars. Professor Flournoy related what followed:

Thereafter every night she described to the listening circle the people of our neighbour planet, their food, dress, and ways of life. At times she drew pictures of the inhabitants—human and animal—of their houses, bridges, and other edifices, and of the surrounding landscape. Later she both spoke and wrote freely in the Martian language. From the writings . . . it is clear that the characters of the Martian script are unlike any in use on earth, and that the words (of which a translation is furnished) bear no resemblance, superficially at least, to any known tongue. The spirits—for several dwellers upon Mars use Hélène's organism to speak and write through—delivered themselves with freedom and fluency, and were consistent in their usage both of the spoken and the written words. In fact, Martian, as used by the entranced Hélène, has many of the characteristics of a genuine language; and it is not surprising that some of the onlookers, who may have hesitated over the authenticity of the other revelations [those contained in the Royal and Oriental Cycles] were apparently convinced that these Martian utterances were beyond the common order of nature. (quoted by Podmore in *Mediums of the 19th Century*, Vol. II, p. 316)

In considering the sensation created by the "revelations" of Hélène Smith, we must remember that all this took place before 1900. Telescopes were many times less powerful than they are today and there were no space probes or satellite photographs. Mars was known principally as a large reddish planet fourth in distance from the sun. In 1877 G. V. Schiaparelli had first described the curious formations he called "canals" on the planet's surface, and at the time of Hélène's séances the most popular theory about the "canals" was that they were the work of some form of intelligent life—in short, of the Martians. The public, therefore, and particularly those spiritualists who had read A. J. Davis' account of his meetings with Martians in the Summer-Land, were prepared to believe that Hélène's description of Mars might be the literal truth. It was the Martian language that was particularly convincing. How, demanded believers, could a young woman with no advanced education have invented a totally strange language that was so complete, so consistent, so logical?

It is greatly to Professor Flournoy's credit that he was able to answer this question where most others could not. This is not to imply that the scientific community was as ready as the public to accept Hélène's recitals at face value. It had certainly occurred to some that even if Martians of a sort did exist they would be unlikely to resemble human beings nearly as closely as they appeared to do in Hélène's drawings. But whereas most of those who were not convinced by her tales about Mars would have put Hélène down as a hoaxer with an overactive imagination, it was Flournoy's contribution to perceive that deliberate fraud could not be the whole explanation.

Ever since the early days of mesmerism it had been observed that persons in trance sometimes seemed to act entirely unlike their normal selves. The silent became talkative, the meek became angry, and so on. Sometimes the personality of the entranced patient changed so much that he could hardly be called the same person. And sometimes these new personalities spoke of lives that were totally different from those actually lived by the patients. These accounts were no more "made up" by the patients than were the hysterical (psychosomatic) illnesses from which some of them suffered and that the mesmerists found they could cure. The patients were genuinely unaware of either the causes of their illnesses or of any difference in their behavior while entranced.

To Flournoy there appeared to be a great similarity between such somnambulistic patients and Hélène Smith. In his account of the case, which was entitled *From India to the Planet Mars* and published in 1899, he convincingly showed that Hélène's séance revelations belonged in the world of psychopathology or mental illness rather than in that of spiritualist phenomena. Today they would probably be called examples of secondary personality of the kind sometimes found in schizophrenia.

The material contained in Hélène's tales of Mars, India, and eighteenth-century France was part of an inner world of fantasy of which she was usually not aware, a world that may have been growing and developing since the period of her vivid childhood imaginings. The unconscious mind, whose nature was just then being revealed through the works of Freud and others, is capable of staggering feats of memory, retaining conversations, scenes, and information that may long ago have been "forgotten" by the conscious mind. However, the unconscious mind has limitations as well; it is not *creative* in the way that the conscious mind is creative. That is, the unconscious has to make do with the materials that come to hand. Instead of discovering new facts, it must rearrange old facts. This, Flournoy showed, was what had been done to produce the Martian language of Hélène Smith.

Weird as the words and letters seemed to most of the sitters, the language contained no sounds that do not occur in French, the medium's native language, although such sounds are abundant in other Earth languages. Likewise, the general structure of Martian was clearly derived from that of French. To take a brief example, English had a single word for the negative (not), while French has two (*ne pas*). Martian, too, had two words for the negative (*ke ani*) and these words were used in the same way as in French, changing their place in the sentence according to fixed rules (as in *ne pas dire*, not to say; *ne dites pas*, do not say). Since there are dozens of possible ways of forming the negative in human languages (not to mention ways unknown to us that might have been thought of by the Martians), this sort of coincidence, repeated throughout the whole language, is striking enough to make it certain that French was the model for Martian.

Studies of mental illness since the time of Flournoy have shown that the invention of a secret, personal language, like the presence of secondary personalities, is not unknown in other cases, though of course not common. The difference is that most people whose unconscious minds harbor other personalities, speak unknown languages, and deliver mysterious messages are not mistaken for mediums. The workings of the unconscious mind will come up again before we have completed our survey of spiritualism. At the moment it is enough to note that this was one of the first cases in which it was proposed that the key to mediumism might lie in the inner world of the medium rather than in the outer world of the "spirits."

A totally different sort of failed experiment in mediumship is represented by the career of Marthe Béraud, a French medium whose materializations are still a subject of controversy. The interesting thing about Marthe Béraud is that it seems she was a fraud from the beginning and hardly cared who knew it. From 1902 to 1904 Marthe was the frequent guest of her fiancé's parents, a General and Mrs. Noel, at their villa in Algiers. The Noels were interested in spiritualism and used to hold séances in their home through the mediumship of a seamstress named Vincente Garcia. Vincente was accustomed to materialize a turbaned figure who described himself as a priest of ancient Hindustan and gave his name as Bien-Boa. He was apparently no more convincing than most full-form materializations, walking around the room, conversing with the sitters, and even drinking lemonade.

In 1904 Marthe's fiancé was tragically killed in the Congo. Whether the shock of his death had anything to do with Marthe's growing interest in the séances is not known, but she began to take part in the sittings and soon displayed a remarkable talent. Shortly she replaced Vincente as the regular medium, although "Bien-Boa" remained on the scene and was later joined by his spirit-sister "Beroglia." Of the antics of this pair a former president of the S.P.R. commented in 1961, "The souls of the departed may conceivably inhabit forms resembling Bien-Boa; if so we must endure the prospect with fortitude." Nevertheless, incredibly, the performances was received with enthusiasm by the Noels and their circle.

Far off in Paris, word of this marvelous new materialization medium reached Professor Charles Richet, the investigator of Eusapia Palladino. Richet hastened to Algiers and there the masquerade should have ended. Astonishingly, it did not. Richet declared himself favorably impressed on the basis of what must seem very superficial evidence compared to the exacting conditions he had imposed on Eusapia. The reason for Richet's belief in Marthe Béraud is of great interest. It was, in his own words, "the absolute honourableness, irreproachable and certain, of Marthe B., fiancée of Maurice Noel, son of the general." We have seen this sort of conviction at work before—in the acceptance of Stainton Moses' phenomena because of his high moral character, in the power of Sir William Crookes to give scientific status to the performances of Florence Cook, and conversely in the respectable S.P.R.'s refusal even to test Eusapia because she had the reputation of a vulgar cheat.

Richet's opinion was all the more amazing when one considers that, according to contemporary testimony, Marthe wasn't even very serious about her deception at first. She seems to have regarded the whole thing as a joke and to have admitted as much to some of her friends, although not to the Noels or Richet. The mysterious "Bien-Boa," Marthe hinted, was no one but the Noels' coachman dressed up in white muslin and probably smuggled into the house with the help of the other servants. It must have been a lot of fun until the great Professor Richet descended from Paris and the game became very real. Did Marthe then wish she had never begun her charade, or did she only regret the light-hearted half-admissions she had made to her friends?

The story now takes a jump of four years and several hundred miles. It is Paris in 1909. At the home of a charming and well-known spiritualist, Madame Bisson, there is a new medium. The young lady is called Eva C., which is understood to be a pseudonym for Eva Carrière. Eva C.'s phenomena include some striking materializations, not of the full form but of the incomplete type, accompanied by the appearance of ectoplasm.

Eva C. was Marthe Béraud. To a young woman deprived of the security offered by her promised marriage, a path had opened and she had walked straight down it. Through her mediumship she acquired friends, attention, and even an adoptive mother in Madame Bisson. Also through Madame Bisson, Eva C. came to the notice of Baron von Schrenck-Notzing (1862–1929), the Munich physician and specialist in psychical research. In 1913 and 1914 both Madame Bisson and Schrenck-Notzing published books on Eva C. Strangely, though the two authors certainly knew that Eva was Marthe, neither mentioned the fact. The cause of the omission was not merely the usual custom of protecting the privacy of the medium with a pseudonym, for the Baron, at least, referred to Richet's investigations of Marthe Béraud as if they provided additional evidence for materialization and without the slightest suggestion that the two cases were one. This curious procedure may have been undertaken because other researchers had not been nearly so eager to endorse the Algiers materializations, particularly after it began to be rumored that the participants themselves had admitted the deception.

On the surface, Schrenck-Notzing's findings concerning Eva C. sounded very impressive. The séances had been held in a red light with the medium seated inside a curtained cabinet that she could open and close at will. In spite of the fact that Eva had been subjected to a "very complete" personal search and was wearing only clothes provided by the investigators, she continually produced mysterious-looking ectoplasm that gave the impression of condensing into faces, limbs, and unidentifiable living shapes. With a battery of eight cameras, two of them stereoscopic, about 225 photographs were taken at various stages of the phenomena.

These photographs of Eva C. are indeed remarkable, but not because they afford us an opportunity to gaze on genuine ectoplasm. What they show, in a number of cases, is "materialized" faces that appear entirely flat and sometimes bear creases as if they had been folded. Quite probably they *had* been folded. Sometime after the appearance of Schrenck-Notzing's book, several of the "spirit faces" were found to be the same as those of perfectly real, living persons whose pictures had recently been printed in the Paris paper *Le Miroir*. It is not up to the skeptic to have to show *how* the newspaper cuttings were smuggled into the séance room in spite of the "very complete" search of the medium, when it is so plain that somehow they *were* smuggled, whether by Eva or by a confederate in the audience.

After 1914 (when German researchers no longer had access to Paris) the investigation of Eva C. was continued by Gustave Geley (1868–1924), director of the Institut Métaphysique in Paris. Again, the world of science declared that Eva's materializations were genuine. But here we encounter something of a mystery. When Dr. Geley was killed in an accident in 1924, his successors found some peculiar papers in his files. Just what these papers were is uncertain, since permission to publish was refused by the Institut Métaphysique. However, it has since been suggested by the writer Theodore Besterman, one of the few persons to have any knowledge of the affair at all, that the items in question were photographs showing that Eva C.'s mediumship was fraudulent. If that were true, then Geley must have known that Eva C. was a fraud and for some reason suppressed the information. However, no full account of the incident has ever been made public, and there are those who maintain that the accusations against Geley are without foundation.

In 1920 Eva interrupted her sessions with Dr. Geley for a trip to London. She had been asked to sit for the S.P.R., a distinction in the spiritualist world something like receiving an Academy Award nomination. Dr. E. J. Dingwall and Dr. V. J. Wooley were the society's chief investigators during the forty sessions that were held in London. Their results, however, were discouraging from any point of view. The phenomena were weak or nonexistent, although the researchers did obtain a small amount of "ectoplasm." On analysis it was found to consist of chewed-up paper.

The conclusion of the committee was hardly a conclusion at all. The phenomena had been too scanty to justify a definitive judgment, they said. The report continued, "If we had not been acquainted with the work of previous investigators we might have felt inclined to draw a negative conclusion from our own observations." Perhaps the committee should have trusted its instincts. The case of Eva C. is a startling example of the cumulative effect of one French professor's belief that the proposed daughters-in-law of generals are above suspicion.

Though not precisely discredited by these events, Eva may have felt that her time was running out. A series of sittings held at the Paris Sorbonne in 1922 was also unproductive, and her career ended shortly afterward when she married a Monsieur Waespé. Unlike many professionals, from athletes to actors, Eva/Marthe knew when to retire.

The same cannot be said of Helen Duncan, a materialization medium who began her career in Dundee, Scotland. Little is recorded of her early mediumship, but by 1931 she was sufficiently prominent in spiritualist circles to be invited to sit for the London Psychical Laboratory (the research department of the London Spiritualist Alliance). Thus it happens that the first entry of Helen Duncan into the annals of psychical research is an exposure.

Helen, like Eva C., specialized in the production of ectoplasm, but was apparently much more imaginative in choosing her materials. "Ectoplasm" obtained from her at various times during the L.P.L. sittings was found to be a mixture of paper, cloth, and white of egg or else surgical gauze soaked in Canadian balsam. The committee's final report concluded that "the material was swallowed by Mrs. Duncan at some time previously to the séance and subsequently regurgitated by her for the purposes of exhibition." If there remained any doubt in the matter, it was dispelled by the medium's husband, who does not seem to have been a model of loyalty. In a final interview he admitted that he had seen his wife swallowing various strange things before her séances. That being so, a very interesting point arises.

First we may be reminded of a chance phrase that occurred in the report of the Sorbonne investigation into the phenomena of Eva C. The sittings, as we said, were largely a failure, but a small amount of "ectoplasm" was seen to emerge from the medium's mouth with what were described as "the very characteristic movements of the effort to vomit." Apparently Helen Duncan was not the first to use this means of deception. There is another possibility to be raised also.

After the L.P.L. sittings the independent investigator Harry Price suggested that Mrs. Duncan might have been one of those rare persons who possesses a "second stomach," or esophageal diverticulum, in medical terms. It is a pouchlike tissue structure in the tube leading from the mouth to the stomach and might indeed be useful for concealing objects too large to hold in the mouth. And although X-rays later taken of Mrs. Duncan did not show such a feature, it remains an intriguing possible explanation for the phenomena of other mediums. Furthermore, the ability to regurgitate at will from the normal stomach, while certainly not a usual one, does sometimes occur naturally and can perhaps be learned with practice. Thus in some cases we may find that the abnormal but certainly real talents of mediums are quite as fascinating as the alleged habits of "spirits." The unaided human body is capable of some amazing feats. We have already mentioned the production of loud raps with the joints, ventriloquism, the stretching of the spine by the muscles, the exceptional agility and muscular control necessary to free oneself from ropes, and the conjurer's astonishing quickness of hand. How many other purely physical talents may have played their part in mediumship unrecognized?

Let us now return to the career of Helen Duncan. We have little choice, since that is what the lady herself did. Undaunted by her exposure at the hands of the L.P.L., she proceeded to give another series of test sittings, this time for the National Laboratory of Psychical Research under the direction of its founder, Harry

Price 1881–1948), otherwise known as "The Ghost Buster" for his work in exposing the real causes of various hauntings and poltergeists, as well as other psychic frauds. It should perhaps be noted that Mr. Price was not a complete skeptic. Although not a believer in spirits, he was of the opinion that some mediums (for example, D. D. Home and Eusapia Palladino) had occasionally produced genuine physical and mental phenomena. Mr. Price was not forced to classify Mrs. Duncan as such an exceptional case, however. Photographs taken at these sessions revealed that the "ectoplasm" she produced was a length of cheesecloth whose bound edges, texture, and creases were clearly visible.

None of these discoveries made any difference to Helen's public. Outside the laboratories her fame continued to grow, and sitters continued to insist that they had recognized departed friends and relatives in the faces she materialized. But in 1933 came proof that not all, at least, of Helen's customers were equally gullible. At a sitting in Edinburgh a member of the circle snatched at one of the "spirit friends" as it fluttered by and found it to be nothing but a torn piece of white underwear. Helen Duncan was taken to court, convicted of fraud, and fined ten pounds. Less than two months later she was back at work. The Spiritualists' National Union had renewed her diploma as an accredited medium.

Eleven years later almost precisely the same thing happened again. Together with her companion Mrs. Brown and a couple named Homer who ran a sort of spiritualist parlor called the Master Temple Psychic Centre, Helen Duncan was arrested, tried, and convicted of "conspiring falsely to pretend that the medium could communicate with the spirits of the dead." The trial created something of a furor in spiritualist circles because the prosecution was carried out under the Witch-craft Act of 1735, a law that was certainly outdated, regardless of the guilt or innocense of the defendant.

Again, "regardless" is the relevant word. Helen Duncan served out her nine months' prison sentence and returned to the séance room quite regardless of past disclosures. Though by this time even the spiritualist press was less enthusiastic about her, she still had a number of faithful followers. She continued to sit, right up until the day in 1956 when the police of the city of Nottingham broke into one of her séances. The medium immediately became ill, possibly from the shock, and died in a hospital five weeks later. The doctors listed the cause of death as diabetes and heart failure, but a certain section of the spiritualist world thought otherwise. "Police brutality"—in the form of disturbing a medium while in trance—was whispered to be the real cause of her death, and some of her more hysterical supporters even used the word murder. If Helen Duncan had been a true materialization medium, would it have been more astonishing than the reality? At her funeral a minister of the Church of Scotland called her the Scottish Joan of Arc. There are still some, including the well-known editor of several British psychic newspapers, who think of her as a martyr to the cause of spiritualism, a victim of the world's stubborn intolerance.

It would be a mistake to conclude that the mid-twentieth century produced no worthy successors to the great mediums of the past. Puzzling manifestations were by no means dead. The next medium to attract the serious attention of the scientific world was the wife of a successful surgeon in Boston, Massachusetts. Her name was Mina Crandon but, like most nonprofessional mediums of the time, she was known to the public under a pseudonym, which in this case was Margery.

Margery's career as a medium began in 1923. Her husband, Dr. LeRoy G. Crandon, had undertaken some semiserious inquiries into the medical aspects of spiritualism, in the course of which he and his young wife made separate visits to a local clairvoyant. According to later accounts, Margery's first session brought forth the revelation that the spirit of her dead brother Walter was present and had a message for her. "Walter," who had been killed in a railway accident in 1911, declared that his sister had great psychic talents and urged her to develop them so that he could prove his existence to her. Mrs. Crandon was naturally excited, and a small circle of friends agreed to join her in testing "Walter's" prediction. Everything came about as suggested.

Mrs. Crandon's mediumship followed the usual course from tiltings and raps to the production of the trance and physical phenomena. It might have remained a purely private matter had it not been for the fact that, in 1922, the magazine *Scientific American* had offered a prize of twenty-five hundred dollars to any medium, professional or nonprofessional, who could produce a phenomenon that would satisfy the judges of its supernormal character. In the year and a half since its announcement, however, the prize had gone unawarded.

Now the Crandons declared that Margery would attempt to succeed where others had failed.

By this time the Boston medium had developed a very interesting range of phenomena. In addition to lifting and tilting of the table and of course the voice of "Walter," there were also apports (once of a live pigeon) the moving and even smashing of pieces of furniture, musical sounds, scents, and moving lights.

The committee selected to investigate these manifestations was made up of five members. They were Dr. William McDougall, professor of psychology at Harvard University; Dr. W. F. Prince, chief research officer of the A.S.P.R.; Dr. Daniel F. Comstock, a physicist and inventor formerly with the Massachusetts Institute of Technology; Hereward Carrington, the psychical investigator whose evaluations of Eusapia Palladino and the Lily Dale camp have already been referred to; and finally Harry Houdini, the great stage magician and escape artist.

It might have been thought that such a collection of experts was ideally chosen for the task at hand, but the composition of the committee caused difficulties almost from the start. Most noticeable was the friction between Houdini and the supporters of Mrs. Crandon, including J. Malcolm Bird, an associate editor of *Scientific American* who had been assigned to the investigation as observer, organizer, and recorder. Bird and others contended that Houdini's record of exposing fraudulent mediums proved that he was biased against the possibility of genuine phenomena and should therefore be disqualified.

In the event, however, the presence of Houdini on

the committee could have had no decisive influence on its verdict one way or the other, since the members found themselves quite unable to agree. Individual opinions ranged from Carrington's belief that some genuine phenomena did occur in Margery's presence, through suspended judgment on the part of McDougall, Comstock, and Prince, to Houdini's assertion that what they had witnessed was a series of very clever tricks. Yet in spite of the fact that the vote would still have been three to one against awarding Margery the prize—even without Houdini—the Crandons and their supporters reacted with outrage to the magician's accusations, published separately in a pamphlet entitled *Houdini Exposes the Tricks Used by the Boston Medium Margery*.

The whole situation got quite out of hand when "Walter" began predicting to all who would listen that Houdini had not long to live, and Houdini countered by claiming that the Crandons, Bird, and Carrington were engaged in a conspiracy to conceal the original fraud. Though this notion could conceivably have been true it had, especially in Carrington's case, not the slightest positive evidence to bolster it. The final scene in the dispute took place when the Crandons accused Houdini of planting evidence of fraud in the séance room in order to discredit the medium. Certainly a folding carpenter's rule (useful for moving distant objects) had been found inside a "fraudproof" box for control of the medium constructed by Houdini, and a pencil eraser was discovered to have jammed the mechanism of a bell that "Walter" was accustomed to ring. However, it will probably never be known who was responsible or whether the objects were intended to discredit the medium's performance or Houdini's exposure of it. The magazine's publisher urged that further sittings be held in order to resolve the deadlock, but though this was done, none of the committee felt inclined to change his opinion, and the prize went unawarded.

However, Margery emerged from the investigation with her credit higher than ever among spiritualists, many of whom had not heard of her before. As a public figure she had much in her favor. She was young, vivacious, financially secure, socially acceptable, and decidedly attractive in a healthy American fashion. From her photographs one might say she looked like a former high school cheerleader, certainly not like a woman of mystery, an accomplished trickster, or a publicity seeker. Whether she was in fact any or all of those things remained to be seen.

During the early part of 1925 Margery was studied by Dr. Eric J. Dingwall, then research officer of the British S.P.R. It is a comment on the difficulty of making satisfactory observations under séance conditions —such as darkness or near darkness, withdrawal of the medium into a cabinet, and the impossibility of completely controlling the medium either by tying or by holding—that at the end of twenty-nine sittings Dingwall was unable either to point to definite evidence of fraud or to declare himself convinced that the phenomena were supernormal.

It was during this period that Margery began to develop a highly unusual manifestation that was to widen her fame even further. On the table in front of her during a séance would be placed two dishes, one containing hot water, the other cold. In the first dish was a piece of dental wax. When the wax was softened, it was claimed that "Walter" could make an impression of his thumb on it, after which the "thumbprint" was put into the cold water to harden. (Naturally the medium was being controlled at these times, as throughout the séances, though it may surprise us to learn that one of the controllers was usually her husband.)

As might be expected, it was not possible to prove that the prints produced actually were the same as those belonging to the dead individual named Walter. What *was* proved on a number of occasions was that the prints were not those of anyone present in the séance room. Margery's supporters argued that this was enough, that as long as the owner of the prints was not in the room at the time it did not greatly matter whether the "thumb" that made them was that of the actual Walter or of some other spirit.

For the modern reader of newspapers or detective fiction it is very hard to separate the idea of thumb-prints from the category of evidence. We are all familiar with the fact that no two persons have identical prints and that fingerprints are often used to prove identity in courts of law. For that reason it is easy to understand why many believers were quite carried away by this manifestation of Margery's. It seemed almost like having a spirit leave a printed calling card, only better. No thumbprint without a thumb, no thumb without a body, no body without survival after death, so ran the reasoning.

The thumbprints, and indeed the whole question of Margery's mediumship, caused a major upheaval in psychical research circles, particularly the A.S.P.R. Many leading members of the society wished to come out in support of the Boston medium, a fact that led to the resignation of Dr. W. F. Prince, the society's chief research officer and a former member of the *Scientific American* committee. Dr. Prince and several others who felt that Margery's phenomena required (at the least) further investigation then formed, in 1925, a separate organization known as the Boston Society for Psychical Research.

It was the *Bulletin* of the B.S.P.R. that published, a few years later, an altogether different view of the thumbprints. In a series of articles by Hereward Carrington and two others, with an introduction by Dr. Prince, it was revealed that the thumbprints did not belong to "Walter" or to anyone else who might be found in the spirit world. They were those of a Dr. Kerwin, Margery's dentist. There could not be any mistake, police experts testified. The prints were Kerwin's, which hardly seems illogical if we ask from what better source one might obtain dental wax and sample thumbprints. Subsequent experiments showed that by this means it was entirely possible to make a die somewhat like a rubber stamp with which thumbprints could be quite successfully forged. The ruse would never have been discovered if a Mr. E. E. Dudley, a former officer of the A.S.P.R., had not undertaken to collect thumbprints from every single individual ever known to have attended one of Margery's séances. By his efforts "Walter" was decisively demoted to the status of a disembodied voice.

Of course spiritualists were quick to point to the example of Eusapia Palladino in defense of the idea that all Margery's manifestations could not be dismissed simply because one had been shown to be fraudulent. There was still another whole class of happenings that was claimed by Margery's supporters to provide irrefutable proof of spirit intervention. These cross-correspondences, as they were called, had been tried before by other mediums (with perhaps more impressive results, as we shall see in a later chapter). However, those carried out by Margery were considerably less complex and therefore much easier to study. They form an excellent introduction to the topic, which constitutes one of the most puzzling and disturbing of all séance phenomena.

The idea behind Margery's cross-correspondences was purely experimental. If the "spirits" could communicate interlocking parts of the same message through two or more different mediums in different places at the same time, then the skeptics would be forced to admit that a single intelligence was engaged in passing information by some supernormal means. The Crandons set out to demonstrate the truth of spiritualism by producing cross-correspondences in messages received through Margery and two other mediums, George Valiantine of New York City and Dr. Henry Hardwicke of Niagara Falls, New York. "Walter" was an enthusiastic participant in these plans. He had always given every sign of being anxious to prove his existence, and it is not surprising that he was the one who devised some of the most striking tests.

It is of course necessary to read the complete record of all the cross-correspondences in order to form a definitive judgment of their value. (It will be found in Volume XXII of the *Journal* of the A.S.P.R., then called *Psychic News*.) For our purposes here it will have to be enough to examine one of the best-known and most representative examples.

During a sitting at the Crandon house on February 17, 1928, "Walter" announced that he had invented a problem that made use of certain materials at hand, and that Valiantine and Hardwicke would each give part of the answer. The materials mentioned consisted of a closed box, a sheaf of calendar pages of the type having one sheet for each day, and a set of cards bearing various symbols such as circles, stars, squares, and Xs. "Walter" was to select from these, while they were inside the box, a few sheets that would form some clue to his message, thus providing a sort of double check on what was later written or spoken by Margery and the others.

On this occasion, after "Walter" had been given time to operate on the sealed box, which sat on the table, Margery emerged from her trance and the party moved to another room at about 9:40 P.M. (The times given are as recorded by Dr. Richardson, a regular member of Margery's circle.) It was customary for the medium to give her part of the cross-correspondence message by automatic writing at this later stage of the sitting. She began to write at 10:05, producing a script that read, "$11 \times 22 =$" and then, "to kick a dead." Though the message was short, automatic writing is often difficult and "Walter" also delivered himself of some general remarks so that it was 10:38 when Margery was finished. The box was then opened and on top of the rest of the contents were found a sheet with the number eleven, a card with the figure X, and another sheet with the number two. Next came a telephone call to New York by Dr. Crandon, during which he was informed that between 9:57 and 9:59 Valiantine had written, "2—No one ever stops to—Walter."

The third part of the message came in by telegram at 11:49. Hardwicke had wired, "Nine forty-five—HO stop R stop SE 2." The meaning was now clear. Together the parts of the message spelled out the sentence, "No one ever stops to kick a dead horse," and the equation, "$11 \times 2 = 22$."

Here, then, is a fairly typical example of what is meant by cross-correspondences. They are, on the surface, one of the most impressive pieces of evidence for survival of the personality, since it would be difficult for even the toughest skeptic to deny that the production of such messages must have been directed by some intelligent mind. That the explanation could be mere chance is too laughable to need discussion.

Suppose, therefore, we accept the idea that Margery's cross-correspondences are the work of "some intelligent mind." The next question is, "Whose?" Of course the Crandons and their party would have us accept that the obvious, the only possible answer is, "Walter's." But is that necessarily so? A highly interesting essay by Theodore Besterman in his book *Some Modern Mediums* points out that "Walter" is not the only candidate for the title of author of the messages. One might, for example, consider the possibility that the intelligence referred to belonged to the medium and her husband.

There are two times at which the whole incident *might* have been engineered without the help of any spirits. First is the time of the séance itself. During the two gaps that occurred in the proceedings—one of

twenty-five minutes between the end of the upstairs
sitting and the beginning of the downstairs sitting, and
one of thirty-three minutes between the beginning and
the end of Margery's automatic writing—there is nothing
in the record to indicate that someone could not have
slipped away to pass a telephone message to New York
City or Niagara Falls. According to Dr. Richardson's
official account of the session there were thirteen persons
present and no attempt was made to pinpoint each one's
movements and activities on a minute-by-minute basis.

Likewise, there is no detailed transcript of Dr.
Crandon's conversation with New York regarding
Valiantine's message—the one contact among the mediums that is admitted to have taken place during the
relevant time. We do not know who listened to the
conversation, whether the doctor was able to ask leading
questions, or even whether his exact words could have
contained a coded message. In the latter connection one
must realize that verbal codes of the type used in
professional mind-reading acts can be incredibly effective
and complex. For examples one need only consult the
books of such famous writers on stage magic as Houdini
and J. N. Maskelyne.

A further objection to the "Dead Horse Message"
is that there is no direct evidence to show that Valiantine
had produced his part of the correspondence as early
as 9:59 (that is, *before* the box was opened and Margery
did her automatic writing). Even if he did do so, there
was still ample time for him to communicate unofficially
with someone at the Crandons' by telephone, supposing
that the message had originated with Valiantine as the
producer of the part of the correspondence that came

first chronologically. (It may be relevant to note at this point that in 1931 Valiantine was to be exposed in the making of "spirit fingerprints" by a technique similar to Margery's; a print alleged to belong to Sir Arthur Conan Doyle was found to be very much like that of the medium's left big toe.)

As between the two methods of arranging the cross-correspondence suggested above, the more likely would seem to be a couple of secret phone calls from the Crandons during one of the time lapses between parts of the Boston sitting rather than the use of a verbal code during the official call, because the latter would still have left Hardwicke's message unaccounted for (since it arrived by telegram). An interesting fact about that telegram is that although Dr. Richardson records in his account that Hardwicke did not begin to sit until 9:50, the message indicated that "Walter" had come through to Hardwicke at 9:45. Was this a simple error, or was the sender of the message trying to make it appear less likely that Hardwicke could have heard from the Crandons after the end of the first part of their sitting at 9:40?

The alert reader has certainly noticed a major objection to the foregoing theories, namely, "What about the calendar pages and cards spelling out 11×2? They were chosen before 9:40 and not revealed until after Margery's part of the message, at least, was complete."

It is certainly true that only the material in the sealed box prevents us from supposing that the whole affair was arranged among the mediums well in advance and without having to go to all the trouble of secret telephone calls. But here again the flaws in Dr. Richardson's records, unintentional though they may be, leave room for doubt about the true situation. He tells us nothing about the previous history of the cards and pages. Could they, for example, have been "marked" beforehand in the way that a cardsharp may mark playing cards so that they can be identified by touch? If so, it would have been a simple matter for either Margery or Dr. Crandon, to name only the two most likely suspects, to have sorted them into a prearranged order in the dark. We are not told, either, exactly what sort of lock or seal was on the box, but it is hard to imagine that any ordinary sort of precaution would have hindered a medium whose tricks Houdini had called "very, very clever."

Finally, if we wish to accept the opinion of the sitters that no trickery was resorted to during the séance itself, we might consider the possibility that the part of the message contained in the box was left to chance. If it was pure accident that caused 11, X, and 2 to be the first three items in the sealed box, all that would have been necessary was that someone open the box secretly during one of the time gaps already mentioned and then reseal it for the official opening. The equation $11 \times 2 = 22$ could then have been passed on to the other mediums along with the parts of the sentence. This procedure is perhaps unlikely since it would require either the co-operation or the carelessness of the person to whom the box had been entrusted, but it cannot be ruled out on those grounds alone.

Clearly the theories put forth here are just that, theories without concrete supporting evidence that what could have happened did happen. Our justification for going into the matter in such detail is that Dr. Richardson and other supporters of the Crandons claimed that the

conduct of the experiment proved that the cross-correspondence "*could not* have been prearranged." (The
italics are the doctor's.) But as we have seen, this
statement means no more than that Dr. Richardson *was
convinced* there was no prearrangement, which is quite
another thing. Opinions may differ as to the likelihood
of conspiracy among the mediums, but it can hardly
be said that such a thing was *impossible,* and therefore
Dr. Richardson and the Crandons have failed to prove
their case.

CHAPTER XI

LAURELS AND LATIN, OR
HOW NOT TO FAKE A SÉANCE

"The famous cross-correspondences of the S.P.R.," as they are usually referred to in histories of spiritualism, seem to occupy a place apart in the minds of most investigators. Perhaps this is partly because even the briefest statement about these interlocking messages—so much wider in scope, longer in duration, and more complex than the correspondences of Margery—sounds frankly incredible. From approximately 1897 to 1910 the British S.P.R. found itself acting as a sort of clearing house for the interrelated utterances of at least seven different mediums around the world. The messages received had unmistakable points of similarity and were moreover alleged to have been written or spoken by spirit controls who were among the S.P.R.'s most famous former members.

For example, we find that both "F. W. H. Myers" and "Richard Hodgson" after their respective deaths in 1901 and 1905 appeared not only to be communicating but to be directing the investigations into their own survival with almost the same vigor as if they were still alive. "Myers" gave his messages through three separate mediums—Mrs. Leonore Piper, Mrs. Helen Verrall, and Mrs. Holland (the last being the pseudonym of Mrs. Fleming, sister of Rudyard Kipling)—and during part of the period in question the three ladies were living as far apart as the United States, England, and India. "Hodgson" communicated through Mrs. Piper and Mrs. Holland.

Though we shall give our main attention to these two cases, it must be made clear that the web of the cross-correspondences was much wider. Other participating mediums were Mrs. Verrall's daughter Miss Verrall, Mrs. Chenoweth, Mrs. Forbes, and Mrs. Thompson, while the alleged communicators included such well-known former psychical investigators as Professor Sidgwick and Edmund Gurney, as well as the deceased relatives and friends of both sitters and mediums.

In order to gain a feeling for the nature of these communications there is no substitute for reading the word-for-word records of the sessions themselves, even in short sections. Only in this way can the difficulty of the problem be gauged. The word "difficulty" refers here not only to our dilemma as interpreters, but to the apparent effort that is being put forth by the communicators. That is a frequent feature of trance messages, it is true, and the fraudulent medium relies on claims of mishearing or misinterpretation to cover up mistakes. However, one can hardly help feeling that one of the most convincing aspects of these cross-correspondences is the tremendously hard work that appears to be involved for all concerned. In an early message the "Myers" control gave this vivid description of the situation. "The nearest simile I can find to express the difficulties of sending a message—is that I appear to be standing behind a sheet of frosted glass which blurs sight and deadens sound—dictating feebly to a reluctant and somewhat obtuse secretary."

The aptness of the above statement is seen in the following script, produced by Mrs. Verrall via automatic writing on February 6, 1907. The communicator is again "Myers," relaying his message through Mrs. Verrall's usual spirit control.

Laura and another
There is some great obstruction this morning
help to remove it.
This must not occur again tell him that.
Put not your light under a bushel

[There follows a very wobbly ink drawing resembling a triangle formed of three round loops above a long vertical line. It is labeled, "K.g. blue riband and five pointed star."]

the great Library has already gone before
Hugh Le Despenser
The branch that should have grown full straight
Apollo's laurel bough
You don't get it right but some of this is
true

[Drawing: a decidedly dagger-like shape with a long blade, pommel, and crossbar. Caption: "I think it is a jewelled dagger." Another caption: "three curved objects and a point." Another drawing: something very much like a shamrock.]

I can't see what all this means but I am told to
say it to you

APOLLOS   LAUREL   BOUGH
There is also some point in the Library
Put together the Library and the bough
Laureatus a laurel wreath
perhaps no more than that

[Drawing: an obvious laurel wreath, perhaps standing on a base of some kind.]

Corona laureata has some meaning here
With laureate wreath his brow serene was crowned.
No more today—await the better news
that brings assurance with a laurel crown.

Without commenting yet on this script of Mrs.
Verrall's, let us continue with extracts of communications
obtained through Mrs. Piper on February 26 and 27
of the same year. The speaker (when not Mrs. Piper
herself) is the medium's usual control "George Pelham,"
who reports the wishes and comments of "Myers." Since
the session was recorded and questions asked by an investigator named J. G. Piddington (J.G.P.), it will be
helpful to use the form of a dialogue. Parentheses indicate Piddington's comments at the time of the session,
while square brackets indicate explanations inserted by
the author, as they do also above.

Mrs. P.:   Fairies (??)
           (hand points) George. —All right.—
J.G.P.:   Say that again.

Mrs. P.:   There is George. Whatever is it? Morehead (?)

J.G.P.:   "Morehead?"

Mrs. P.:   Morehead (?) (or some such word)

[In a later commentary Piddington said he believed it possible that the word was meant to be Lauread, not Morehead. How much of this sort of interpretation is hindsight we can never know.]

    laurel for laurel

J.G.P.:   Say that again.

Mrs. P.:   for laurel. I say I gave her that for laurel. Goodbye. (addressed apparently by Mrs. Piper to the spirit).

J.G.P.:   No, before you say goodbye ask him to repeat that.

Mrs. P.:   I gave her that for laur-el. (. . .)

J.G.P.:   Spell it.

Mrs. P.:   Laur-el (or Laur-ie, the second syllable being again indistinct)

J.G.P.:   L-a-u. Is that right?

Mrs. P.:   Aphasia, aphasia

[At this point there is a brief digression not related to the cross-correspondence.]

J.G.P.:   Do you remember what George said?

Mrs. P.:   Well, let me think. You're Mr. Piddington, aren't you? Something—I think he said something about—let me see. Well, I think it was something about lau-rel wreaths he tell her.

J.G.P.:   (mistaking the last three words for a proper name) "Hetella?"

Mrs. P.:   (irritably) He tell her. He would tell her. Oh! you make me so cross. . . . Tell her about.

More material concerning this correspondence came through in the next day's session, when "Myers" himself appeared to be the communicator and the message was written rather than spoken.

Myers: listen.
J.G.P.:   Yes.
Myers: I gave Mrs. Verrall
Laurel wreath
J.G.P.:   Yes, quite right; she got it.
Myers: and I said Hodgson.
J.G.P.:   "Hodgson?"
Myers: yes would give the next.
J.G.P.:   I don't know about that, I'll look.
Myers: she may not have received it but
J.G.P.:   No; but she got "laurel wreath" *clearly.*
Myers: I (written while J.G.P. was speaking)
yes I gave her that
and as the spirit of the light
Returned to its body (that is, during the waking stage of the trance) I tried to grasp it (Pencil breaks.)
Rector: [another of Mrs. Piper's spirit controls] You must keep the machine (i.e. the pencil) in order when the I (?) don't like them when they (scrawl) (Hand tries to write beyond the margin of the paper.)
R.
Myers: Grasp the spirit. so as to give it to you last time.

> J.G.P.:   I heard it quite well: "laurel wreath."
> Myers: Yes all right   I go now
>   I cant think more my thoughts wander
>   Farewell
>   Myers.
> (All the above portions of the "Laurel" correspond-
> ence appear in the *Proceedings* of the S.P.R., Vol.
> XXII, 1908, pp. 94–103)

The foregoing is only a tiny sample of incidents whose complete records occupy thousands of pages. What are we to make, then, of even such a minor piece of the puzzle? Quite obviously the connection of the messages goes beyond the mere repetition of the word "laurel." During his lifetime F. W. H. Myers had been a noted classical scholar, and so also was Mrs. Verrall. It is therefore not surprising that the Verrall scripts contain numerous learned allusions to Greek and Roman traditions such as the use of laurel for the wreath used to crown winners of the Olympic games and the fact that laurel was the sacred plant of the god Apollo. The scripts also contain quotes from poems referring to the topic of laurel and some Latin words related to "laurel"—*laureatus*, one who has been crowned with laurel, and *corona laureata*, the laurel crown or wreath of the victor. But quite apart from the depth of scholarship required to pinpoint all the possible interconnections of the messages, one thing is indisputably clear—the two mediums *are* talking about the same thing, however confusedly.

An equally important aspect of the cross-correspond-ences is the question of personal recognition. Several of the investigators, such as Sir Oliver Lodge, William James, Mrs. Sidgwick, and Richard Hodgson had of course been well acquainted with the alleged communicators Gurney, Myers, Professor Sidgwick, and (later) Hodgson. In a few cases the mediums, too, had known the communicators during their lifetimes. For example, Mrs. Piper had worked very closely with Richard Hodgson for eighteen years before his death.

These relationships among the participants made the verification of identity both easier and more difficult. On the one hand, the sitters were often able to say that the communicators sounded "like themselves." Thus the "Edmund Gurney" who gave messages through Mrs. Piper (we may call him Piper-Gurney) was judged recognizable by Lodge but not recognizable by James, while both Verrall-Gurney and Forbes-Gurney were agreed to be colorless and rather neutral with regard to personality. The handwriting of Thompson-Sidgwick was strikingly like that of the late professor, although the ideas expressed sounded less like Sidgwick's than like Mrs. Thompson's. (The medium's statement that she had never seen Sidwick's handwriting could neither be proved nor disproved.)

Mrs. Verrall had been a close friend of F. W. H. Myers, and Verrall-Myers was agreed to be much more lifelike than either Piper-Myers or Holland-Myers. Nevertheless, Verrall-Myers was unable to give a correct account of a sealed letter that Myers had instructed Lodge to open after his death. And finally, as if to add to the confusion, a series of sittings with Piper-Hodgson in England yielded much true factual material but little feeling of the real presence of Hodgson, while another set of sittings with the same entity, held later in the United States, was pronounced very authentic and convincing.

Clearly we cannot know how much of their own knowledge and impressions the mediums in the cross-correspondence cases may have put into the mouths of the alleged communicators, whether consciously or unconsciously. One has only to watch a skilled stage comedian or impersonator to know how easily a few mannerisms of speech or expression can conjure up a well-known public figure. In a case where most of those involved must have been acquainted with each other by reputation and through the psychic press, if not personally, it becomes very difficult to judge how much weight should be given to spontaneous feelings of recognition on the part of the sitters.

The cross-correspondences would be much easier to dismiss if they contained nothing but classical references and lifelike personal impressions. That they also contain a wealth of facts that apparently could not have been known to the mediums adds an extra dose of bafflement.

As we have said, the volume and complexity of the material available are staggering. The most useful examples of the sort of thing under discussion come from the mediumship of Mrs. Piper, though from a slightly earlier period than that of the cross-correspondences. At this time Richard Hodgson was still alive and was the chief organizer and director of Mrs. Piper's research sittings. One of her sitters had for some time been a young man, a friend of Hodgson's, who had been introduced to the medium under the pseudonym of George Pelham. Pelham died rather suddenly, and shortly afterward a "George Pelham" announced himself as one of the communicators in Mrs. Piper's trance. (We have already seen "Pelham's" role in the first part of Mrs. Piper's contribution to the "laurels" correspondence.)

Over a period of some months Hodgson then arranged to introduce various friends of Pelham's into the sittings, unknown to Mrs. Piper. In twenty-eight of thirty cases these individuals were recognized by "Pelham." There were only two who were not recognized, and "Pelham" never claimed acquaintance with anyone who had not been known to the real Pelham. In one of the numerous tests devised by Hodgson during this period "Pelham" was asked whether he could observe what a certain friend of his, a Mrs. Howard, was doing at the time of the séance. The reply contained a detailed description of Mrs. Howard at her desk. She was said to take some violets and press them in a book, to write a letter to Pelham's mother, and another to someone named Tyson. She also went upstairs to hunt for something in a drawer, came back down, and finished one of the letters, having put two pictures of Pelham on her desk.

On being told of this experiment, Mrs. Howard reported that she had done none of the things described *at the time of the séance,* but all of them on the afternoon and evening before, as was corroborated by her daughter. Not only was "Pelham's" account true in almost every detail (the exception being that the violets were put into a drawer rather than into a book), but Mrs. Howard remarked that some of the actions reported had not been usual ones for her. For example, she had not written to Mrs. Tyson, whom she knew only slightly, for a period of weeks or even months before the day in question.

Thus, in the perverse manner so common in psychical research, the experiment ended neither in success nor in failure but only in presenting another problem.

On another occasion Sir Oliver Lodge brought to a session with Mrs. Piper a gold watch that had belonged to his deceased Uncle Jerry. The watch had come into Lodge's hands by that morning's mail and he had kept its arrival and origin secret until giving it to the entranced medium. "Uncle Jerry" then proceeded to give a detailed account of his boyhood sixty years earlier. It concerned a near-accident while swimming in a creek, killing a cat in a certain field, the finding of a long skin (perhaps a snakeskin), and so on. None of these events was familiar to Sir Oliver, whose father was very much younger than the uncle in question and had only known him as a grown man. The facts given through Mrs. Piper by "Uncle Jerry" had to be verified by writing to two surviving uncles, now very old men, who had grown up with Jerry. Between them they confirmed the entire story, though neither one alone had knowledge of all the events described.

This type of mediumship, as displayed by the S.P.R. group, is very different from that of the great physical mediums. Here we find no spirit lights, no tipping tables, no ghostly fingers, only a group of persons who appear to speak with the voices and write with the hands of others and to possess information that could not possibly have come to them by normal means. In fact, mental phenomena of one sort or another have always been a part of mediumship, from the moment when Kate and Margaret Fox induced "Mr. Splitfoot" to enumerate names, ages, and histories of the Foxes' neighbors in Hydesville, some of which were claimed to be beyond the children's knowledge.

There has been no great medium who failed to astonish his or her sitters over and over with personal information, even when the sitter had remained anonymous, thus ruling out any such device as Mr. Pidgeon's useful list. The interesting thing is that mental phenomena were so much less popular than the more spectacular, but much more easily faked, physical effects. Perhaps the reason is that to those who accepted the spiritualist belief in survival there was no mystery about such information. The spirit is of course expected to remember everything about his past life and is also thought to have access to knowledge from other spirits and from his (invisible) observation of events in the real world.

If we are to search for an explanation of the S.P.R. cross-correspondences, the obvious place to begin is with this theory of spirit intervention, which the spiritualists would have us accept as the only adequate answer. Does the evidence of the cross-correspondences (and of the other phenomena described in this book) make it reasonable to conclude that the individual personality survives after death? If so, it will upset many of our basic ideas about the universe, contradict the teachings of some of the world's major religions, and even cast doubt on the meaning of such common words as "life," "time," "space," "fact," "real," and "proof." It will contradict all the testimony of our five senses, which tell us that objects do not move by themselves, that dead bodies cannot be brought back to life, and that two physical objects cannot occupy the same space at the same time. Surely we will be justified in applying here the excellent principle that the simplest explanation is the best one. Before we take the great leap into believing in spirits, we must examine and reject every other less extreme point of view.

One possible solution, of course, is universal fraud. Suppose the whole affair of the cross-correspondences was concocted by overzealous spiritualists in a desperate attempt to stifle criticism once and for all? What stands in the way of this notion is not so much the undoubtedly high reputations of the S.P.R. mediums and investigators (since the cases of Sir William Crookes, Marthe Béraud, and the Crandons have shown that *no one* can be considered above suspicion in this field); rather, it is the number of people and the length of time involved.

Conspiracies have a way of coming to light through the sheer inability of the plotters to keep the secret. (What would we now think of Florence Cook if she had not boasted to Anderson about her affair with Crookes?) If the cross-correspondences were fraudulent —that is, if they were invented beforehand and divided among the various mediums in order to provide proof of survival—it is rather remarkable that not one of the dozen or so people who must have been in on the scheme has confessed or left behind some incriminating evidence. Furthermore, though it may be possible that the material for the cross-correspondences was assembled through extensive research into the lives, thoughts, and writings of the alleged communicators, the mere task of organizing the hoax would have been stupendous.

Also in favor of the S.P.R. material, perhaps, is the fact that it has none of the convenient patness of the Margery correspondences. Instead, its three thousand pages, compiled during a period of well over ten years, are fragmentary, confusing, and exasperating, but somehow more convincing for that reason. Not only would the preparation of so much material have been horrifyingly complicated, it almost seems like more trouble than it was worth. If the S.P.R. group were engaged in faking evidence, they might have found a less tortuous method.

The same problems apply to the notion of individual fraud, as opposed to group fraud. First of all, no single person had access to all the participants or all the data produced. Not even Mrs. Piper, whose work has justly had the starring role in this account, was involved in every correspondence or gave messages from every communicator. Furthermore, Mrs. Piper may be the single best-investigated medium in the history of spiritualism. From 1887 until she entered semiretirement in the 1920s she was under the constant, direct supervision of the S.P.R. and Richard Hodgson (1855–1905).

Hodgson, as the society's research officer, was exceedingly well qualified for such an investigation. He was a lawyer by training and had, only three years before being introduced to Mrs. Piper, been responsible for the exposure of the notorious but fascinating Madame Blavatsky (1831–91), an adventuress, pseudomystic, and imaginative mediumistic trickster who founded the Theosophical movement.

Hodgson's personal opinion was that "nearly all professional [that is, usually, physical] mediums form a gang of vulgar tricksters, who are more or less in league with one another." Hodgson was determined not to be taken in by any sort of trickery, and upon being introduced to Mrs. Piper in Boston by William James he immediately set out to discover whether she collected information about her sitters. For a period he even went to the length of having the medium followed by detectives, and he made it standard practice never to tell her who was coming to sit with her or to allow sitters to use their correct names.

Of the results of Hodgson's efforts William James wrote, "Dr. Hodgson considers that the hypothesis of fraud cannot seriously be maintained. I agree with him absolutely. The medium has been under observation, much of the time under close observation, as to the conditions of her life, by a large number of persons, eager, many of them, to pounce on any suspicious circumstance for fifteen years. During that time, *not only has there not been one single suspicious circumstance remarked, but not one suggestion has ever been made from any quarter* which might tend positively to explain how the medium, living the apparent life she leads, could possibly collect information about so many sitters by natural means." From a man of the intellectual stature of James, himself not a spiritualist, such a statement is bound to carry weight.

Fraud, then, must be said to be unlikely as an explanation of the cross-correspondences. But there is another possibility, or rather, combination of possibilities, for us to consider. During the period covered by the cross-correspondences, psychologists were developing a new view of the human mind, based partially on the work of the early mesmerists, that would at last offer a workable theory not only of such cases as that of Hélène Smith but of the genuine mediumistic trance in general. (The theory did not, however, necessarily explain the alleged paranormal phenomena that accompanied the trance.) The main feature of this view is that a large and important portion of what goes on in the mind takes place at a level below our normal awareness, known as the unconscious.

We have already mentioned the role of the unconscious mind in producing some physical illnesses of the type that may be cured by mesmerism or the power of suggestion and also in the elaborate trance imaginings of such mediums as Hélène Smith. In the trance the conscious mind and will are temporarily out of action, while the person's awareness and actions are dominated by the unconscious. The entranced person or somnambule is thus not responsible for what he does while in the trance state and may perform actions that he would otherwise regard as either wrong or foolish, although most authorities agree that the power of the hypnotist does not extend to making his subjects do things they feel to be deeply repellent, such as committing murder. It is also known that the trance state may in certain persons provide an opportunity for the appearance of "secondary personalities"—aspects of the personality that have become divided from the everyday self and may think and act very differently.

Now, the important thing about these facts from the point of view of spiritualism is that any aspect of the trance that can be induced by a mesmerist or hypnotist may also be self-induced. The medium may not only produce his or her own trance by means of suggestion (either consciously or unconsciously), he may also display a variety of secondary personalities through the power of suggestion, the positive belief that spirits will speak through him. It may well be that these secondary personalities are what we have been referring to as spirit controls, all products of the medium's unconscious mind.

There are several striking ways in which an entranced person, in this case the medium, may act differently from other people or from his waking self. As we mentioned in connection with Hélène Smith, the entranced person has access to his entire subliminal memory, only a tiny portion of which is generally available through a conscious "effort to remember." Therefore if "spirit controls" are really secondary personalities of the medium they may well know things that the medium honestly believes he has forgotten or never knew. There are many well-documented cases of hypnotized patients who have recalled whole pages of forgotten books that they had merely glanced at in the distant past.

Clearly, the task of saying what an entranced medium could or could not know has become much more difficult. Any educated person who reads widely encounters a staggering amount of useless information during a lifetime, and although most of this material is not consciously remembered, it is still lodged in the subliminal memory and its appearance in a trance statement cannot be used to prove that the entity who is speaking is not the medium.

In the case of the cross-correspondences, it is unfortunately impossible to say what general information the mediums may have possessed about the communicators. The two individuals concerned might never have met, but that must not obscure the fact that all the parties were members of the same "circle" in its broadest sense—the circle of spiritualism and psychical research. Passing remarks by third parties, chance references in the literature of spiritualism, and ordinary "shop talk" could have supplied a surprising amount of personal information, later to appear as evidence of identity in a trance communication. This is a form of unintentional fraud for which the medium can in no way be blamed. The unconscious mind is by definition a mind without a conscience. It takes any information that comes to hand, without the slightest regard for the source of that information, and uses it to back up the medium's expectation that "spirits" will manifest themselves.

Such self-suggestion may also be the source of some physical phenomena. For example, if the medium believes that tables will tip, he may unconsciously satisfy his belief by slipping one foot under a table leg (a very common method of producing fraudulent raps and tips) if the opportunity arises. It is this possibility that makes it so difficult to assess a mediumship like that of William Stainton Moses. The often repeated conviction that such a man *could not* have been guilty of fakery has no relevance at all when we are talking of Moses' unconscious actions. Because Moses sat only with friends and fellow believers and was never subject to any sort of adequate control, it is impossible to say that one of the most famous mediumships of all time was not the entire result of unconscious faking, although the medium in his waking state may have been totally sincere in proclaiming his honesty.

It ought to be noted, however, that unconscious fraud is probably much rarer than the old-fashioned, deliberate kind. Some of the most obviously fraudulent commercial mediums, who have probably never experienced a genuine trance, have been known to excuse themselves when exposed with an argument that might be put in the words of Mr. Sludge:

> I don't know if I move your hand sometimes
> When the spontaneous writing spreads so far,
> If my knee lifts the table all that height,
> Why the inkstand doesn't fall off the desk a-tilt,
> Why the accordion plays a prettier waltz
> Than I can pick out on the piano-forte,
> Why I speak so much more than I intend,
> Describe so many things I never saw.

Nevertheless, when trickery is detected in physical phenomena, at least, one may be reasonably sure that it was intentional.

Subliminal memory and self-suggestion are not the only kinds of unconscious fraud that may affect the happenings in the séance room. The early mesmeristic doctors were among the first to observe that entranced patients sometimes seemed able to see, hear, or feel things much more acutely than was normally possible, a condition often called hyperesthesia. However, it required several decades of further study before it was recognized that entranced persons were using their sharpened senses to gather information as to the intentions and state of mind of the mesmerist.

The tiniest physical reaction of the doctor—an indrawn breath, an expression of surprise, a glance at the part of the body to be treated next—had become for them as clear as a list of instructions. The doctors then found that their patients "knew" what was wanted of them before the words were spoken, as if by reading their minds.

Hyperesthesia is similar to a technique used by professional mind readers. These stage performers, who seldom seriously claim to get their information from spirits, can bring incredible perfection to the art of muscle reading, as it is called. They have learned that nearly everyone gives out a constant series of involuntary reactions to the world around him. Tiny movements of the face and body reveal when the individual is lying, when he is surprised or angry, when he recognizes a familiar name, and so on.

Some people even engage in subvocal whispering; that is, they move their larynxes or lips soundlessly as if they were about to respond aloud to a suggestion. This, of course, may be a great help to the muscle-reader (or medium) who is looking for information. The only difference between the skill of the performer and the hyperesthesia of an entranced (or occasionally an unentranced) person is that the professional has to undertake years of study before he becomes expert enough to "read" with a high degree of accuracy.

This faculty is not confined to human beings, astonishingly enough. There have been various "animal geniuses" who have made fortunes for their owners by signaling answers to complex questions thought to be beyond the reach of nonhuman minds. The famous Elberfeld Horses, for instance, stupefied the scientific world at the turn of the century by appearing to give instantaneous answers to such mathematical problems as 375×821 or the square root of $73,891$. The horses, of which there were at one time five, signaled their answers by pawing for each digit in order, so that 372 would be three strokes, pause, seven strokes, pause, two strokes.

Much has been written about them, some of it both pretentious and absurd, but there seems little doubt that the horses were merely responding to their trainer's unconscious physical signals (so minute that they were never noticed by the human spectators), which told them each time the proper number of strokes had been given. This answer was discovered by accident when it was found that the horses could not respond when the trainer was out of sight. Amazingly, one still finds this case listed on the contents pages of books describing "Great Unsolved Mysteries of the World."

To return to our more genuinely mystifying subject, there is no doubt that unusual but by no means supernormal factors such as hyperesthesia, subliminal memory, and secondary personality could account for some, at least, of the knowledge exhibited by the mental mediums of the S.P.R. and others. Anything to which the medium can be shown to have had access, no matter how briefly or how long ago, is now unacceptable as proof of survival. The same may be true of anything that is known to the sitters, on the grounds that they may be giving unconscious clues discernible to someone in a state of hyperesthesia. Against this last conclusion it has been argued that experienced researchers such as those who worked on the cross-correspondences are trained to guard against revealing themselves in this fashion and that in any case hyperesthesia is not very common even among mediums. For the sake of argument, however, we may agree to define the problem as above. Then we must ask, "Is there anything in these cross-correspondences for which we still cannot account?"

To the discomfort of skeptics, the answer plainly must be yes. None of the explanations outlined above takes us any closer to knowing why Mrs. Piper was apparently able to tell Sir Oliver Lodge facts about his uncle that were not only unknown to him but were not known as a whole to any single living person. Similarly, in the case of "George Pelham," no one in the séance room knew or had any reason to wish to know what Mrs. Howard had been doing the *day before* the test. Where, then, does the rare medium like Mrs. Piper get such information, and get it repeatedly?

It will not do for us to dismiss these incidents as isolated cases (though of course few are as massively documented as the cross-correspondences). Mrs. Verrall, an active researcher herself as well as an automatist, once made a detailed analysis of 238 definite statements that occurred in the communications of Mrs. Thompson, another of the S.P.R. mediums. Of them she found that thirty-three were false and sixty-four could not be verified, usually because they concerned persons who were dead or unavailable. The remaining 141 were established as true, and it was further found that ninety contained information not available from public sources such as newspapers, official records, parish registers, and tombstones. That is approximately 59 percent accuracy, a record few political analysts or stockbrokers can equal. Yet a careful reading of the literature of mediumship forces one to the conclusion that such things do occur.

At this point the person who is totally opposed to all except the most conventional scientific explanations may well give up in disgust. If he cannot prove fraud he will take refuge in a variety of suppositions like the following:

1. Coincidence—"Anyone can guess right once in a while."

2. Honest error—"Sir Oliver's surviving uncles were so old that they couldn't remember what had gone on in their youth; they only said what they thought would please their famous nephew."

3. Biased interpretation—If the spirit of your sister "Katie" remembers owning a red Plymouth that was really a red Ford, does the researcher count the statement as right or wrong?

These points of view are undoubtedly perfectly valid in some cases, and are firmly held by a good many people, even some psychical researchers. There is, however, a third possible position concerning séance-room phenomena—one that falls somewhere between belief in spirits and total skepticism. If one allows oneself to admit the existence of those mysterious mental powers called psychic, much of the problem disappears. The ability to "read" another's thoughts (telepathy), to discern the history of an object by holding it in one's hand (psychometry), to see or in some cases hear in the mind events distant in time or space (clairvoyance and clairaudience) have been part of our folklore since prehistoric times. More recently, under the name of extrasensory perception (ESP), they have been the subject of intensive research at such places as Duke, Stanford, and Harvard universities, as well as by the S.P.R., A.S.P.R., and related organizations.

Without going into the methods and results of that research in detail, it can be said that since the 1930s many people have come to believe that ESP is a proven reality. For them it is hardly necessary to theorize about spirits in order to account for the mental phenomena we have described here. The "Case of Sir Oliver's Uncle," for example, becomes a simple instance of psychometry, while "George Pelham's" description of Mrs. Howard can be put down to clairvoyance on the part of Mrs. Piper (though that still does not explain why the events seen took place the evening before the sitting).

Believers in ESP suggest that the trance state may be favorable to the appearance of psychic abilities just as it may be favorable to hyperesthesia and is certainly favorable to the exercise of subliminal memory and influence by suggestion. That would explain why mediums produce so many more instances of supernormal knowledge that the rest of us. It also explains why research into the question of survival has become incredibly difficult. How can one devise an identity test for a communicator in which the facts asked for were known to him in life and are not known to anyone else still living (in order to rule out the possibility of telepathy), yet can still be verified *after* being received via the medium? Some people even insist that the facts must not be recorded in any way, either, otherwise the medium might discern them clairvoyantly. But how can one verify what isn't known and isn't recorded? We shall have more to say later about recent efforts to get around this difficulty.

In the meantime the poor skeptic, the man who wants a full and complete explanation based only on known principles of science, is no better off than before. The existence of the ESP theory may relieve him of the necessity to believe in disembodied spirits, but replaces it with the idea that every thought or experience ever recorded by any human mind is to be found in a sort of vast, Universal Free Library where the only motto is, "Ask, and it shall be opened unto you." In short, the skeptic is invited to trade one mystery for another and may be excused for thinking that both are equally unsatisfactory.

Naturally each of us must decide for himself to what extent factors such as deliberate fraud, unconscious fraud, mere coincidence, and ESP may be used to explain trance phenomena in general and the cross-correspondences in particular. In doing so, he will certainly have to give serious thought to two human tendencies that have played a major role in the development of the spiritualist movement, as in that of many other movements. "The will to believe" and "the will to disbelieve" —how much influence do they have in the life of even the most logical person?

Man considers himself to be a marvelously intelligent creature, but the truth is that he frequently believes what is most reassuring rather than what is most logical. A person whose whole life is built on his love for another may simply refuse to believe that the one he loves is dead. Similarly, a devoted disciple of a great teacher, priest, political leader, or healer (or medium) may cling to his belief long after his idol has been shown to be wrong, incompetent, or dishonest. (Of the last we have seen some examples in earlier chapters.) In both cases the mind simply refuses to disrupt its deepest habits and deny its deepest needs for the sake of mere facts.

Probably none of us is free of similar tendencies, and though some individuals may rise above self-delusion it is always necessary to be watchful, especially when judging a new and startling proposition. The scientist whose whole life work and reputation among his colleagues might be shattered if he were forced to admit the truth of survival should be very suspicious of his own unbelief, just as the spiritualist must take account of the shock he would feel if his faith were to be unarguably refuted. The only advice that can be offered to those who set out to form an opinion is: Distrust most deeply those facts that seem to confirm your private opinions and secret hopes.

CHAPTER XII

MORE MUMMERY AND SOME MODERN "MIRACLES"

During the past forty years the spiritualist movement has in general continued to develop in the directions established for it earlier. Like most other human undertakings, however, it has been somewhat affected by changing technology on the one hand and changing styles on the other. Thus home activities such as table tipping and the use of the ouija board are less popular now than they once were, while the road-show variety of spiritualist exhibition presented by the Davenport brothers has virtually vanished from the scene.

The products of science and invention have made life both easier and more difficult for the would-be spiritualist faker. Easier because many happenings formerly termed miraculous are now simple to produce in any living room, for what is a phonograph or a radio but a disembodied voice, or a motion picture image but an apparition? Further, the engineer who triggers a dynamite blast with a radio signal is producing action without contact very much like telekinesis, and atomic physicists have repeatedly recorded the conversion of energy into matter, which can surely be termed materialization if only on the level of subatomic particles.

The secret use of electronic devices can produce very startling effects, as was recently shown in the case of a British professional medium who had astonished his sitters with his knowledge of their affairs, complete with names, dates, and addresses. The man was exposed when it was revealed that he received his information from an assistant with a short-wave radio transmitter, who sent him a rapid-fire stream of information obtained from the contents of visitors' coat pockets, handbags, briefcases, and so on, which they were requested to leave in an adjoining room. The medium's supposed hearing aid was nothing but a miniaturized receiver.

On the other hand, methods of detection have become as easy to obtain (and to conceal) as methods of deception. One unlooked-for-effect of the development of infrared photography for night-time military use was that physical mediumship, particularly full-form materialization, suffered a definite and probably permanent decline. Apparently there were too many cases in which the infrared camera recorded the all too solid form of the medium moving about the room instead of the hoped-for spirit. Although the modern period has produced its share of internationally famous mediums, very few of those specializing in physical manifestations have invited the investigation of scientific committees.

Margery (Mrs. Mina Crandon) was perhaps the last really important medium whose principal claims were based on the production of raps, lights, touches, and the more complex phenomena such as thumbprints and ectoplasm. However, in later years, and particularly after the exposure of the famous "thumbprint of 'Walter'" in 1932, the Crandons kept very close control over those who attended their sittings and never again attempted a public demonstration of any kind. Margery still had many supporters among spiritualists and investigators alike, even including for a time the leading members of the A.S.P.R., following the resignation of Dr. Walter Franklin Prince.

The Crandons' private circle ceased to be active in 1938 with the death of Dr. Crandon, although the medium herself lived on until 1941. Skeptics have suggested that it may have been more than grief for her husband that caused the medium to abandon her séances, for the single most suspicious circumstance of Margery's mediumship was undoubtedly the fact that her husband was not only present at every session but actually served as one of the two controllers.

Another important factor in the decline of physical phenomena (at least among the more serious students of mediumship) was the unfavorable final conclusions about them that had been reached by some of the most influential and dedicated psychical researchers. Thus after a lifetime of investigation, Frank Podmore found himself unable to point to a single authentic physical phenomenon, and this conclusion has been largely echoed by later specialists such as Dr. E. J. Dingwall.

Nowadays physical phenomena appear most often in settings that are not designed to inspire confidence in their genuineness. The spiritualist Camp Chesterfield in Chesterfield, Indiana, is an institution that has been in operation each summer for over seventy years. The camp operators claim to play host to fifty thousand "pilgrims" each season, making available to them the services of more than twenty "tested and approved" mediums— specialists in every phase of mediumship, from spirit photography through apports and materialization.

In 1965 a visit was made to Camp Chesterfield by the Canadian spiritualist, writer, and broadcaster Allen Spraggett, a man who is far from being a skeptic about survival and spirit return. Spraggett was impressed with nothing about the camp except the simplemindedness of its mediumistic trickery and the slanderous and sometimes racist nature of some of the "spirit revelations" produced there. He found himself in agreement with another disillusioned former patron of the camp, the late Tom O'Neill, an editor and publisher of a psychic newspaper who resigned his credentials as a minister of the Spiritualist Church because of his experiences at Camp Chesterfield. Mr. O'Neill's summary of the operation was, "It's simply a gigantic shill game—fraud through and through."

There is one type of physical (or at least not purely mental) mediumship whose popularity has increased rather than declined in this century. Spiritual healing, though always a part of the mediumistic scene, has become a major activity, particularly in Britain. Probably the most famous spiritual healer in the world at the present time is a white-haired ex-printer in his seventies named Harry Edwards. For more than thirty years Mr. Edwards has been using his "spirit gift" on patients with every sort of complaint from toothache to tumors, and thousands have testified to his success. At his healing sanctuary in the town of Burrows Lea, Edwards and

four assistants conduct three public healing sessions each
week and also see numerous private patients. So great is
the demand for the healer's time (partly because his fame
has been spread through television appearances), that the
organization reputedly employs forty-four full-time typ-
ists to deal with the more than forty thousand pieces
of mail received each month. According to Edwards'
supporters, the entire operation is financed by voluntary
donations and no fee is ever charged.

The spiritual healing of Harry Edwards and others
is different in at least one respect from the "faith healing"
that has been practiced by many great religious figures
of all denominations. The spiritual healer is a medium
whose "spirit controls" identify themselves as physicians,
sometimes famous physicians of the past, who wish to
use the superior knowledge of the spirit world for the
benefit of mankind. Thus two of the entities claiming
to work through Harry Edwards are Louis Pasteur
(1822–95), the discoverer of the bacterial theory of
disease, and Joseph Lister (1827–1912), founder of
antiseptic surgery. It is the belief of Edwards and his
colleagues that they are merely instruments in the diagnosis and treatment of disease, the skill and knowledge
being those of their "controls." This attitude was once
nicely expressed in a short conversation between a patient and another spiritual healer, Ted Fricker.

> Patient: Are you a faith healer?
> Fricker: Not exactly.
> Patient: Do I need to have faith in you?

Fricker: I don't care whether you have faith or not. I
            have all the faith that is necessary.
(Quoted by Maurice Barbanell, in *Spiritualism Today*,
p. 76)

Needless to say, the patient in question, a man allegedly
almost immobilized by a spinal injury, later added his
name to the list of those who testify to the marvels
of spiritual healing.

It is not surprising that this aspect of spiritualism has
been the one that arouses the greatest opposition among
skeptics, especially doctors and scientists. Though believers have argued that no one is better qualified than
the patient to know whether he has been helped and
that what is important in both spiritual healing and
faith healing is that the patient feels better, not the
reason for his improvement, the medical profession has
been steadfast in its opposition to spiritual healing.

Doctors insist that consulting a spiritual healer may
harm the patient by keeping him from seeking orthodox
medical help until it is too late and that even in "hope-
less" cases it is often crueler for the patient and his
family to live on false hope. They point out further
that it is well known that in a certain small percentage
of "incurable" cases of such diseases as leukemia and
cancer the patients experience "spontaneous remission,"
which is to say that they get well for no known reason.
There has been considerable hostility between doctors
and advocates of spiritual healing because doctors often
claim that patients who are "cured" by spiritual healers
fall into four categories: those who would have gotten
well anyway; those whose illnesses were psychoso-

matic in origin (like some of the early mesmeric patients) and were therefore healed by suggestion on the part of the healer; those who convinced themselves they felt better while possibly dangerous conditions went untreated; and finally, fakers who were seeking publicity, with or without the co-operation of the healer.

Obviously, the root of the argument is whether patients show genuine *physical* as well as mental improvement after spiritual healing. On this question it seems unlikely that the scientific and the spiritualist worlds are going to agree in the near future.

In Britain spiritual healing has advanced to the point where the National Federation of Spiritualist Healers, of which Harry Edwards is president, has been permitted by a large percentage of hospital committees to send its members to see patients whenever the physician in charge does not object. The decision was a victory for spiritualists since it was obtained over the vigorous opposition of the British Medical Association. In 1969 the National Federation claimed to have fifty-seven hundred spiritual healers on its membership rolls.

Since the British have always been known as animal lovers, it is not surprising that some spiritual healers in that country have turned their attention to nonhuman patients. One of the best-known animal healers was the late George Tomkins, who numbered among his patients not only dogs and cats, but a racehorse, a cow, and a marmoset. Another famous animal healer, still practicing, is Hazel Ward. Like most spiritual healers, whether their patients are animal or human, Ward offers healing at a distance, or "absent healing," as well as healing by contact. One of her most famous cases concerned the healing of a sixteen-year-old dog named Nickie, who lived in Queensland, Australia, thirteen thousand miles from the medium.

In spite of the popularity of spiritual healing, however, the main trend of spiritualism in recent years has undoubtedly been toward the more purely mental types of mediumship. Although they were not directly concerned with the question of spirit survival, the experiments of Dr. J. B. Rhine and others at Duke University during the thirties and forties opened a controversy among psychologists that has had great influence on spiritualist belief and is certainly far from finished. Briefly, Dr. Rhine and his assistants asserted that they had established scientific proof of the existence of ESP, the supposed mental faculty through which human beings could perceive objects or events distant in time or space without the use of the "normal" senses. Dr. Rhine's results were attacked, and continue to be attacked, from three principal points of view. Some opponents argue that his methods of testing—in which volunteers generally attempted to guess which of five designs appeared on the concealed faces of so-called ESP cards or Zener cards taken in series of hundreds or even thousands of tries—were not sufficiently safeguarded against cheating by the participants. Another group maintains that the flaw in Rhine's procedure is the manner in which he uses the complex mathematical theory of probability to interpret his results. In other words, one side says Rhine's results would be meaningful if they were accurate, while the other admits the results may be accurate but contends they are not really meaningful. The third, and perhaps most valid objection to

Rhine's experiments is that other researchers in other places have not been able to get the same results.

The importance of repeatability in science is very great since it is the reason why, for example, oil can be refined by the same method in New Jersey or India, and the same recipe will produce the same cake in Alaska or Zambia. If one cake turns out chocolate and the other orange, or worse still, if one turns out to be a cake and the other a kettle of stew, something is very wrong indeed. Naturally, Dr. Rhine and his colleagues have offered answers to these objections, and it is fortunate that we do not have to take sides in the controversy. All we must understand is that the Duke experiments gave a considerable lift to the spiritualists. For the first time it appeared that the mediums' claims to possess supernormal knowledge might be taken seriously by the world of science.

A great many spiritualists (and others) adopted the point of view that the fact of ESP has now been proved beyond any doubt. The only thing that was in question, according to this group, was whether the phenomena of the séance room were to be explained by the spirit theory or the ESP theory, a dispute that had been building up since the time of the S.P.R. cross-correspondences.

On the other side of the coin, vigorous and outspoken opponents of spiritualism have continued to make themselves felt in recent years. One of the most persistent was Joseph F. Rinn, whose career as an active debunker of mediums stretched from the later days of the Fox sisters (the 1880s) all the way to the early 1950s. Rinn was a man of independent financial means and a great friend of the magician Harry Houdini. Together they unmasked dozens of fraudulent mediums, mind-readers, and other "miracle mongers," as Houdini called them, people who claimed to be able to walk through walls, breathe under water, handle fire, and so on. As a magician Houdini of course had no objection to such performances (many of which he duplicated himself) as long as they were admitted to be just that—performances. However, he was firmly opposed to all claims of supernatural intervention and devoted a considerable amount of time to investigation and exposure, as we have seen in the case of Margery.

Rinn's contribution to their joint enterprises, in addition to his considerable knowledge of stage magic and fraud, was to offer a series of very substantial prizes to anyone who could give a genuine demonstration of mind-reading or any other psychical phenomenon. After the withdrawal of the *Scientific American* prize for which Margery and others had unsuccessfully competed, Mr. Rinn added ten thousand dollars of his own money to a sum of eleven thousand dollars offered by the magazine *Science and Invention* for the same purpose. The offer stood for some years, but although several attempts were made, no one ever carried off the prize.

This public failure undoubtedly contributed to a moderate decline in the popularity of American spiritualism after 1930. The Duke experiments, although they were encouraging to spiritualists, did more to promote other areas of psychical research and did not offset a general feeling that the spirits were not proving to be as exciting as had once been hoped. Several critics of the movement had pointed out that humanity had never received a single piece of useful information from the "spirit world" in spite of all the mediums who claimed to have communed with the great scientists and thinkers of the past, and the publicity attending various exposures of fraud had not helped the situation.

Although accurate figures are hard to come by, it seems that the number of active spiritualists in the United States and Europe reached its peak shortly after the First World War, declined slightly for the next two decades, and then leveled off at about one-half to two-thirds its highest point. That is not to say, however, that the movement ceased to attract public attention. There was, for example, the affair of Arthur Ford and the spirit of Harry Houdini.

After the unexpected death of the great magician (stricken down by appendicitis in 1926) it became known that Houdini and his wife had made a private pact about spirit communication. Although he did not believe in mediums, Houdini had vowed that if he found it to be at all possible to return from the spirit world he would make every effort to get in touch with his wife Beatrice. Mrs. Houdini had for years been her husband's stage partner in his famous mind-reading act, using a code that they had never revealed. To prevent any sort of fraud in the matter, the Houdinis agreed that the message Harry would try to send would be the code for the word Believe, as it would have appeared in their old act. For some years after Houdini's death, Mrs. Houdini continued to hope for a message from him, but although she attended several séances she never heard the vital code words. Then, in January 1929, the New

York *Times* carried the story that Beatrice Houdini had received her long-awaited message at a private sitting with a medium named Arthur Ford.

In the course of his mediumistic career, which began just after the First World War and continued until his retirement in the late 1960s, the Reverend Arthur Ford was to become one of America's best-known mental mediums. At his sitting with Beatrice Houdini, he produced his most sensational achievement up to that time. Unfortunately, the question of the source of the message soon became a matter for furious debate. Before the day when she received the message Mrs. Houdini had been ill for some time as the result of a fall, sometimes delirious and constantly in the care of a nurse. Although she at first announced to the newspapers that the message was undoubtedly genuine and that she was now convinced of her husband's survival, she later withdrew the statement and declared she did not believe that the message (which was unquestionably the one agreed upon) came from her husband at all. What brought about such a change of mind? The story now becomes a matter of two conflicting sets of testimony, neither of which seems to be exactly unbiased.

According to Houdini's old friend Joseph Rinn in his book *Sixty Years of Psychical Research*, the whole affair was made possible by the fact that Mrs. Houdini had accidentally revealed the code and the message expected during one of her bouts of delirium. Rinn claims that the message became known in New York psychic circles a whole day before the séance. In support of this story, a tabloid newspaper later published an account of how one of its reporters had trapped Ford into admitting (before hidden witnesses) that he had learned the message without the aid of the spirits and used it to carry out a fraud on Mrs. Houdini. (The widow had offered ten thousand dollars to anyone who gave her the correct message; however, Arthur Ford neither claimed nor received the money.) Rinn contends that someone, either an attendant at the hospital where Houdini died or more probably the nurse who was caring for Mrs. Houdini after her fall, overheard a mention of the code and the message and gave the information to Ford or an agent of Ford, probably for money. Before accepting this view of the matter we must note that his account clearly reveals both his own prejudice against spiritualism and the dubious nature of the evidence.

Arthur Ford's version of events is of course quite different. In his autobiography he asserts that the "confession" was staged by the newspaper involved, using an impersonator to discredit him. He also maintains the genuineness of the message and of Mrs. Houdini's first reaction to it, hinting that she was later persuaded to change her mind by the enemies of spiritualism. The medium then goes on to suggest that the tremendous (and, in spiritualist circles, largely favorable) publicity he received from the event had been engineered by "Houdini" as an apology for his former disbelief. The evidence boiled down to Ford's word against the newspaper's (and Rinn's), thus leaving members of the public free to believe whatever they liked.

No such sensationalism attended the career of Eileen Garrett, an Irishwoman who, until her death in 1970, was one of this century's greatest mental mediums. Perhaps her only rival in the field was Mrs. Piper, and, like her, Mrs. Garrett spent the larger part of her time under strict scientific supervision and never engaged in public mediumship of any sort. For more than fifty years Mrs. Garrett participated in tests and experiments of all kinds, as much for the purpose of answering her own questions about her "voices" as for the benefit of science. She spent hours sitting inside a curious metal cage, which had been developed by one group of researchers in order to see whether the metal's effect of blocking out electromagnetic radiation would make any great change in the medium's powers of clairvoyance.

She spent hundreds of other hours on the symbol-calling experiments of Dr. Rhine, in which she achieved an average of 13.4 correct guesses out of twenty-five when chance alone would only have given five. The fact that these results were not repeated in later sessions under the direction of Mr. S. G. Soal in London did not dismay her, any more than her previous success had prompted her to make inflated claims for her powers. As she once remarked, "There may be nothing in it. Nothing at all. Who knows?" Yet the voices continued to speak and the documents relating to her mediumship continued to pile up.

In 1930 Eileen Garrett was the central figure in one of the simplest, most baffling of all cases of alleged survival. While giving a sitting for the investigator Harry Price in London on October 7, Mrs. Garrett's usual control unexpectedly announced the presence of someone named Irwin or Irving. The original purpose of the sitting had been to attempt to contact the spirit of Conan Doyle, but nevertheless "Irwin" insisted on being heard. On the previous day news had reached London of the crash in Beauvais, France of the British experimental dirigible airship *R 101*. Now "Irwin" proceeded to give the sitters in a London séance room a rapid and dramatic account of the crash.

What was astonishing about the communication was the very specific and highly technical nature of the tale. "Irwin," who identified himself as the dirigible's captain, killed in the crash, described the conditions of the flight using the following statements: "bulk of the dirigible was too much for her engine capacity"; "engines too heavy"; "useful lift too small"; "gross lift computed badly"; "flying too low altitude"; "load too great for long flight"; "cruising speed bad and ship badly swinging"; "severe tension on fabric, which is chafing"; "starboard strakes started"; "never reached cruising altitude"; "impossible to rise"; "cannot trim"; "this exorbitant scheme of carbon and hydrogen is entirely wrong."

Every one of those statements was later confirmed as correct by the official inquiry into the disaster, and there was something else. Although it was barely conceivable that the medium, with only twenty-four hours' warning and no previous knowledge of airships, could have boned up on the technical literature of aeronautics sufficiently well to make the report sound authentic, it was judged close to impossible that the information she uncovered should have contained a closely guarded official secret as well.

Yet the "scheme of carbon and hydrogen" was exactly that—an experimental proposal for a new fuel source whose disclosure in a séance created official confusion and even some wild accusations of "treason by telepathy." No one has ever come forward to explain how or why such information could have come into Mrs. Garrett's hands by normal means, and the whole story is certainly a remarkable instance of *something*, whether one supposes it to be the spirit return of Captain Irwin, ESP from the disaster's survivors, highly efficient but purposeless espionage, or an extraordinary coincidence.

Mrs. Garrett's contribution to psychical research was not limited to her own mediumship. She was also the founder and president of the Parapsychology Foundation in New York City, a small but influential organization that encourages serious professional research and conducts its own publishing program. Because she competed for no prizes, and made no startling claims, and perhaps because she herself was not a spiritualist, Eileen Garrett was not as well known to spiritualists as some other contemporary mediums. Yet she was almost alone among mediums in being willing to consider with detachment the question of whether the voices that spoke during her trances were those of genuine surviving spirits, secondary aspects of her own personality with exceptional psychic powers, or even the unconscious means used to conduct extensive frauds. Perhaps the work of the Parapsychology Foundation will eventually help to establish the truth.

Among the organizations largely concerned with research relating to spiritualism at the present time, the two most important and enduring are the Society for Psychical Research in Britain, and its counterpart, the American S.P.R.

Still a part of the scene also are the psychic press and the spiritualist camps such as Camp Chesterfield and Lily Dale, which now affords a permanent site for the

Fox house, moved there from Hydesville. The Spiritualist churches are now united under the banner of the International General Assembly of Spiritualists (founded in Buffalo, New York in 1936), whose membership in the United States was recorded as 164,072 in 1956.

In addition to these (relatively) more conventional groups, there are also a few like the remarkable Aetherius Society of Great Britain. Organized in 1954 by the medium George King, the society resembles some others in that its purpose is to spread the teachings of a particular group of spirit controls. These entities show their modernism, as well as their originality, by allegedly residing in flying saucers, however. According to the medium, his controls transmit to him communications from other planets. They appear also to have access to the most exalted individuals in the history of Earth, if we believe the report of the medium's mother that she was once transported bodily into another sphere, where she had tea with Jesus Christ.

Most spiritualists of course reject such absurdities as firmly as would most skeptics. The obvious eccentric has always had a place in spiritualism and will probably continue to do so, since spiritualists are in general a tolerant lot. Their early difficulties with the laws concerning spirit communication as a form of religion encouraged them not to be bigoted about the views of their fellow spiritualists. Fortunately, however, the laws applying to mediums have been considerably reformed in most English-speaking countries, although spiritualists still feel there is room for improvement. The old witch-craft-inspired English statutes against which Sir Arthur Conan Doyle fought so determinedly were finally replaced in 1951 by the far more lenient Fraudulent Mediums Act, and the situation is even more liberal in the United States (with some variations from state to state) and New Zealand.

Revision of the laws has not led to the disappearance of startling exposures of fraud. The year 1958 saw the unmasking of William Roy, the medium who employed the ingenious trick with the radio mentioned at the beginning of this chapter. In the confession he published in the English *Sunday Pictorial*, Roy revealed that in addition to about fifty thousand pounds in fees and donations he also received expensive presents and favors from rich supporters. When not using modern communications techniques Roy relied on such standbys as collapsible rods and "ectoplasm" made of cheesecloth to achieve the physical effects for which he was famous.

His mental feats were helped along by an extensive card-index containing information on sitters and likely sitters (prominent persons known to be interested in spiritualism). The information on the cards was carefully compiled from revelations made (and perhaps later forgotten) by the sitters themselves at previous séances, from voters' lists, from newspaper stories, and from government records of births, deaths, and marriages. Another source was fellow mediums, showing that the organization that furthered Charles Pidgeon's career lives on in spirit. "We phony mediums traded information—like swapping stamps," declared Roy. It is hardly any wonder that many of the estimated one hundred thousand persons who attended Roy's séances over the years went away mightily impressed.

His most striking trick, aside from his mental mediumship, was judged to be the production of the direct voice by means of microphone relays. This device gave the impression of two spirit voices talking together, an effect that could not possibly have been achieved by ventriloquism, the usual method of faking direct voice.

Today there are undoubtedly still fraudulent mediums to be found as well as those of a more serious cast, like Eileen Garrett. More and more there seems to be a split between the religious, faith-oriented branch of spiritualism and the scientific, proof-oriented branch. Though the two still overlap in many areas, it is definitely the scientific branch in which the most lively debate occurs, particularly with regard to the argument over the spirit theory versus the ESP theory.

A very recent development in that debate is the Combination Lock Test for survival conceived by Dr. Ian Stevenson and announced in the A.S.P.R. *Journal* for July 1968. The difficulty of securing proof of survival that is not also attributable to ESP on the part of the medium is, as we have already seen, very great. Dr. Stevenson, a prominent psychical researcher and member of the department of psychiatry of the University of Virginia School of Medicine, suggests the problem might be approached by equipping a number of individuals with ordinary combination padlocks. Each person participating in the test is directed to set his lock to a combination known only to himself, leaving no written record of his choice. The combination may be either a series of six numerals (since most combination locks use numerical combinations) or a six-letter word (which, experts suggest, might be easier to remember and transmit after death). If letters are used, they are made to correspond with the numerals on the lock by assigning values in this manner:

A B C D E F G H I J K L M N
1 2 3 4 5 6 7 8 9 0 1 2 3 4
O P Q R S T U V W X Y Z
5 6 7 8 9 0 1 2 3 4 5 6

Thus if you want the key to your combination to be WE LIVE you will set your lock to 3-5-2-9-2-5. At present Dr. Stevenson already has several such locks in his keeping and has undertaken to bring each lock to the attention of a qualified medium after receiving word of the death of its owner. The hope is that the lock's combination will appear as part of a trance communication, whose accuracy can of course be tested by trying to open the lock.

Dr. Stevenson's scheme is certainly one of the most imaginative methods for testing survival yet proposed. However, the opposing camp is still not prepared to concede that the test is conclusive, even if mediums should produce the correct combinations in all cases. The contention is that the combinations could be gotten by clairvoyant perception of the lock's owner at the moment when he set the combination. For those who regard ESP and survival as equally unproved, however, it would certainly be a great event if even one medium were to succeed in opening one lock in this way. Projects using the Combination Lock Test are now also under way in England, but it will probably be a good many years before evidence becomes conclusive one way or the other.

During recent decades interest in spiritualism, as in all phases of the occult, has undergone something of a revival in Western countries. How long this will last no one can say, but it is clear that those who prophesied in the 1940s that the movement would fade away like a dematerializing spirit hand were being a little premature. Spiritualism has been many things—ridiculous, awe-inspiring, irritating, eccentric, devout, theatrical, trivial, and puzzling. Its basic idea appeals so deeply to man that it will probably remain a part of the scene as long as human beings experience the fear of death.

EPILOGUE

THE BISHOP'S TALE

They say that those who ignore history are doomed to repeat it. Since the history of spiritualism is nothing if not a long series of errors and deceptions (on the part of both skeptics and believers), let us see whether what we now know of it will help us to avoid the mistakes of the past in analyzing a modern case. Only by attempting to play detectives ourselves can we judge the real virtues or drawbacks of the case for survival.

No incident in modern spiritualism has been more widely publicized and debated than that of the late James A. Pike, Bishop of the Episcopal Church. In 1966 Bishop Pike, already a well-known and controversial figure because of his liberal religious views, became the center of a considerable sensation when the press learned that he believed he had received authentic spirit messages from his son Jim. The background of the story, as later related by Dr. Pike in his book *The Other Side*, may be summarized as follows.

For several months before Jim's death he and his father had been sharing an apartment in Cambridge, England. The young man had been going through a period of depression and restlessness in which he felt that life was meaningless and that he could not make contact with other people. He had taken a variety of drugs, including LSD, in the apparently vain hope that the experience would help him to sort things out, and his father had not tried to forbid him because he believed that Jim, at the age of twenty, had a right to solve his own problems and needed support and understanding rather than criticism.

Tragically, however, the improvement in Jim's outlook that seemed to have begun in Cambridge did not last, and on February 4, 1966, Jim Pike committed suicide in a New York hotel room, during what was to have been a short trip back to the United States.

Because of this sad event it was nearly two weeks until Bishop Pike returned to the apartment the two had shared in Cambridge. Shortly afterward he and the two colleagues who were now staying there with him began to notice a series of strange happenings. According to his account, Dr. Pike had never up to this time entertained the idea of spirit return and was strongly disinclined to accept supernatural stories at face value, even those that play a role in the Christian gospels. Nevertheless, he gradually found himself becoming convinced that something out of the ordinary was occurring.

On various occasions books, postcards, and opened safety pins were repeatedly discovered lying in such a position as to form an angle of about 140 degrees, while a clock that had been stopped for months at 12:15 was found reset to 8:19. In that position the clock's hands were at the same angle as that of the books and cards and might easily, the observers noted, have represented the English equivalent of the time of Jim's death in New York, although the exact hour was unknown.

Later, freshly delivered milk mysteriously went sour, partially legible yellow crayon marks were found on a glass door, a picture of Jim's sister was moved from its usual place, a missing book turned up in plain sight, postcards associated with Jim were found attached inside books with some sort of adhesive, and, strangest of all, on three mornings Dr. Pike's assistant, Mrs. Maren Bergrud, awoke to find that part of the hair of her bangs had apparently been singed off. (It was a hair style that Jim had thought unbecoming to her.)

Each case was attested to by all three witnesses and was agreed not to have some simple explanation such as carelessness on the part of the woman who came to clean. Sometimes the circumstances were such that it would have seemed difficult (but not, perhaps, impossible) for any one of the three persons involved to have arranged the "manifestations" deliberately.

It was at this point that Dr. Pike asked the advice of a friend, another clergyman, who suggested he consult a medium. The reasoning behind this recommendation was that in "poltergeist cases" such as that described it is thought that the spirit of a person recently dead is attempting to draw attention to itself in hopes of communicating with the living. It is, to cite a commonly made comparison, like the ringing of a telephone bell, which tells us that someone on the line has something to say to us via the telephone mechanism. In this instance the "telephone mechanism" through which Dr. Pike hoped to receive a message, or at least an explanation of the disturbances in his apartment, was Mrs. Ena Twigg, one of Britain's best-known living mediums.

The consultation was a success in the sense that Mrs. Twigg was able to "get through" to "Jim." Speaking sometimes under the direct control of "Jim," sometimes in the voice of her own control, Mrs. Twigg at this first séance (March 2, 1966) conveyed to Jim's father a considerable amount of specific information. In addition to voicing the sort of reassurance and continuing affection common in such messages, "Jim" referred to the August birthday of Dr. Pike's assistant, Maren Bergrud; mentioned by name (and somewhat critically) a New York couple who were friends of the Pike family; approved of the fact that the flowers at his funeral had been limited to two bouquets in the church sanctuary; and addressed his father as "Dad" (rather than as "Father" or "Pop," for example).

All of the information given was correct and in character, with the exception that neither of the young man's grandmothers was "on the other side" although "Jim" had mentioned meeting his grandmother. Perhaps more significant to Dr. Pike was his own intuitive feeling that it was indeed his son who was speaking. Such impressions are perilously easy for those who have been recently bereaved, but it must be admitted that "Jim's" words sound psychologically appropriate in the light of his state of mind before death, as recorded by his father. Thus in describing his suicide "Jim" said, "It wasn't intentional—everything snapped—too many pills." He also gave the impression that he continued to be abreast of his father's affairs and wished to support him in his fight for freedom of belief within the Episcopal Church.

Knowing that his time in England was coming to an end, Dr. Pike later attended a second session with Mrs. Twigg for the primary purpose of asking the name of someone in the United States through whom he could continue to communicate with "Jim" if it seemed desirable. The last was an important condition, as Pike had no particular feeling that "Jim" had anything more to say to him and considered it possible that the whole incident (whatever its meaning) was closed. However, at the second session "Jim" advised his father to consult "Spiritual Frontiers—a Father Rauscher—priest of the Church—in New Jersey" in case further communication was desired. Unfortunately, the detailed notes of this session were subsequently lost, but one of "Jim's" other remarks that stuck in the bishop's memory was particularly significant. It was the then seemingly pointless promise, "I'll be with you come August."

This séance marked the end of the first phase of Bishop Pike's experiences with mediums. There followed an interlude marked only by one seemingly chance event. One day after preaching a Holy Week sermon at St. Thomas Episcopal Church in New York City, Dr. Pike was introduced to a fellow minister who had been in the congregation. The man was the Reverend Arthur Ford, the same medium who had delivered the code message to Mrs. Houdini thirty-seven years earlier.

Mr. Ford mentioned to Dr. Pike that he had clairvoyantly seen the figures of a young man named Jim and an old man named Elias (the name of Pike's wife's deceased father) standing behind him as he preached his sermon. Perhaps the bishop would be interested to know that they were encouraging him. Pike thanked his colleague for the information and inquired (purely out of politeness, he later admitted) with which church or organization Ford was connected. "The Spiritual Frontiers Fellowship" was the answer. So much for coincidence.

The Spiritual Frontiers Fellowship did not crop up in Dr. Pike's life again until almost four months later in Santa Barbara, California, near the end of July. Then the name was mentioned to Pike in a casual conversation with a friend and was coupled with that of the Reverend George Daisley, member of the Fellowship who, like Ford, happened to be a medium. At almost the same time Dr. Pike received a telephone call from one of the friends who had been with him in Cambridge the previous winter. The caller related that there had been another series of happenings, particularly the finding of opened safety pins arranged in the now familiar 8:19 position.

Dr. Pike took this to mean that his son was once more trying to get in touch with him. He decided to telephone the Mr. Daisley who had been mentioned as a member of the Spiritual Frontiers Fellowship and who was also located in California. Surprisingly, Mr. Daisley appeared to have been expecting the bishop's call, and explained that he had "heard from 'Jim'" two weeks before. It seemed to Pike that this must certainly be what had been meant by the earlier message, "I'll be with you come August."

Accordingly, an appointment was made for a sitting with Mr. Daisley a few days later. "Jim" succeeded in coming through in much the same way he had with Mrs. Twigg. He mentioned the incident in Cambridge when the supposedly lost book had been found and also the fact that his father had that day made a wrong turn in driving to Mr. Daisley's house. It happened that Mrs. Bergrud was also present, and she was very much surprised when "Jim" remarked that her present hair style was an improvement—she had never grown back the bangs that had apparently been singed from her head during the manifestations in Cambridge.

Correct reference was also made to the fact that Mrs. Bergrud had been "discussing going to the dentist with a lady in the hall" (her landlady) the day before. Another interesting remark, this one addressed to Dr. Pike, was that his "Uncle Will" was on "the other side" or about to arrive there. Pike considered this to be an error until the following October, when he learned of the death of an uncle by that name with whom he had had little contact for some years. Naturally, in this sitting as in almost all such sittings, there was also a considerable amount of conversation that was not specific enough to be verifiable or of more than general interest. The foregoing can only be a sampling of the sort of remarks that might be considered "evidential," that is, evidence of survival.

The third phase of Dr. Pike's experiences with "Jim," the phase that was to bring his activities to public notice, began on September 3, 1967 when the bishop appeared on Canadian television with the medium Arthur Ford and Allen Spraggett, the journalist whose exposure of Camp Chesterfield has already been mentioned. It was only in connection with the program that Dr. Pike learned of Ford's mediumship, although of course he remembered their meeting in New York in the spring of 1966. The television program, which had been conceived by Mr. Spraggett, was to consist of two parts, a general discussion of psychic phenomena and an attempt at a sitting in which Mr. Ford was to try to make contact with Jim Pike. There was some uncertainty as to whether the medium would be able to become entranced in the brightly lit and unfamiliar television studio, but as things turned out there was no difficulty at all. Mr. Ford quickly began to speak in the voice of "Fletcher" (his usual spirit control), and the séance was under way.

"Fletcher" immediately announced the presence of two spirits who wished to get in touch with the bishop, a young man and an elderly one. After some probing it was established that they gave their names as "Jim" and his grandfather "Elias," the same pair that had been perceived by Ford in New York. An interesting detail was that "Fletcher" appeared to be uncertain of the name Elias, first producing Elisha, whereas Arthur Ford already knew from his encounter with Pike in New York that Elias was the correct name of Jim's grandfather. This might indicate that "Fletcher" was not simply using facts known to Ford. On the other hand, the slip might have been made for the purpose of producing just that impression.

In the conversation that followed it was indicated that Jim Pike had had a Slavic background and that he had had some association with a man named Martin Halverson who was now "on the other side" also. The first item was correct, as Dr. Pike's wife's family had come from Russia. As for the second, although Dr. Pike himself dimly remembered a person of that name, he had no notion that Halverson had been acquainted with his son, a fact that was only verified later.

During the remainder of the séance a number of other spirit entities seemed to "come through" via "Fletcher." Most of them claimed to be people who had known Dr. Pike at one time or another during his career in the church—former teachers, colleagues, and assistants. In most cases correct names were given and also some description of the time, place, and nature of the person's former association with Pike. This was not the first time other personalities had made themselves known in Dr. Pike's séances. Earlier, entities claiming to be the great theologian Paul Tillich and the famous psychic Edgar Cayce had also taken part, although little of what they said could be considered evidential.

The session had been a long one, but now it became clear that the medium was coming out of his trance. The program was over and soon the news services of the world were buzzing with the story that America's most controversial bishop had appeared on television in support of the belief in spirit return.

The list of Dr. Pike's major experiences with the spirit world contains one more item. A few months later he participated in a second session with Mr. Ford, this time accompanied by his assistant, Diane Kennedy (soon to become the second Mrs. Pike). The occasion produced one of the most important and baffling pieces of information in the whole affair. When questioned about the details of his last day alive, "Jim" gave an account of meeting some acquaintances from the West Coast who, it was implied, had given him the drugs under whose influence he had killed himself. Unfortunately, though for obvious reasons, Dr. Pike's book does not give the names of these individuals or any verifiable details of their alleged meeting with Jim, an event that would certainly be of great interest if we had better evidence for it than Pike's word that the story checked out.

Another noteworthy remark at this séance concerned a California friend of Dr. Pike's. "Tell George Livermore —you'll be seeing him soon—that, as I get it, Caroline will be coming over soon." According to Pike, he had no particular reason to expect to see Mr. Livermore in the near future and was not even sure who Caroline might be, although he had a vague idea that that was the name of Mr. Livermore's mother, a woman prominent in church affairs in Pike's diocese. The bishop was therefore taken aback to encounter George Livermore at a Christmas Eve midnight service only a few days later and even more taken aback to learn of Mrs. Livermore's death the following February. Her name, he discovered, had been Caroline.

Dr. Pike's reaction to the experiences outlined above is best expressed in his own words.

> Both for personal and intellectual reasons I wanted to be sure I was not being taken in. I am not naturally of a suspicious nature in personal relations, in spite of my training as a lawyer and service in World War II in Naval Intelligence. Yet I gave special attention to analyzing possibilities of deception in this whole matter, not only because of the quite unusual character of all that had happened but also because, I must confess, I shared the quite widespread presumption against the honesty and/ or stability of mediums and the like. . . .

> An easy way of escaping the need to deal with data which do not fit one's system of thought about the

universe is to brand as fraudulent those who uncover the data. But the data still remain, and if we are sincere about our search for truth we will seek to adjust our hypotheses to accommodate them.

(*The Other Side*, pp. 338–39)

Following his own advice, Dr. Pike "adjusted his hypotheses" to the point of admitting the possibility of spirit communication. He did not, however, become a Spiritualist in the religious sense, as some have claimed. Nor did he take much further interest in the psychic world before his untimely death after becoming lost in the Israeli desert in September 1969. The bishop's statements make it clear that he had not been carried away by his experiences and that he had reached his conclusion about survival only after attempting to give all due weight to opposing theories. It is only fair that we should do likewise.

The "Bishop Pike affair" was undoubtedly the biggest news story dealing with psychic or spiritualist phenomena of the last ten years. It immediately raised a storm of public debate in which no possible (or impossible) view was left unvoiced. Basically, however, there are only four conceivable explanations of the story. One of these four theories, or some combination of them, must contain the truth of the matter.

First, of course, is the possibility that Bishop Pike was simply lying about his experiences. If the history of spiritualism teaches us anything, it is that no one is above suspicion. There are those who believe that the whole thing was the act of a publicity-seeker who craved attention and that the only point at issue is whether Pike was a criminal or merely insane. They point out that the witnesses to the Cambridge phenomena and most of the séance revelations were either Dr. Pike's employees and subordinates or the mediums themselves, who were naturally ready to go along with the conversion of an important public figure. Against this view one can only place one's own assessment of a man whose career attracted at least as much admiration as opposition and who must have been extraordinary indeed if he managed to involve so many in his deception without being exposed.

At the opposite extreme from the view that the whole thing was a lie is the acceptance of Pike's conclusions at their face value: that the spirit does survive after death and that therefore "Jim" was Jim. The case for this conclusion has already been presented briefly above and can of course be found complete in *The Other Side.*

In between lies the great gray area of delusion and deception. Our third possibility is that Dr. Pike may have been mistaken about the evidence for his son's survival. It can be argued that the young man's death was bound to bring to his father not only sorrow but some sense of guilt. He, a bishop, a man whose concern is the welfare of others, had not been able to save his own son from despair. And the more deeply he felt that he had failed, the more he might have wished to believe that his son was *not* "dead," that in one sense the terrible event had never happened. It will have to be a matter for our individual judgment to decide how much of Dr. Pike's conviction could have resulted from the familiar "will to believe." In particular, some of the happenings in the Cambridge apartment could have been ordinary oddities or coincidences that seemed to be especially significant once the idea of the poltergeist had been broached.

The other area in which self-delusion is to be watched for is as always in the sitter's personal conviction of identity—the feeling that "Jim" the voice in the séance room was the same as Jim the son of Bishop Pike. As we saw in the S.P.R. cross-correspondences, this is an exceedingly difficult question to resolve. To use the comparison with the telephone once again, the sitter is in the position of receiving a call from someone who identifies himself as a friend or relative. In ordinary life, in about 999 cases out of a thousand, it never occurs to us to question the identity of the person on the other end of the line. But once identity has been made questionable by the fact that the "caller" is known to be dead, no assumption is safe.

One cannot say, "Why, I'd know So-and-so's voice anywhere," because under séance conditions the actual voice one hears almost never claims to be that of the individual. The mechanism through which the person spoke while living (his tongue, larynx, lips, lungs, and so forth) is no longer in existence, so that we should hardly expect him to sound the same even if he is in direct control of the medium's voice mechanism. But the more usual situation is that the medium (who in this case serves merely as the telephone) is being controlled or "spoken into" by his or her usual spirit control, who merely passes on the words and ideas of the alleged communicator.

This is like having a conversation with a friend who can't come to the phone in which a stranger tells you things like, "Sally wants me to say she misses you." Either way, there is little chance that the sitter will really be able to recognize the communicator's voice. Proof of identity therefore has to rely on factual information. Furthermore, such information most often seems to be transmitted, if at all, by a device that is more like an old-fashioned crystal-set radio than a modern telephone. It is as if the conversation were constantly being interfered with by static, bad weather, and a failing power source, as well as mechanical flaws in the apparatus. Each of us ought to consider how certain we could be of the identity of even our closest friend under such conditions and how tempting it would be to give in to our own desire to believe that the caller was indeed the person he claimed to be.

It is only fair to say that in minimizing the importance of the "will to believe" Dr. Pike always maintained that he had no sharp sense of guilt about his son's death since he felt, both as a minister and as a person who had gone through psychoanalysis, that no individual's problems can be wholly blamed on another and that he personally had not failed to give his son support and understanding.

Finally, we must consider the possibility that Dr. Pike was deceived by others, rather than merely deluded. For example, could the events in Cambridge have been "arranged" by someone in the household? If so, that person *could* have been Mrs. Maren Bergrud, the assistant whose bangs were scorched and who was to commit suicide herself a little over two years later. Such things have been done by persons of unbalanced mind, although needless to say, there is no positive evidence that Mrs.

Bergrud or any other particular individual *was* behind the disturbances.

With regard to the séances themselves, it is hardly surprising that Dr. Pike found his way into the hands of a medium, since anyone who was at all familiar with psychical research would know that "poltergeisting" of the Cambridge sort is generally looked on as an attention-getting device on the part of a departed spirit. If we are to suggest that the séances were part of an organized deception, we shall certainly have to suspect some communication among the mediums involved. We must also ask how much, if any, of the material revealed *could* have been researched in advance (although neither here nor later is it our intention to claim that any of the mediums *did* conduct such research).

There is no doubt that some of the relevant information was quite simple to come by. The fact of Jim Pike's suicide had been reported in major newspapers only a month before the first séance, and it would not have required much imagination on the part of Mrs. Twigg to guess whom it was that the bishop expected to contact. Furthermore, the medium had ample warning of Dr. Pike's visit, since the first appointment was made for him under his own name two days beforehand. (This fact has been denied in some later reports in the psychic press, but Pike states it specifically on page 111 of *The Other Side*.) Even if Mrs. Twigg had made no special effort to investigate her famous sitter, it would have been a little odd if she had known nothing about his professional position, since she was an active member of Dr. Pike's church and would probably have heard his visit to England discussed in church circles, even if she had not attended any of the numerous services he had conducted at neighboring churches during his stay.

If "Jim's" remarks on that occasion were very appropriate ones for a young man who had just committed suicide to make to a father known to be a liberal and controversial clergyman, we may ask ourselves how easy it might have been for a clever psychologist to predict the attitudes shown. Is it, for example, very startling in these days that a son should urge his father not to give in to pressure, not to conform blindly to church doctrine but to keep fighting the church establishment? In short, it is hard to see in the sessions with Mrs. Twigg any revelations that *could not* have been the product of shrewd guessing and a little advance research in the newspapers and Dr. Pike's own books.

What is harder to explain, what in fact Dr. Pike found it impossible to explain on any other basis than spirit survival, is his continuing contact with members of the Spiritual Frontiers Fellowship after his return to the United States. Although the bishop did consider the possibility that there had been communication between Mrs. Twigg and the Dr. Rauscher whose name was mentioned at the second sitting, he rejected the idea of conspiracy.

First, he said, all the mediums involved struck him as thoroughly honest and sincere individuals (but this, one recalls, is from a man who labeled himself "not naturally of a suspicious nature"). Second, Dr. Pike suggested that if Dr. Rauscher's was the name given him it would have been logical that Rauscher be the one to carry through. The point is a valid one, but of course we have noticed that if Dr. Rauscher himself failed to get in touch with Dr. Pike, his organization did not. Arthur Ford, a member of the Fellowship, showed up "by chance" at a sermon of Pike's in New York. And if "Jim's" remark about renewing contact "come August" had been relayed to members of the Fellowship in general, it might have required no presence of mind at all for Mr. Daisley to say he had been expecting to hear from the bishop.

On the other hand, one need not imagine that a deliberate conspiracy was *necessarily* called for in order that spiritualist circles should have been talking about the visit of a nationally known bishop to a prominent British medium. Mrs. Twigg was, as we said, well aware of the identity of her sitter, and it would hardly be surprising if word of the séances had spread across the Atlantic. In that case, of course, and assuming Mrs. Twigg was not practicing fraud, one could only expect the most general account of the séances to circulate, because the genuinely entranced medium is quite unaware of what is said.

As with the English sittings, the material produced through Mr. Daisley contained a good deal that might be the result of shrewd guessing. For example, the fact that Dr. Pike and his party were noticeably late for the appointment might have been the basis for the fact that "Jim" knew they had taken a wrong turn en route. Dr. Pike himself points out that the medium's house was difficult to find, so that Mr. Daisley must have been used to having his visitors miss the turn-off. Less easy to dismiss as good guesses or the result of possible research are items such as "Jim's" remark about the improvement in Mrs. Bergrud's hair style, which represents the kind

of trivial knowledge of Pike's affairs that would be unlikely to come up in inquiries about his background.

The same mixture of kinds of information is to be
found in the séances with Arthur Ford. There, however,
we observe a little more emphasis on specific statements
and less on the sort of hopeful sentiments Dr. Pike
rightly termed "filler," that is, harmless but unverifiable
chitchat that seemed intended to fill up gaps in the conversation. At first sight, the reference to "Jim's" Slavic
background is impressive; even more impressive are the
list of associates of the bishop's who were mentioned in
the televised session, and the prediction of the death of
Caroline Livermore.

But as to the latter one may ask whether there is
really any great skill involved in predicting the death of
a woman in her eighties. And likewise, with regard to
the former, any professional researcher or journalist
would be quick to note that a considerable amount of
this material was available to anyone who cared to
look at the pages of *Who's Who in America* and the
equally useful but less widely known *Yearbook of the
Episcopal Church*. Thus the "Slavic background" item
could easily have been deduced from the *Who's Who*
entry, which gave Jim's mother's maiden name as
Yanovsky. Names, dates, and places of Pike's past associations could certainly have come from the *Yearbooks*
for the relevant years, also, although there again we find
some material that would be less easy to look up.

For example, one woman was referred to (correctly, as
Dr. Pike admitted) as "a thorn in your side." This item
would not have been likely to appear in a *Yearbook*.
Was it (and the other bits of information like it) the

result of a lucky conversation between Ford or an assistant and some person who had known Dr. Pike? And if so, how much of that kind of digging can we suppose a medium could do without having someone notice his interest and report back to the subject? It is always safe to assume that an experienced investigator can find out more than the general public believes possible; otherwise there would be no spies or police detectives. On the other hand, there is a limit to the most searching inquiries, and one must draw the line somewhere.

Apparently the same is hardly true of the use of the ESP hypothesis in such cases. Those who believe in the reality of ESP would find no difficulty in explaining this otherwise puzzling material. Once one admits ESP, it allows one to suppose that the medium may know virtually anything and everything. If it is possible to perceive thoughts and memories from the conscious mind of the sitter, there is nothing particular to prevent us from thinking that the conscious minds of others, whether present or absent, may also be "read." And if the conscious mind is thus open to the medium, why not the unconscious mind also, with its vast stores of information not ordinarily "remembered" by the individual? As we said, it is impossible to draw the line. A believer in unlimited ESP could therefore explain Dr. Pike's whole experience in terms of unconscious fraud on the part of the various mediums, who merely fished out a netful of relevant material from the great psychic ocean and handed it out in the form of messages from "Jim" because it had been suggested that that was what was wanted.

It is clear by now that no single explanation will do

for *all* the facts presented (unless one takes the extreme view that the entire story was the invention of a mental case or a publicity-seeker). We did not undertake this discussion in order to provide, as the headlines would put it, The Key to the Mystery, but rather to show the kinds of questions that may be asked by an inquiring person in his approach to the contemporary spiritualist scene. Fact, fraud, phantasm, or possibly a mixture of all three? By now the reader has probably made his own decision. But it is not surprising that on that subject, as on so many others, our constant companion Mr. Sludge will have the last word.

Fine, draw the line
Somewhere, but, sir, your somewhere is not mine!
Bless us, I'm turning poet! . . .

Enough of talk!
My fault is that I tell too plain a truth.
Why, which of those who say they disbelieve,
Your clever people, but has dreamed his dream,
Caught his coincidence, stumbled on his fact
He can't explain, (he'll tell you smilingly)
Which he's too much of a philosopher
To count as supernatural indeed,
So calls a puzzle and problem, proud of it
Bidding you still be on your guard, you know,
Because one fact don't make a system stand . . .
Whereas I take that fact, the grain of gold,
And fling away the dirty rest of life,
And add this grain to the grain each fool has found
O' the million other such philosophers,—
Till I see gold, all gold and only gold,
Truth questionless though unexplainable,
And the miraculous proved commonplace!

GLOSSARY OF TERMS

animal magnetism—Franz Anton Mesmer's name for the force by which he accomplished his mesmeric cures, based on the idea of a continuous magnetic fluid filling the spaces of the universe, the supposed medium of the doctor's influence on his patients. Later discredited.

apparition—general term for a supernormal appearance, whether of the dead or of the absent living.

apport—a materialized object, especially in the séance room or in connection with a haunting.

automatism—unconscious muscular movement such as that producing automatic writing or the messages of the ouija board or planchette (which see).

cabinet—a curtained recess or other small enclosure opening off the séance room often used by mediums for the purpose of "condensing the psychic force" when materialization is being attempted.

clairaudience—the faculty of "hearing" information about an object or event by supernormal means; a form of ESP.

clairvoyance—the faculty of "seeing" an object or event by supernormal means; a form of ESP.

control (*of the medium*)—any method of ensuring that the medium does not consciously or unconsciously produce "phenomena" by normal means; tying, holding, and instrumental checks.

control (*spirit*)—See: *spirit control*.

direct voice—voice of an alleged spirit control coming from outside the body of the medium.

direct writing—writing allegedly produced by the hand of the spirit or other entity, rather than by the hand of the medium as instrument. The best-known form is slate writing.

divination—any method of discovering the future or "the will of the gods" by reading signs such as tea leaves, the flight of birds, etc.; not to be confused with methods of communication with the spirits of the dead.

ectoplasm—a substance supposedly extruded by a medium and used to form materializations, usually said to be whitish and thready or vaporous.

ESP (extrasensory perception)—general term for the acquisition of knowledge without the use of the normal senses.

ghost—popular term for the appearance of a deceased person or his image to the living; an apparition of the dead; usually associated with a particular person or place haunted.

hallucination—a vivid and convincing visual perception that does not represent the true present, thus usually a false perception; however, a veridical hallucination may represent true events elsewhere in time or space.

hyperesthesia—unusual acuteness of the senses experienced by some entranced persons and occasionally by those not entranced.

hypnotism—term first used by James Braid in 1841, a variety of trance characterized by increased sensitivity to suggestion and now usually used in place of the older name "mesmerism" (which see).

levitation—lifting of the medium or occasionally a sitter during a séance, also applied to lifting or floating of mystics, saints, and ecstatics.

magnetization—the process by which Mesmer claimed to employ *animal magnetism* (which see).

materialization—the creation of matter "out of thin air," especially the production of full-form or partial "spirit figures" during a séance.

medium—one who claims power to communicate with the spirits of the dead.

mesmerism—the trance-producing procedures of Anton Mesmer, chiefly used in the eighteenth and nineteenth centuries. (See also: *hypnotism* and *magnetization*)

muscle reading—a device used by professional mind-reading performers (and perhaps mediums) by which the thoughts and reactions of the subject are "read" from his tiny, unconscious muscular movements.

object reading—See: *psychometry*.

oracle—a prophet or a site where prophecy is practiced, especially the oracles of ancient Greece, some of which were mediumistic.

ouija board—a device for obtaining messages by automatism, having a pointer that moves to spell out words under the hands of the operator or operators.

phantasm—generally, an *apparition* (which see) but sometimes restricted to an apparition of a living person.

planchette—a device for writing out messages by automatism, having two wheels or rollers and a writing instrument that moves under the hands of the operator or operators.

poltergeist—from the German, "a noisy or rattling spirit"; or a variety of psychic phenomenon characterized by the unexplained and usually destructive movement of physical objects.

possession—also called *demonic possession;* formerly used to denote various types of unusual behavior, including mediumism, seizures, and some kinds of insanity and thought to be the work of a demon inhabiting the subject's body.

precognition—supernormal foreknowledge of a future event; a form of ESP.

psychical research—the unbiased, scientific investigation of all allegedly supernormal phenomena, physical and mental.

psychometry—the "reading" of an object by a medium or psychic; a form of ESP.

reincarnation—the belief that the individual spirit may return to inhabit more than one body.

séance—a sitting with a medium.

secondary personality—a portion of the personality that becomes "split off" from normal consciousness, most usually found in schizophrenics but also in at least some cases of mediumism, when it is referred to as a *spirit control* (which see).

shamanism—the tribal magic of a variety of peoples of arctic and subarctic regions of Asia and North and South America, having many features in common with spiritualism.

somnambulism—a state of sleep or half-waking dominated by the unconscious mind; most often used of the spontaneous or mesmeric trance as opposed to the mediumistic trance.

spirit control—an apparent spirit entity that takes control of the body of a medium for the purpose of transmitting messages or producing phenomena by allegedly supernormal means; thought by many to be secondary personality of the medium.

spiritualism—the belief that the individual human soul survives after death and can communicate with the living.

Spiritualism—the religious sect that professes the above belief as part of its creed.

subliminal memory—the portion of the memory lodged in the unconscious mind and not usually "remembered" except in trance, hypnosis, or other states of automatism.

subvocal whispering—a particular form of the activity assessed in *muscle reading* (which see) in which the subject unconsciously makes soundless motions of the lips and larynx, as if to "give away" the answers to his own questions.

telepathy—perception of the mental state or mental activity of another by supernormal means; a form of ESP.

teleportation—(or *telekinesis*) the movement of objects without contact, such as séance-room furniture, by supernormal means; not usually applied to movement of persons. (See: *levitation*.)

trance—general term for abnormal mental states dominated by the unconscious mind including, loosely, hypnosis, catalepsy, ecstasy, somnambulism, some forms of hysteria, and especially the mediumistic trance.

ventriloquism—the art of speaking with little or no lip movement and of throwing the voice so that the sound does not appear to come from the actual speaker; often used to counterfeit the *direct voice* by fraudulent mediums.

BIBLIOGRAPHY

Barbanell, Maurice, *Spiritualism Today*. London: Herbert Jenkins, 1969.

Besterman, Theodore, *Some Modern Mediums*. London: Methuen & Co., 1930.

Bird, J. Malcolm, *"Margery" the Medium*. London: John Hamilton, 1925.

Bridges, E. Lucas, *The Uttermost Part of the Earth*. New York: E. P. Dutton & Co., 1948.

Campbell, Joseph, *The Masks of God: Primitive Mythology*. New York: The Viking Press, 1969.

Carrington, Hereward, *Personal Experiences in Spiritualism*. London: T. Werner Laurie (undated).

———, *The Story of Psychic Science*. New York: Ives Washburn, 1931.

Christopher, Milbourne, *ESP, Seers, & Psychics*. New York: Thomas Y. Crowell Company, 1970.

———, *Houdini: The Untold Story*. New York: Thomas Y. Crowell Company, 1969.

Curtis, Natalie, *The Indians' Book*. New York: Harper & Brothers, 1907.

Davis, Andrew Jackson, *Death and the After-life*. New York, A. J. Davis & Co. and the Progressive Publishing House, 1876.

———, *The Principles of Nature, Her Divine Revelations, and a Voice to Mankind*. New York: A. J. Davis & Co., Progressive Publishing House, 1875.

Dingwall, Eric J., *How to Go to a Medium*. London: Kegan Paul, Trench Trubner & Co., 1927.

——, *Some Human Oddities.* New Hyde Park, New York: University Books, 1962.
——, *Very Peculiar People.* New Hyde Park, New York: University Books, 1962.
Doyle, Arthur Conan, *The History of Spiritualism.* New York: George H. Doran, 1926.
Edmunds, Simeon, *Spiritualism: A Critical Survey.* Letchworth, England: Aquarian Press, 1966.
Eisenbud, Jule, *Psi and Psychoanalysis.* New York: Grune & Stratton, 1970.
Estabrooks, G. H., *Spiritism.* New York: E. P. Dutton & Co., 1947.
Feilding, Everard, *Sittings with Eusapia Palladino.* New Hyde Park, New York: University Books, 1963.
Flacelière, Robert, *Greek Oracles.* New York: W. W. Norton & Company, 1965.
Flournoy, Théodor, *From India to the Planet Mars.* New York: Harper & Brothers, 1900.
Fodor, Nandor, *Encyclopedia of Psychic Science.* New Hyde Park, New York: University Books, 1966.
Ford, Arthur and Bro, Marguerite Harmon, *Nothing So Strange.* New York: Harper & Row, 1958.
Fornell, Earl Wesley, *The Unhappy Medium: Spiritualism and the Life of Margaret Fox.* Austin: University of Texas Press, 1964.
Garrett, Eileen J., *Many Voices: The Autobiography of a Medium.* New York: C. P. Putnam's Sons, 1968.
Hall, Trevor H., *New Light on Old Ghosts.* London: Gerald Duckworth & Co., 1965.
——, *The Spiritualists: The Story of Florence Cook and William Crookes.* London: Gerald Duckworth & Co., 1962.
——, *The Strange Case of Edmund Gurney.* London, Gerald Duckworth & Co., 1964.
Hill, J. Arthur, *Spiritualism: Its History, Phenomena, and Doctrine.* New York: George Doran & Co., 1919.

Home, Mme. D., *D. D. Home: His Life and Mission*. London: Kegan Paul, Trench Trubner & Co., 1921.

Houdini, Harry, *Miracle Mongers and Their Methods*. New York: E. P. Dutton & Co., 1920.

Jaspers, Karl, *General Psychopathology*. Chicago: University of Chicago Press, 1963.

Jastrow, Joseph, *Fact and Fable in Psychology*. Boston and New York: Houghton Mifflin Company, 1900.

Nelson, G. K., *Spiritualism and Society*. New York: Schocken Books, 1969.

Noss, John B., *Man's Religions*. New York: The Macmillan Company, 1964.

Pidgeon, Charles (pseud.), *Revelations of a Spirit Medium*. H. Price and E. J. Dingwall, eds.; London: Kegan Paul, Trench Trubner & Co., 1922.

Pike, James A. and Kennedy, Diane, *The Other Side: An Account of My Experiences with Psychic Phenomena*. Garden City, New York: Doubleday & Company, 1968.

Podmore, Frank, *Mediums of the Nineteenth Century*. New Hyde Park, New York, University Books, 1963. (orginally entitled *Modern Spiritualism*)

——, *The Newer Spiritualism*. New York: Henry Holt & Co., 1911.

Price, Harry, *Fifty Years of Psychical Research: A Critical Survey*. New York: Longmans, Green & Co., 1939.

Prince, Morton, *Dissociation of a Personality: A Biographical Study in Abnormal Psychology*. Westport, Connecticut, Greenwood, 1969.

Progoff, Ira, *The Image of an Oracle: A Report on Research into the Mediumship of Eileen J. Garrett*. New York: Helix Press, Garrett Publications, 1964.

Rhine, Joseph B., *Extra-Sensory Perception*. Somerville, Massachusetts: Humphries, 1962.

Rhine, Louisa E., *Hidden Channels of the Mind*. New York: William Sloane Associates, 1961.

Rinn, Joseph F., *Sixty Years of Psychical Research*. New
    York: The Truth Seeker Company, 1950.
Spence, Lewis, *An Encyclopedia of Occultism*. New Hyde
    Park, New York: University Books, 1968.
Spraggett, Allen, *The Unexplained*. New York: New
    American Library, 1967.
Underhill, A. Leah, *The Missing Link in Modern Spirit-
    ualism*. New York: Thomas R. Knox, 1885.

INDEX

Adare, Viscount (*later* Earl of Dunraven), 98–101, 102, 103, 104

Aetherius Society, 249

Afterlife, spiritualism and belief in, 1, 3–8, 44–47, 72ff. *See also* survival and communication

Agriculturalizers, 54

Alexander II, Czar, 96

American Society for Psychical Research (A.S.P.R.), 162, 173–74, 194, 197–98, 199, 230, 248, 251

Ames, Julia A., 170

Anabaptists, 23

Ancestor worship, 3, 7–9

Anderson, Francis G. H., 128–29

Angels, 73, 168

"Animal geniuses," 226–27

Animal healers, 239–40

Animal magnetism, 24–30, 67, 275, 276. *See also* Magnetism

Apparition(s), defined, 275

Apportation (apports), 20, 46, 50, 63, 137, 174, 194, 275

Association of Beneficents, 54

Associations (organizations; societies), spiritualist, 61, 112, 135, 159–76, 248, 249. *See also* specific organizations by name

Automatic writing (automatism), 63–64, 112, 134, 170, 178, 200, 202, 276. *See also* Cross-correspondences; Planchette; Slatewriting

Baggally, W. W., 152–56, 157, 158

Barbanell, Maurice, 238

Beneficents, Association of, 54

Béraud, Marthe (Eva C.), mediumship of, 183–88, 189

Bergrud, Mrs. Maren, 258, 261, 268–69, 271

Bertrand, Alexandre, 27, 29

Besterman, Theodore, 188, 201

Bezely, Almira, 51–52, 56

Bible, 10–12, 20, 71–72, 81, 166

Binding. *See* Tying (binding) of mediums

Bird, J. Malcolm, 194, 195

Bisson, Madame, 185–86

Blackburn, Charles, 112–13, 124, 126, 128, 129–30

Blavatsky, Madame, 220

Bois, M. H. A. Jules, 129

Boston Society for Psychical Research (B.S.P.R.), 198

Bottazzi, Professor, 151
Brewster, Sir David, 89–91
Bridges, E. Lucas, 16–18
British National Association of
  Spiritualists, 135, 162
Brittan, Reverend S. B., 83
Britten, Mrs. Emma Hardinge,
  167
Brougham, Lord, 89, 90
Browning, Elizabeth, 92
Browning, Robert, 92–95
Bryant, William Cullen, 35, 88
Bulwer-Lytton, Sir Edward, 89
Burial (graves, tombs), belief in
  afterlife and, 4–6
Bush, George, 68, 69–70, 72, 89

Cabinet(s), and mediumship,
  109ff., 136ff., 275. See also Ma-
  terialization(s)
Cagliostro, Count, 178
Camps, spiritualist, 173–74, 235–
  36, 248
Cantlon, Mrs. Claire, 163–64
Carrington, Hereward, 152–56,
  157–58, 173, 194–95, 198
Catholic Church, and spiritualist
  movement, 19, 23–24, 164. See
  also Christianity
Cayce, Edgar, 263
Chambers, Robert, 97
Chenoweth, Mrs., 208
Chiaia, Ercole, 137–38
China, ancient, 6, 7–8, 9
Christ. See Jesus Christ
Christianity, and spiritualist move-
  ment, 19–24, 36–37, 56, 57, 72,
  83–84, 160, 164–70
Christian Rationalist, The, 84
Churches, spiritualist, 60, 61, 160,
  166–70, 249, 278
Church of the New Jerusalem,
  81

Civil War era, spiritualism and,
  58–59
Clairaudience, 20, 21, 23, 66, 275
Clairvoyance, 13–14, 20, 23, 66,
  67, 81, 160, 252, 275
Clay imprints, 138–39
Clodd, Edward, 165
Collins, B. Abdy, 110–11
Combination Lock Test, 251–52
Communication after death. See
  Survival and communication
Comstock, Dr. Daniel F., 194–95
Conan Doyle, Sir Arthur, 161–
  62, 164, 167, 203, 246, 249
Consciousness (human self-con-
  sciousness), 2–3. See also Un-
  conscious mind
Control (of the medium), de-
  fined, 275. See also Tying
  (binding) of medium; specific
  aspects
Control(s), spirit. See Spirit con-
  trol(s)
Cook, Emma, 126–27
Cook, Florence, mediumship of,
  110–30, 131; Crookes' investi-
  gation of, 119ff.
Cook, Kate, 127, 129–30
Cooper, James Fenimore, 35
Corner, Edward Elgie, 18, 128,
  129
Courtier, Jules, 151–52
Cox, Edward, 123
Crandon, Dr. Leroy G., 193–205,
  234–35
Crandon, Margery, 193–205, 234–
  35; and cross-correspondences,
  199–205, 206, 234–35
Crandon, Walter, 193–205
Crime(s), spiritualism and, 51–
  53, 56
Croesus, King of Lydia, 13–14

Crookes, Sir William, and mediumship investigations, 105–7, 119ff.

Cross-correspondences: British S.P.R. and, 206–32; Crandons and, 199–205, 234–35; possibility of conspiracy and fraud in, 218–32

Cures. *See* Healing, spiritual; Mesmerism

Curtains, cabinet, movement of, 140, 143, 149, 153, 154

Curtis, Natalie, 15

Daisley, Reverend George, 260–61, 271

Dalston Association, 112

Damianis and Eusapia Palladino, 137

Dante, 74–75, 81

Davenport, Ira Erastus, 131–33

Davenport, William Henry, 131–33

Davies, Reverend C. Maurice, 114–16

Davis, Andrew Jackson ("Poughkeepsie Seer"), 55, 66–84, 166, 169; classification of spirits by, 72ff.; *Death and the After-life* by, 76–84; Great Harmonia system of, 72, 81, 83; *Principles of Nature . . .* by, 67ff.; and spiritualist periodicals, 82–84; Summer-Land of, 74–81, 180; *Univercoelum* of, 69, 82–84

Davis' Revelations Revealed (Bush), 62

Death, spiritualism and belief in afterlife and, 1, 3–8, 44–47, 72ff. *See also* Afterlife; Survival and communication

Death and the After-life (Davis), 76ff.

De Gloumeline, Julie (the second Mrs. D. D. Home), 90, 99, 107–8; biography of husband by, 90, 99, 107–8

De Kroll, Alexandrina (the first Mrs. D. D. Home), 96, 97

Delphic oracle, 13–14

Demonic possession, 21–22, 30, 51–53, 277

De Morgan, Augustus, 61

Devil (evil), 21, 36, 56, 74. *See also* Demonic possession

Dingwall, Dr. Eric J., 94, 103, 144, 188, 196, 235

Direct voice, defined, 276. *See also* Trance speaking (trance voices)

Direct writing, defined, 276. *See also* Automatic writing; Slate-writing

Discarnate entities, 44–47, 63–64

Divination, 9, 276. *See also* Fortune-telling; Prophecy

Dreams, 8–9, 15, 20

Dudley, E. E., 198

Duke University, and ESP research, 229–30, 240–41, 242

Duncan, Helen, 189–92

Dunlop, Bessie, 22

Ectoplasm, 18, 47, 110, 117, 174, 186–87, 188, 189–90, 191, 235, 250; defined and described, 18, 276

Edmonds, John Worth, 59, 88

Educationizers, 54

Edwards, Harry, 236–38, 239

Egypt, ancient, 5–6, 24

Elberfeld Horses, 226–27

Electrizers, 54

"Electro-biology," 60

Electronic devices, séance phenomena and, 234

Elementizers, 54

Elongation (stretching) of body, mediums and, 47, 88, 139, 190

Ely, Miss description of D. D. Home by, 91

Encyclopedia of Occultism, An (Spence), 26

Encyclopedia of Psychic Science (Fodor), 139

Endor, King Saul and woman of, 10–13, 14

England: history of spiritualism and, 59–64, 89ff., 160ff., 248, 249–50; laws and mediumship in, 163–64; spiritual healing in, 236–40; spiritualist societies in, 160–72; S.P.R. cross-correspondences and, 206–32

ESP (extrasensory perception), 1, 160, 229–32, 240–41, 242, 246, 248, 251–53, 273. *See also* specific aspects, phenomena, individuals, organizations

Eugénie, Empress, 96

Europe, and history of spiritualist movement, 19–30, 60–64. *See also* specific aspects, countries, organizations

Eva C. *See* Béraud, Marthe (Eva C.)

Evangelicals, 23

Faraday, Michael, 62–63

Feilding, Everard, 152–56, 157, 158

Ferguson, J. B., 131

Fingerprints, spirit, 197–98, 203, 234–35

Fish, Mrs. Leah Fox (*later* Mrs. Underhill), 33, 34, 35, 37, 38, 41, 60, 62, 65, 71, 109

Fishbough, Reverend William, 67

Flammarion, Camille, 147

Flournoy, Theodore, 148, 179–83

Flying saucers, 249

Fodor, Nandor, 130, 139

Forbes, Mrs., 208, 214

Ford, Reverend Arthur, 243–45; and Bishop Pike affair, 259–60, 261–64, 271, 272, 273; "Fletcher" spirit control of, 262–63

Fortune-telling, 163–64. *See also* Divination; Oracles; Prophecy

Fox, Katherine, 31–42, 60, 62, 65, 71, 217–18, 214, 249

Fox, Leah. *See* Fish, Mrs. Leah Fox (*later* Mrs. Underhill)

Fox, Margaret, 31–42, 60, 62, 65, 71, 217–18, 241, 249

Fox, Mr. and Mrs. John, 31–42, 60, 62, 65, 71

Franklin, Benjamin, 26–27, 30

Fraud(s), 87, 118, 233–34 (*see also* Scientific investigations; specific aspects, individuals); Bishop Pike affair and, 265ff.; cross-correspondences and, 218–32 (*see also* Cross-correspondences); and decline of mediumship, 177–205, 233ff.; Eusapia Palladino and, 139–58; Helen Duncan and, 189–92; legislation and, 58–59, 163–64, 192, 249–50; Margery Crandon and, 193–205, 234–35; Marthe Béraud and, 183–88; medium organizations and, 174–76; spiritualist camps and, 173–74; unconscious mind and, 181–83, 222–27

Fraudulent Mediums Act, 250

Freud, Sigmund, 182

Fricker, Ted, 237–38

From India to the Planet Mars (Flournoy), 181–83

Galen, 67

Garcia, Vincente, 184

Garrett, Mrs. Eileen, 129, 245–48, 251

Geley, Gustave, 187–88

Ghosts, 1, 6–7, 276

"Gifts of the Holy Spirit," 20, 168

Governmentizers, 54

Graves. *See* Burial (graves, tombs)

Great Britain. *See* England

Greater World, The (newspaper), 171

Greater World Spiritualist League, 171

Greece, ancient, 13–14, 24

Greeley, Horace, 35

Grimes, Dr. S. J., 66

Gurney, Edmund, 208, 214

Hall, Trevor H., 100, 103–4, 115, 126, 127

Hallucination(s), psychic phenomena and, 143–44, 152, 155, 276

Halverson, Martin, 262

Hands (and arms), spirit, 46, 88, 92, 97, 109, 138, 142, 149, 151, 153–54

Hardwicke, Dr. Henry, 199–201

Harvey, Reverend C. H., 58

Hayden, Mrs. W. B., 59–61, 89

Healing, spiritual, 15–16, 20, 21, 24–30, 236–40. *See also* Mesmerism

Healthfulizers, 54

Herald of Progress (periodical), 84

Herne, Frank, 113

Herod, King, 20

Hodgson, Dr. Richard, 144, 162, 206, 214–16, 220–21

Holland, Mrs. (pseudonym of Mrs. Fleming), 208, 214

Holy Man (Oglala Sioux Indians), 15

Holy Spirit, 20, 168

Home, Daniel Dunglas, mediumship of, 85–107; and Ashley Place levitation, 98–107; Browning and, 92–95; and founding of Spiritual Atheneum, 98, 105; *Incidents in My Life* by, 97; scientific investigations of, 100–8

Hope (spirit photographer), 161

Houdini, Harry, 104, 194–96, 202, 203, 242, 243–45; question of death and communication from, 242, 243–45

Houdini, Mrs. Harry (Beatrice), 243–45

Houdini Exposes the Tricks Used by the Boston Medium Margery, 195–96

Houshken (shaman), 16–18

Howard, Mrs., 216–17, 228, 230

Hunt, Amos, 52–53

Hydesville (N.Y.) rappings, Fox family and, 31–42, 249

Hyperesthesia, 225–28, 276

Hypnotism, 28–30, 60, 222, 276. *See also* Mesmerism

"Imperator" (spirit control), 73

Incidents in My Life (Home), 97

Indians' Book, The (Curtis), 15

Infrared photography, 234

Institut Metaphysique, 188

International General Assembly of Spiritualists, 249

Irwin, Captain, 246–48

Israel, ancient, 13. *See also* Old Testament; specific individuals

James, William, 161, 214, 221
Jeanne d'Arc, 21
Jencken, H. D., 102
Jesus Christ, 20, 72, 83, 111, 171, 172, 249
Joseph (biblical), 20
Judaism, 170, 172. *See also* Israel, ancient
Julia's Bureau, 70

Kant, Immanuel, 82
Kennedy, Diane (*later* Mrs. James A. Pike), 263
Kerwin, Dr., 198
King, George, 249
Koons, Jonathan, 50, 74

Lavoisier, Antoine L., 26–27, 71
Lee, Dr. Charles Alfred, 39, 40
Legislation (laws), and spiritualism, 58–59, 163–64, 192, 249–50
Levitation, 20, 50, 63, 88, 112, 134, 139, 153, 160; defined, 276; D. D. Home and, 98–107
Lie detector (polygraph), 63
Lights, spirit. *See* "Spirit lights"
Lily Dale (N.Y.) spiritualist camp meetings, 173, 248–49
Lincoln, Abraham, 36, 59, 61
Lincoln, Mary Todd, 36
Lindsay, Master (*later* Earl of Crawford), 98–101, 102, 103, 104
Lister, Joseph, 237
Livermore, Caroline, 264, 272
Livermore, George, 264
Lodge, Raymond, 167–68
Lodge, Sir Oliver, 143, 144–45, 162, 167–68, 214, 217, 228, 229, 230
Lodge, "Uncle Jerry," and British S.P.R. cross-correspondences, 217, 228, 229, 230
Lombroso, Cesare, 137–38, 140
London Society for Psychical Research, 100
London Spiritualist Alliance (L.S.A.), 135, 162–64, 189–90
Luigi, Prince (of Naples), 96
Lyceum Movement, 169–70
Lyon, Dr., 67
Lyon, Mrs. Jane, 104–5

McDougall, William, 194–95
Magic, shamanistic, 14–18
Magnetism. *See* Animal magnetism
Magnetization, defined, 276
Marie Antoinette, Queen, 178
Mars (Martians), 79, 179–83
Maskelyne, J. N., 202
Master Temple Psychic Centre, 191
Materialization(s), 18, 109–30, 131–55, 174 (*see also* specific aspects, mediums, phenomena); defined, 277; frauds and decline of mediumship, 177–205 *passim;* full-form, 109ff.; science and inventions and, 233–34
Matthews, Justus, 52–53
Mediums (mediumship), 1–2, 7, 10–18, 31ff., 44–47, 67ff., 85ff., 109ff. (*see also* Spiritualism; Survival and communication; specific aspects, mediums, phenomena); and cross-correspondences, 206–32 (*see also* Cross-correspondences); defined, 277; frauds and decline of, 177ff., 233ff. (*see also* Scientific investigations); and healing, 15–16, 236–40 (*see also* Healing, spiritual); history of, 1–18, 19ff.

(*see also* specific aspects, individuals, places); organizations and, 159–76; physical and mental, differences between, 85; and physical phenomena, 31ff., 47, 85–107, 108–30; religion and, 19–24 (*see also* Religion); science and, 233–34 (*see also* Scientific investigations); séances and, 233–34 (*see also* specific aspects, mediums); shamanism and, 14–18

"Mediums' Benevolent Society," 176

Mediums of the 19th Century, 180

Mental illness, mediumship frauds and, 181–83

Mesmer, Friedrich Anton, 24–30

Mesmerism, 24–30, 41–42, 66, 67, 221, 222, 225–27 (*see also* Animal magnetism); defined, 277

Mettler, Mrs. Semantha, 54–55

Mind reading, 226–27, 234, 243, 250

Minerva Scientific Circle, 149–50

Miracles, biblical, and spiritualist movement, 20–21

"Mr. Sludge, 'The Medium'" (Browning), 93–95, 119, 158, 225, 274

"Mr. Splitfoot," 32–33, 36, 41, 83, 217–18

Morselli, Enrico, 150

Moses, William Stainton, mediumship of, 133–35, 146, 162, 185, 224; "Imperator" spirit control of, 134–35

Moyes, Winifred, 71

Murder, spiritualism and, 51–53, 56

Muscle reading, 226–27, 277, 278

Music (musical instruments), spiritualist phenomena and, 46, 132, 134, 136, 139, 149, 153

Myers, F. W. H., 143, 144–45, 147–48, 157, 162; and S.P.R. cross-correspondences, 206ff.

Napoleon III, 96

National Federation of Spiritualist Healers, 239

National Laboratory of Psychical Research, 190–91

Neanderthal Man, 4–5

New Motor movement 49, 54–56, 57, 74

Newspapers. *See* Press (newspapers, periodicals)

New Testament, 20, 72. *See also* Bible

Noel family, 183–85

Ochorowicz, Dr. Julijan, 142, 143

Old Testament, 10–13, 72. *See also* Bible

Ona people, and shamanism, 14, 16–18

O'Neill, Tom, 236

Oracles, 13–14, 43–44, 277

Organizations. *See* Associations

Other Side, The (Pike), 255, 265, 266, 269

Ouija boards, 10, 233

Owen, Robert, 61

Owen, Robert Dale, 59, 61

Palladino, Eusapia, mediumship of, 136–58, 191, 198; scientific investigations of, 139–58

Parapsychology Foundation, 248

Paris General Psychological Institute, 151

Pasteur, Louis, 237

Paul, St., 20

"Pelham, George" (spirit control), 210, 215–16, 228, 230
Pentecostals, 23
Phantasm, defined, 277
Phillmore, Mercy, 163–64
Philosophy, and spiritualism, 66–84; Davis and, 67–84
Photographs (photography), 19, 117, 121, 123, 174, 187, 191; infrared, 234
Physical Phenomena of Spiritualism, The (Carrington), 52
Piddington, J. G., 210–13
Pidgeon, Charles F. (pseudonym), 175–76
Pike, Bishop James A., 255–73
Pike, Jim (son), 255–73
Piper, Mrs. Leonore, 208, 214, 215, 216, 217, 220–21, 228, 230, 245–46
Planchette, 9, 63, 277
Podmore, Frank, 100–3, 106–7, 108, 124, 126, 162, 180, 235
Poltergeists, 257, 267, 269, 277
Polygraph (lie detector), 63
Possession. *See* Demonic possession
Precognition, defined, 277
Press (newspapers, periodicals), 82–85, 112, 248. *See also* individual publications by name
Price, Harry, 190–91, 246
Primitive Baptists, 23
Prince, Dr. W. F., 194–95, 198, 235
Principles of Nature, Her Divine Revelations, and A Voice to Mankind (Davis), 67–74
Prophecy, 20, 71, 160. *See also* Divination; Fortune-telling; Oracles
Protestantism, and spiritualism, 23, 65, 83, 164–65. *See also* Christianity
Psychical research (*see also* ESP; Scientific investigations; specific aspects, individuals, organizations, phenomena); defined, 278
Psychic News, 111
Psychometry, 161, 170, 229, 230, 278
Psychosomatic illnesses, 27, 28–29, 238–39. *See also* Healing, spiritual; specific aspects, *e.g.* Suggestion (self-suggestion)
Pythagoras, 10
Pythia (Delphic oracle), 13–14

Quarterly Journal of Science, 122

Rapport, Mesmer's cures and, 25
Raps (rappings), spirit, 49, 51, 60, 62, 132, 136, 138, 141, 153, 174, 190, 224; Fox family and, 31–42; Home and, 87, 90, 92, 122
Rasputin, 28
Rauscher, Dr., 259, 270–71
Reid, Thomas, 22
Reincarnation, 4, 278
Religion, and spiritualist movement, 19–24, 36–37, 42, 56, 57, 65, 72–73ff., 159, 164–70, 251. *See also* Bible; Christianity; specific aspects, denominations
Revelations of a Spirit Medium, 174–76
Rhine, Dr. J. B., 240–41, 246
Richardson, Dr., 200, 202–5
Richet, Charles, 140, 142–43, 144–45, 147–48, 157, 184–85, 186
Rinn, Joseph F., 241–42, 244–45
Roberts, Mrs. (medium), 6, 89

R 101 (dirigible) crash, 247–48
Rosicrucianism, 172
Roy, William, 250–51

Saints, and spiritualist movement, 19–21
Samoyeds, and shamanism, 14, 18
Samuel (biblical prophet), 11–13, 14
Saul (biblical king), 10–13, 14
Schiaparelli, G. V., 180
Schizophrenia, 182
Schrenck-Notzing, Baron von, 143, 186–87
Science and Invention (magazine), 242
Scientific American (magazine), 194–95, 198, 242
Scientific investigations (scientific method; scientific research), and spiritualism, 24–30, 61–64, 144, 151–52, 153–56, 159–76, 241, 251; and cross-correspondences (*see* Cross-correspondences); and decline of physical mediumship, 177ff., 233ff. (*see also* Fraud(s); specific aspects, investigations, mediums, organizations)
Scotland, witchcraft in, 22
Séances, 10–13, 19, 21, 30, 31ff., 44–47, 109ff., 136ff., 174, 177ff., 255ff., 278 (*see also* Mediums; specific aspects, mediums, phenomena); and frauds and decline of mediumship, 177ff., 233ff.; growth of spiritualist movement and, 50ff., 59ff., 65ff.; and survival after death (*see* Survival and communication)
Secondary personality, 182–83, 222, 227, 278

Seventh-Day Adventists, 23
Shakers, 23
Shamans (shamanism), 14–18, 43–44, 278
Shockle, Charles E., 59
Siberia, shamanism and people of, 4, 18
Sidgwick, Professor and Mrs., 143–45, 162, 208, 214
Sioux Indians, and shamanism, 15
Sittings with Eusapia Palladino & other Studies (Feilding), 153–56
Sixty Years of Psychical Research (Rinn), 244–45
Slate-writing, 46–47, 276. *See also* Automatic writing
Sly, Samuel, 53
Smith, Hélène (Catherine Elise Muller), mediumship of, 177–83, 221, 222; Oriental Cycle of, 179–80; Royal Cycle of, 178–79, 182
Soal, S. G., 246
Society for the Diffusion of Spiritual Knowledge, 167
Society of Psychical Research (S.P.R.), British, 125, 135, 143, 144–45, 146, 147, 148, 149, 152, 155–56, 188, 230, 248; and cross-correspondences, 206–32; founding of, 160–62
Some Modern Mediums (Besterman), 201
Somnambulism, 27–30, 222, 278
Soul(s): Davis on afterlife and, 72ff.; and survival (*see* Survival and communication)
Speaking in tongues, 20. *See also* Trance speaking
Spear, John Murray, 53–56, 57
Speer, Mr. and Mrs. Stanhope, 134–35

Spence, Lewis, 26

"Spirit circle," 2; Fox family and growth of, 41–47

Spirit control(s), 22, 30, 34ff., 44–46, 60, 73–74, 170–71, 178, 237–40, 245–48 (*see also* specific aspects, controls, mediums, phenomena); and cross-correspondences, 223 (*see also* Cross-correspondences); defined, 278; and survival and communication, 1–18, 44–47, 255–73 (*see also* Survival and communication; specific individuals, mediums)

Spirit Electronic Communication Society, 50–51

"Spirit lights," 46

Spirit Messenger (periodical), 84

"Spirit teachers," Davis on, 73, 74

Spiritual Atheneum, 98, 105

Spiritual Frontiers Fellowship, 259, 260, 270, 271

Spiritualism (spiritualist churches), 60, 61, 160, 166–70, 249, 278

Spiritualism (spiritualist movement, spiritualists), 1ff., 31ff., 233ff. (*see also specific* aspects, individuals, mediums, organizations, phenomena); and belief in survival and communication (*see* Afterlife; Survival and communication); criticism of and opposition to, 56–59, 110ff., 165, 240–53 (*see also* Scientific investigations; specific aspects, individuals, mediums, organizations); definitions, 1ff., 278; fraud and (*see* Fraud[s], specific aspects, individuals); history and

growth of, 1–18, 19ff., 31ff., 49ff., 86–108, 109ff. (*see also* specific aspects, individuals, places); and mediumship (*see* Mediums; specific aspects, phenomena); organizations and, 159–76 (*see also* Associations; specific organizations); recent trends and revival of interest in, 233–53; and religion and philosophy (*see* Philosophy; Religion); science and (*see* Scientific investigations)

Spiritualist, The (newspaper), 112, 113, 118

Spiritualist National Federation (*later* Spiritualist National Union), 167, 168–69, 191; Seven Principles of Spiritualism and, 168–69

Spiritualists, The (Hall), 115

Spiritual Telegraph (periodical), 84

"Splitfoot." *See* "Mr. Splitfoot"

Spraggett, Allen, 236, 261, 262

Stead, W. T., 170

Stevenson, Dr. Ian, 251–52

Stone, and Mrs. Hayden, 60

Stowe, Harriet Beecher, 35

Strand (magazine), 165

Subliminal memory, 227, 278

Subvocal whispering, 226, 278–79

Suggestion (self-suggestion), and mediumistic phenomena, 29, 223, 224–25, 239. *See also* Hypnotism; Mesmerism

Sumer, royal tombs in, 6

Summer-Land, Davis and, 74–81, 169

Super-rays, Zwann and, 49, 50–51

Survival and communication, 1–

18, 44–47, 59, 60–61, 63–64, 159, 165, 243–45, 246–48, 255–73 (*see also* Afterlife; Mediums; Spirit Control[s]; specific aspects, individuals); cross-correspondences and, 218–32 (*see also* Cross-correspondences); ESP and (*see* ESP); fraud and, 218–32 (*see also* specific aspects, mediums, phenomena); tests for, 251–52

Swedenborg, Emanuel, 67, 82

Table tipping, 43, 49, 62–63, 106, 135, 174, 195, 224, 233; Cook and, 111–12; Home and, 88, 106; possible explanation of, 62–63

Telekinesis, 155, 233–34. *See also* Apportation; Teleportation

Telepathy, 160, 227, 230, 279

Teleportation, 134, 137, 140, 141, 143–44, 153, 154, 155, 160, 279. *See also* Apportation; Telekinesis

Thompson, Mrs., 208, 214, 228

Thumbprints. *See* Fingerprints, spirit

Tillich, Paul, 263

Tolstoy, Alexis, 97

Tolstoy, Leo, 97

Tombs. *See* Burial (graves, tombs)

Tom Fools' knot, binding of mediums and use of, 131–32, 151

Tomkins, George, 239

Trance(s), mediumistic, 12, 13, 27–30, 43–47 (*see also* Medium(s); Séances; specific aspects, individuals); defined, 279; and frauds and decline of mediumship, 177–205, 218–

32; unconscious mind and (*see* Unconscious mind); "will to believe" ("will to disbelieve") and, 231–32, 266–67, 268

Trance speaking (trance voices), 12, 13, 20, 23, 31ff., 44–47, 49, 53, 63, 66ff., 245–48, 250–51, 267–68 (*see also* Spirit control[s]; specific individuals, mediums); direct voice, 276, 279

Treatise on Somnambulism (Bertrand), 27

Trollope, T. A., 89, 95

Trumpets, 46, 136

Tungus people, and shamanism, 14, 18

Twigg, Mrs. Ena, 258, 259, 269–70, 271

Tying (binding) of mediums, 18, 190, 275; Davenports and, 131–33; Eusapia Palladino and, 139, 151; Florence Cook and, 112, 114, 115–16, 117, 118; use of Tom Fool's knot in, 132–33, 151

Tyson, Mrs., and S.P.R. cross-correspondence, 216

Unconscious mind, and spiritualist phenomena, 8, 29, 62–63, 181–83, 222–28, 229, 279

United States, spiritualism in, 30, 31ff., 45–59, 65ff., 162, 172–76, 248–49, 250, 251–53. *See also* specific aspects, individuals, events, organizations, places

Univercoelum (periodical), 82–84

Uttermost Part of the Earth, The (Bridges), 17

Valiantine, George, 199–201, 202–3

Ventriloquism, 276, 279. *See also* Trance speaking (trance voices)

Verrall, Miss (daughter), 208

Verrall, Mrs. Helen, 208ff., 228

Voices(s), spirit. *See* Trance speaking (trance voices)

Volckman, William, 118–19, 127

Wagner, N. P., 142

Wakeman, Mrs. Rhoda, and Wakemanites, 52–53, 56, 57

Ward, Hazel, 239–40

White Eagle (spirit control), 73

White Eagle Lodge, 171–72; six principles of, 171–72

Willard, Clarence E., 47

Williams, Charles, 113

"Will to believe" ("will to dis-believe"), mediumistic phenomena and, 231–32, 266–67, 268

Witchcraft Act of 1735, 192

Witches (witchcraft), 21–22, 192

Wooley, Dr. V. J., 188

World War I era, spiritualism and, 165

Written messages, 46. *See also* Automatic writing (automatism); Cross-correspondences; Planchette; Slate-writing

Wynne, Captain Charles, 98–99, 103

Yorkshire Spiritual Telegraph, 61

"Zodiac" (spirit control), 73, 171

Zwann, N., 50–51

GEORGESS McHARGUE is a free-lance writer and former book editor who lives in New York City. A graduate of Radcliffe College, she has a special interest in oddities and unusual lore, from monsters and mythology to mediums. When not engaged in writing, she likes to spend her vacations on horseback in Montana.